Behavior Change through Guidance

Behavior Change through Guidance

Henry Weitz

Director, Bureau of Testing and Guidance
and Associate Professor of Education
Duke University

John Wiley & Sons, Inc., New York · London · Sydney

Library of Congress Catalog Card Number: 63-23368

Printed in the United States of America

Library of Congress Catalog Card Number: 64-23865
Printed in the United States of America

To Ellen

Preface

◆◆

M any years ago, Dr. Louis Cohen, in his presidential address to the North Carolina Psychological Association, raised a painful question, which has been troubling many of those who heard him ever since. After describing some of the therapeutic steps he had taken with one of his disturbed patients and indicating that the patient seemed to get well, Dr. Cohen wondered aloud before his professional colleagues what he had done to facilitate the recovery of this disorganized and distressed individual. This seemed to be a strange display of modesty for so accomplished a therapist. Yet he meant every word of it. He did not know with any certainty how he had contributed to the well-being of his patient. He was not, in fact, entirely sure that he had had anything to do with the recovery.

In guidance, as in psychotherapy—and, one suspects, in all the so-called helping professions—one is never absolutely sure that what he does has any intimately causal relationship to the improvement of the person receiving the help. Even when we have a kind of faith, as most of us do, that we are somehow contributing to the easing of another's burden, we have little in the way of clear knowledge of how we might enhance our effectiveness. As guidance practitioners, we want to help; we want to believe that by reason of our intervention, this man is more productive and that one more socially effective. We should like to believe that because of our professional skills, which have been directed toward the modification of human behavior, some individuals have been enabled to apply their new-found talents to socially creative enterprises that will make this a more satisfactory world. But we do not have this kind of reassurance about guidance.

We appear to know less about how to help a student choose the best possible program of courses in high school than we know about how to blow up the student, the school, and the world in which he lives. The explosion can be managed with magnificent certainty. Regardless of the arrogance with which it is often done, guidance cannot be practiced with the same certainty. Yet it is precisely this sort of certainty that we think we require in guidance if the profession is to develop and to make its contribution to the lives of those it seeks to help.

We are frequently informed that what is required to force guidance into a more intimate alliance with perfection is more research—more and better. This melancholy adoration of research confronts us at every turn of a professional journal's page. It takes the form of ritualistic hymns extolling the virtues of research as the solitary road to salvation. (What thesis, dissertation, or experiment report does not conclude with the statement: "Further research is required to . . . ."?) Some guidance practitioner-scholars, having convinced themselves of this virtue, have desisted from the hymn-singing long enough to devise little experiments that document some subatomic particle of truth or to contrive yet another psychometric instrument with which to observe such particles.

Consider for a moment that as this is being written some folks called Catholics and some folks called Buddhists are slaughtering each other and themselves with frightening enthusiasm for reasons that to many observers of the Vietnam scene seem murky. One is inclined to speculate about the amount of assistance or comfort one of the victims or perpetrators of these "disorders" would get from a Q-sort or a semantic differential in understanding what motivates him to choose this curious means of resolving a problem in human intercourse. This debacle in a place presently known as Vietnam is not such a far cry from the problems faced by a high school freshman trying to select an appropriate program of studies that will determine in many crucial ways how he will live out his life. The student, the bhikkhu, and the Vietnamese private with a bayonet in his hand are all faced with environmental forces that disrupt their serene progress toward constructive and satisfying goals; they are all confronted with their own limitations in skill, talent, knowledge, and self-understanding, which become obstacles to their achievement of socially creative objectives. They all require some guidance, some behavior modification, that will permit them to make self-directed, rational, responsible decisions leading to personally satisfying and socially valued consequences. Unfortunately, our research into the subatomic particles of human behavior and our curious little psychometric instruments give almost as little help to one of these deserving clients as they do to the others.

Perhaps the reason that we have reached such an impasse in our guidance research and instrumentation is the fact that we have attended so rigorously to our methodological problems that we have lost sight of the entity we are trying to observe and understand. The central entity in guidance, as we see it, is social, global, human behavior. But not behavior in general, not the behavior of human beings as a class. Instead we need to look at the behavior of man$_1$, a specific, unique, and somewhat terrifyingly wonderful individual specimen. Not only do we need to focus our attention on the observation and understanding of the behavior of single individuals, but we need to view that behavior as it is performed in the rich and varied environmental context that shapes its meaning and significance.

In this book we have attempted to achieve just such a focus. Here we have tried to examine the structure of idiosyncratic human behavior, to see the interactions between a unique biographical history and a unique configuration of circumstances, and to relate this behavioral interaction to that crucial human activity of collaborative problem solving that we have come to call guidance. This is no fully formed theory of behavior (would that it were!). It is, however, a sincere attempt to indicate trails leading to vantage points from which behavior may be viewed and to suggest particularly interesting vistas that may begin to give a new perspective to guidance.

This book is designed for the scholar and the practitioner. There is, particularly in the behavioral sciences and in their applications, a continuum of scientific activity, which ranges from "pure" science on the one hand to technology and practice on the other. Greenwood differentiates between pure science and practice in the behavioral sciences in the following way:

> The purpose of scientific activity is the description and explanation of nature in all of its manifestations. . . . The primary aim of science is an understanding of nature better than common sense can yield us. . . . The term technology refers to all disciplines designed to achieve controlled changes in natural relationships by means of procedures which are scientifically based. . . . The scientist's prime aim is the description of the social world; the practitioner's prime aim is the control of that world. (Greenwood, 1961, p. 74.)

Both scientist and practitioner in the area of guidance will, if our attempts here have been fruitful, find approaches to the understanding and control of behavior that may enhance their scholarly research and their efforts to facilitate the acquisition of more effective behavior by their clients. The scientific process, especially that aspect of it involving theory formulation, has been aptly described by Greenwood:

> . . . The derivation of empirical generalizations can be operationalized, but I have yet to find a textbook that will operationalize the theorizing

process. The interpretive process, the development of formulations which account for a series of facts, is essentially a free-wheeling speculative one. It is an inferential process whereby the inquiring mind churns the available information over and over employing all the logical devices and bringing to bear upon it any and all kinds of relevant knowledge. The process allows for considerable play of the imagination and the final formulation bears the imprint of the formulator. (Greenwood, 1961, p. 77.)

The notions described in the pages that follow are intended as a goad to the reader, both practitioner and scholar, to stimulate him to some of this free-wheeling speculation, which the field of guidance so sorely needs.

This book is also intended equally for the beginning and the advanced student in the field. It can be used with equal profit in a beginning course in the principles of guidance or in an advanced course in counseling and guidance techniques. But this is no how-to-do-it manual. Such illustrative material as is presented is designed to illuminate a principle or to suggest a type of application and not to indicate a cookbook formula for guidance. We have been concerned throughout with a way of understanding behavior and with the principles for achieving behavior modification through guidance. The guidance practitioner who has a firm grasp of these formulations will find ample assistance in developing techniques for applying them in the many excellent textbooks that center their concerns on such matters as methods and instruments. Or, better still, the practitioner who understands human behavior in its broadest social context and who appreciates the problem-solving focus of guidance will devise applications and practices that suit his own style of life and his own personality.

A word, perhaps, needs to be said at this point about the use of the term *guidance*. We have used this term to label the kinds of behavior changes considered in this book. In recent years, this good old term has fallen on evil days. Status-conscious practitioners who have fought their way up the academic ladder to a doctorate degree with some psychological content prefer to be called psychologists and to practice psychological counseling. They are inclined to reserve the term *guidance* for some amateur endeavors (as they view them) undertaken by a lower order of practitioner in the secondary schools. These high-school guidance workers (as they used to be called) are doing with high-school students precisely what their more highly degreed colleagues are doing with college students and adults: helping them solve problems . . . all kinds of problems. Meanwhile, all sorts of educational fauna have become counselors. Deans whose training and disposition fit them best for instructional and administrative functions see themselves and present themselves as counselors. There are admissions counselors, extracurricular counselors, attendance counselors (remember the old truant officer?), health counselors (the school nurse), and even diet counselors (school-cafeteria managers). A.P.A. Division 17 to the contrary, the term *counseling* has lost a good bit of its charm, if not its meaning.

We have chosen, therefore, to return to the old term *guidance*. Not vocational guidance, just plain guidance. And we mean by it what it used to mean: professional assistance in solving problems and in acquiring generalized problem-solving behavior. We have made some effort to differentiate guidance from instruction (Chapter Three), and we hope to have disposed of that two-headed monster, the teacher-counselor, or at least to have stunted its growth. Even the casual reader should have no difficulty in differentiating between guidance work as described here and pupil personnel administration. No special attention is given to this latter activity because it appears now to have become so clearly a clerical-administrative enterprise as to be self-evidently excluded from the professional guidance function that holds our interest.

Throughout the argument we have called the professional guidance practitioner a counselor. This is not to suggest that all of guidance is counseling. The counselor may use counseling as one means of carrying on guidance. Counseling is probably the most widely used guidance technique, but it is by no means the whole of guidance. Other forms of intervention are used by the counselor to achieve the problem-solving goals of guidance: providing information, group conferences, direct manipulation of the environment, and the like. In the main, however, problems are solved and general problem-solving behavior is acquired in the face-to-face collaborative effort of the counseling consultation.

In an effort, then, to answer the painful question raised by Dr. Cohen many years ago, we introduce this approach to guidance. We are concerned, throughout this formulation, with a modification of behavior, especially that aspect of human behavior concerned with seeking the solutions to very human problems. The end product of this change in problem-solving behavior is an individual who is capable of making mature, rational, responsible decisions and is thus able to achieve a state of dynamic serenity.

The source of one's ideas is not always identifiable. Insofar as the ideas presented in this book were identifiable, however, they have been acknowledged with gratitude in the bibliography and text. I should like here to express my appreciation to the authors and publishers who were kind enough to grant me permission to quote from their publications. There remains, however, a large number of people, not so easily identifiable, who have been kind enough to share their thoughts with me: my former teachers, my students, my colleagues, and especially those writers of the past and present whose ideas were so forceful as to be assimilated into my own thinking in such a way as to make it impossible for me to say where, outside my own head, these thoughts originated. I can only say, "Thank you!"

A special kind of appreciation is expressed here to Rex B. Cunliffe and Oscar K. Buros, who, more years ago than any of us cares to count, started me wondering about some of the notions I have tried to formulate in this book. Neither of these fine teachers, however, should be burdened with the responsibility for the points of view expressed in what follows.

I wish to express appreciation also to the editors and publishers of the *Personnel and Guidance Journal,* the *Journal of Counseling Psychology,* and the *Educational Forum* for permission to use portions of essays of mine that they had previously published. Certain sections of this book represent revisions and expansions of these earlier essays. These sections are specifically noted in the text and bibliography.

How does one thank adequately those long-suffering workers who struggled through the typing and proofreading of many drafts of this manuscript? My gratitude to Mrs. Walker, Mrs. Reskovac, and Mrs. Lewis of the Duke University Bureau of Testing and Guidance and to Mr. Heyn of the University of Ceylon!

HENRY WEITZ

Peradeniya, Ceylon

Contents

◆◆

Contents

One

The structure of human behavior

◆◆◆

Human experience is a continuous, unsegmented stream of behavior. Each behavioral event is intimately united with and
derived from every earlier act; at the same time each, as it occurs,
establishes itself as an element in some future experience. A response
performed at one point on this continuum becomes a part of some
subsequent stimulus pattern capable of evoking new responses at
some later point. All previously performed acts merge and blend to
form a reservoir from which new stimuli and responses emerge as
they are required. Even birth and death are inseparably linked, for
human life, as we know it, has the process of dying stamped upon it
before the moment of birth. The past, the present, and even the
future participate in the kinds of responses an individual performs at
any given instant, and this immediate behavior influences both his
future actions and the ways in which he interprets his former experiences. This state of affairs appears to derive, in a major way, from
the fact that, as Cohen (1961, p. 502) puts it, "brain function, as
nearly all biological phenomena, is basically repetitive and conservative."

This intimate interaction of behavioral events and the shifting role
of behavior from response to stimulus acts may be seen in the familiar
experience of a child's reactions to a flower blooming in the garden.
A brightly colored object, swayed by a passing breeze, catches the
eye of a small child toddling in the garden. The child sees the object.
This is to say, she turns her head in its direction; she adjusts the
lenses of her eyes to bring it into sharp focus; she attends to it, reducing
the impact of other competing stimuli. This focus of attention produces
new stimuli within the child. The lens-focusing act and the turning
of the head produce muscle tensions which make the child aware

1

of the object's size, shape, position, and distance from her. The depth of focus of her vision, that is, the foreground and background area brought into sharp focus, provide stimuli which evoke perceptions of the flower's setting. These stimuli arising from the child's own responses blend with light stimuli arriving from the outside and produce sensations of color. Pollen particles attach themselves to the sensitive membrane of the child's nose and evoke other physiological responses which, in turn, stimulate perceptions of a sweet scent.

These events of alternating and interacting stimuli and responses—which Mowrer (1960a and 1960b) calls response-correlated or response-produced stimuli—become for the child a perception of a state of affairs, an awareness of the flower. The speed with which these events and acts occur is very rapid indeed. So rapid, in fact, that the child, or even a highly sophisticated observer, would be unable to measure and catalogue readily the elements of behavior being performed.

As these events unfold, they become clothed in meaning for the child. She classifies each act in terms of her total previous experience. Thus, as the child senses the flower, a rush of remembrance of things past, of other swaying, brightly colored, sweet-scented objects in similar settings instantaneously wells up within her to reveal the nature and meaning of this particular event which has caught and momentarily held her attention. She recalls her earlier delight in grasping the attractive object. She remembers her mother's pleasure as she carried the object toward her face and her father's saying over and over, "Flow-er, flow-er," and tenderly showing her how to smell it. This object, in the past, came to mean welcomed and pleasant attention from those who were most dear to her. These images, these "reference signals" (Powers, Clark, and McFarland, 1960) from the past become part of the meaning and part of the behavior of the moment; and our little girl runs to the flower, plucks it, and carries it to her nose. Whereupon a bee, who up to this very moment has been going about his own private business, expresses his distaste for the intrusion by stinging the little girl.

This experience, new and painfully startling as it is, becomes a part of the next sequence of events in which the child participates. The child is startled. She cries out. She runs to her mother, who is alarmed by the event. And so it goes. The bee sting, a painful consequence of what appeared initially to be a pleasant sequence of events, becomes embedded in the behavior system of our little girl forever. Perhaps, later, when she is a debutante, her pleasure in receiving a corsage from her escort of the evening is diluted by the recollection—

vague as it may be—of that earlier bee sting. The present event lodges itself in the matrix of the future and shapes its structure.

This familiar occurrence in the life of a child illustrates the inextricable relationship among the events in an individual's life and suggests the interchangeability and essential unity of stimuli and responses. No segment of behavior can be detached and viewed separately from its antecedents and consequences. In the life of an individual, behavior seems to have no beginning and no end. This continuity of behavior, moreover, extends beyond the confines of an individual's life into the lives of others with whom he establishes some sort of affiliation. Isolated human behavior cannot exist. The isolated HUMAN being is a contradiction. Biological considerations aside, the individual owes his HUMANNESS to his society.

(Man has been shown to be a social being, nourished and shaped by the culture of the society in which he lives.)Far from being endowed by nature, apart from society, with intelligence, personality and inalienable rights, he is, without the benefit of the culture built by the cooperative efforts of countless generations of men, little more than a mere brute, devoid alike of language, reason, conscious selfhood, or any sense of moral right. (Stanley, 1953, p. 192.)

The individual's behavior, his acts, his thoughts, his feelings, are inextricably fused with the acts, thoughts, and attitudes of the culture which shaped him and which he in turn determines. Nor are these influences bounded by the temporal limits of the life of an individual. Today's responses may be evoked by events which occurred centuries ago in a distant land. The meaning derived by the reader from the words printed here is determined in a major way by the historical events which fashioned our language. The attitudes which these words call up are modified by the philosophies and value systems which sprang from one man's contemplative vigil on a mountain top and another's death on a cross. The responses now being made by the reader will become a part of his behavior tomorrow, while this behavior may extend into the infinite future as it has some impact on those who follow. Thus, acts performed today have their source in the infinite past and flow forward into the infinite future.

1. Modification in the flow of behavior

Although the flow of behavior which makes up human life may be continuous, it is not uniform. Some parts of the stream are clear and swift, filled with energy and highly productive. In other terrain, the stream spreads to a broad, quiet lake. In still another environmental context the flow becomes a turbulent, rampaging current, murky, disturbed, and destructive. Yet regardless of the circumstances, it moves forward inexorably. Into this continuous, unsegmented stream, there may be introduced, from time to time, events which modify its direction, accelerate or decelerate its flow, deflect it from its course, or harness its energies to new and more demanding tasks. Some of the events which change the course of a life may have deleterious consequences: reduced productivity, loss of status, withdrawal of love, or mental or physical illness. These are the consequences of such intervening events as war, depression, and public or private folly. On the other hand, certain experiences may modify the flow of behavior and bend it to more effective channels: heightened productivity, more satisfying interpersonal relationships, a greater recognition of beauty, and a sense of serenity. Educational experiences both contrived and fortuitous have such salutary influences. Certain religious and spontaneous aesthetic stimulation can redirect behavior into new socially and personally productive channels. Affiliation, affection, and love represent experiences which may provide stimuli to new responses of unanticipated desirable direction and energy.

Guidance, too, may be this sort of favorable experience. Guidance may be thought of as one of those processes which can redesign the psychological terrain through which the behavioral stream flows in such a way as to create more productive experiences. Effective guidance can reshape the course of a life. THUS, GUIDANCE INVOLVES BEHAVIOR CHANGE.

Changing behavior by means of guidance requires the application of techniques, devices, and processes to a stream of behavior to produce some new pattern of responses. Thus, the practice of guidance demands an understanding of three essential elements: the behavior to be changed, the methods of effecting the changes, and the goals to be achieved by the change. The practice of guidance-like activities without these understandings becomes a frivolously automatic routine resembling a tribal ritual at its worst. An understanding of these essential elements of guidance permits the practitioner to be both more efficient and more effective, thus making the total undertaking more rewarding not only to the client but also to the practitioner himself. In the end, the changes in the behavioral flow accomplished through guidance should lead to a state of meaningful, rational, and purposeful serenity in the client.

2. *Descriptive language and human behavior*

The science of human behavior and its application in guidance both require that the concepts, thoughts, reasons, and attitudes which comprise our knowledge be arranged in some manageable order. This order, generally expressed as a set of principles, is given form in one kind of symbol or another, usually verbal, often mathematical. Herein lies one of the major difficulties in the investigation of human behavior. This difficulty requires that a warning be sounded at the outset of our discussions. As indicated earlier, psychological behavior is a continuous, unbroken stream of events. It is impossible, in objective reality, to detach a segment and at the same time examine the flow. If we take a bucket of water from a swift-running brook, we have only the bucket of water to analyze and evaluate. We can learn about the fluidity of water, its temperature, its color and odor. We can separate it into its components of hydrogen and oxygen. We can estimate the number of molecules and atoms. But we have lost the magic bubbling of the brook; the sparkle and sound are gone. What is left is no longer the brook we sought to understand.

So it is with human behavior. Observation, recording, and analysis of the continuous events of human life are impossible in objective reality. The events which may make up psychological behavior merge one into the other in such a way as to be one moment stimulus and the next moment response, one moment cause and the next moment effect. Analysis of these events as they occur in objective reality is impossible, because they have no beginning and no end, whereas the analytic tools we use, the symbols and the processes we apply, require that the events they symbolize remain fixed and constant.

The idea of love, for instance, plays an important role in many discussions of human needs and drives. The word-sound *love*, even narrowly interpreted, can be and is applied to relationships between parent and child, husband and wife, friend and friend, mistress and lover, grandparent and grandchild, boy and girl, depraved psychopath and victim. Nor does the word apply exclusively to need-satisfying relationships between persons; objects and abstractions can become a part of an interaction labeled *love*. A man can love a painting, a piece of music, his country, power, wealth, success, and the like. Many of the bits and pieces of behavior performed in one love relationship are readily observable in the others. Yet somehow, the symbol *love* does not quite tell us what is going on. Even with modifiers and amplification this word can not capture the essence of the behavior being performed. A great deal is lost in translation from the behavioral language of objective reality which is continuous, unsegmented, and dynamic to the symbolic language of words and signs which must be fixed, static, and conventional to communicate.

Yet only through the medium of symbolic language is it possible to stop the continuous flow of behavior momentarily and to examine it, not in objective reality, but in symbolic reality. Throughout this book we shall explore human psychological behavior as it can be made to exist in the symbolic reality of our minds and our language. But we shall try to be mindful of the bucket of bubbling brook, remembering that it becomes the brook again only when we empty our bucket back into the stream.

3. *Events, symbols, and structure*

Psychological behavior has thus far been described as an intimately interrelated, continuous stream of events. An understanding of this concept of behavior requires some elaboration of the nature of an event. In common usage, *event* is taken to mean an occurrence, an incident, a circumstance, an occasion, a transaction, a happening, and so on. Involved in each of these terms which suggest the meaning of *event* is the notion of activity and movement. In an event, something is moving, hence changing its relationship to something else. An event, then, involves at least two objects acting in relation to each other, since movement and relationship embody a change in position of one object relative to another. The notion of a single object in isolation changing its position is a meaningless concept, for change involves direction with respect to other objects in the time-space matrix.

Yet the objects which make up events are themselves events. Consider for a moment a piece of furniture, a chair, for example. This chair, made of wood, has size, color, weight, and a kind of internal organization of its parts which we see as form. Even on this macroscopic level, these characteristics of the chair depend for their meaning upon an observer. Its form, color, size, weight, and so forth, emerge as a consequence of the interaction between this hunk of matter and the person contemplating it. Thus the observation process, involving as it does the changing relationship between the chair and the observer, qualifies as an event. When we go below the macroscopic level of observation, however, the EVENT characteristics of an object become even more obvious. The surface characteristics of a chair are determined, in a large measure, by its submicroscopic composition. The molecules, atoms, and subatomic particles are the objects of which the chair is made. Yet these objects are themselves in constant motion relative to each other. What appears to be a chair is, in reality, empty space traversed by minute particles moving at fantastic speeds and interacting with one another. A chair, then, encompasses more empty space than it does matter. It owes its existence to the ordered movement of its particles in relation to each other. The chair, this object, may thus be viewed as an event.

Objects and events are similar in that they are both composed of elements in dynamic relationship to each other. In order to facilitate further discussion of these matters, however, we shall, from time to time, need to differentiate between objects and events. The differentiation will be made on the basis of the rigidity of the structure. Structural relations which are relatively stable, constant, persistent, and rigid on the macroscopic level of observation will be labeled *objects;* those which are flexible, fluid, unstable, and varying will be labeled *events*. Thus a chair, for all its submicroscopic activity, would in this nomenclature be called an *object,* whereas the situation of a weary man using the chair as a resting place would be labeled an *event*. This is not too far from common usage. It is brought into the discussion at this point, however, to alert the reader to the concept of dynamic structure as a changing but ordered complex of multidimensional relationships. The existence of objects and events and our ability to talk about them leads us quite naturally to a consideration of several concepts of reality. It must be perfectly obvious that the word *chair,* even when it is carefully described and modified, is not the same thing as the chair itself. When I speak of the Victorian chair with the horsehair upholstery standing in the northwest corner of my study, and even when I further specify that it is made of walnut of the finest grain, I find it difficult to relieve my fatigue by resting on this description, although the object itself has frequently served this purpose. The difference, the absolute NON-IDENTITY of the object and its symbol must be reasonably clear to most sane people.

A symbol, roughly, is a sign which stands for something. The word *chair,* the picture 🪑, or a cabinetmaker's working drawing may all stand for an object and be meaningful to most English-speaking people who are familiar with chairlike objects through personal experience. These signs stand for meaningful, experienced objects and, hence, are symbols. The road sign ⟨S⟩ is a symbol for curves ahead and is ignored at the driver's peril. Words, verbal symbols, that stand for objects and events are, perhaps, the most widely used of these meaningful signs. Mathematical signs, graphic and plastic signs, nonverbal noises such as cheers and music, and gestures may become symbols, PROVIDED they stand for something so far as the receiver of the message is concerned. Signs may, however, be used as if they were symbols and yet stand for nothing. Such signs are meaningless. Korzybski (1948) illustrates the meaningless sign in the following question: If the temperature of this pencil is 60 degrees, what is the temperature of one of its subatomic particles? Here we see that although *temperature* is a perfectly good symbol when applied to the pencil as a whole, it is meaningless when it is applied to one of the subatomic particles, because temperature is a function of the speed of interaction of these particles and hence has no meaning when it is applied to a single one of them.

This relationship between symbol and object provides a clue to the existence of at least two different kinds of reality. Objects and events may occur in what we shall call *objective reality* as well as in what we shall hereinafter refer to as *symbolic reality*. Consider the chair, the physical object, as it stands in the corner. Consider also the word *chair* as we may say it or write it. Both have a kind of reality. The physical chair may be moved, refinished, reupholstered, sat upon, and put to a variety of uses. It may stub our toe in the dark, or it may bring us an unexpected financial windfall when it is sold as an antique. This object, the chair, exists *out there* in objective reality on what Korzybski (1948) calls the *unspeakable level*. By this he means NOT that we cannot speak about it, for we can—in fact, we just have. He means that the words we use to speak about the chair are not its existence. These words are not the chair's characteristics; they represent but are not the things we do to the chair or the things the chair can do for us. The words we use to speak about the chair are simply symbols. They form a reality of their own, but they are not the objective reality of the chair *out there*.

The words we use to speak about the chair may be organized into a dynamic structure which we label *symbolic reality*. Now within this structure of symbolic reality we may discuss the chair. We may consider whether to have it reupholstered or to sell it as an antique. We may feel that it has such sentimental value, ugly as it is, that we wish to keep it. We may reach some conclusions about the chair in symbolic reality. We may then decide to act upon these symbolic conclusions and perform some objective behavioral operation on the chair, but this can be performed only by moving into the arena of objective reality on the unspeakable level.

4. *Interaction of symbolic and objective reality*

This translation of symbolic reality into objective reality has certain basic implications for guidance. The counseling process, which is one of the major devices used in guidance, depends in a large measure on the fact that symbolic reality and objective reality interact and on the capacity of human beings to make the necessary translations from one to another. Just as a poet can translate an ode to his lady fair into a kiss for the lady herself and reverse the process by translating the ecstasy of the kiss into another publishable ode, so the guidance practitioner can facilitate the conversion of the client's problem stated in symbolic reality into a symbolic solution which the client then translates into objective behavior in objective reality. This differentiation of symbolic from objective reality is essential to an understanding of human behavior and to a grasp of guidance practices which are designed to enhance it.

The distinction between symbolic and objective reality and between symbolic and objective behavior remains fairly clear so long as we are talking about physical things such as chairs, tables, trees, or people on the one hand and words and symbols on the other. The distinction loses some of its clarity, however, when we begin to consider thoughts, feelings, dreams, and the like. What are these events?

To consider this issue we must return to our ideas about events. An event has been described as an occurrence in which two or more objects change their relationship to one another. Let us consider such an occurrence. Let the reader imagine a group of young children marching around the block of a suburban residential area. Some of the children have toy drums which they beat in a more or less regular cadence; others have toy horns which they blow with agonizing irregularity. The leader of the marching column carries a flag. A few ride on bicycles or tricycles which have had red, white, and blue crepe paper laced through the wheel spokes. All march in a solemn, disorganized fashion, herded along by a few proud parents who carry the little ones too small to toddle. It is a bright sunny morning: the Fourth of July.

Here we have an event. Before the march started, this group of children was an unstructured aggregate of individuals participating in events of their own. Through the efforts of the adults they were organized into new relationships with each other and became a new event, an event an observer might label *a parade*. The marching column of children is an event in objective reality. The physical facts of the column, its movement, its noise, all represent objective behavior of the children and are elements of an event in objective reality. The label *Fourth of July Parade* which may be given to it by the observer is, however, a symbolic event.

The energy of the sound and reflected light from the parade as well as the energy of the sounds and reflected light from the small segment of the suburban world surrounding the children impinges upon the nervous systems of the ears and eyes of the observer and stimulates electrochemical activity throughout his total nervous structure. He becomes aware of the exaggerated strut of that little boy and of the panicky hustling of the little girl in the red pinafore who can't keep up with the crowd. All of these sights and sounds energize the observer's receptor mechanism, causing new relationships to be established therein. On the microscopic and submicroscopic levels these neural activities become events in objective reality. This neural behavior activates muscular, glandular, skeletal, and other changes in the observer. These too are part of objective reality.

At this point, however, other behavioral mechanisms participate in the event. Memories of other parades are etched on the response systems of the observer; not only the memories of the physical circumstances of earlier parades, but also recollections of earlier feelings and attitudes of the observer. Emotional and intellectual responses to earlier experiences with Fourths of July, patriotism, and the naive enthusiasms of children, to political speeches and saluting the flag each morning in elementary school, have also been stored in the memory apparatus of the observer. The neural activity generated by the present passing parade of children energizes these stored memories in such a way as to involve them in the total experience.

The observer now begins to think about the parade and its meaning. He not only thinks about it as an intellectual exercise, but he simultaneously feels about it. It becomes an emotional experience. Both cognitive and affective responses are linked at one end to the current objective event and at the other to the reservoir of intellectual and emotional memories. The flood of thought and feeling images which are thus evoked represent a kind of no man's land of reality. If we view only the physical, organic changes which take place in the observer as being the event, we may consider what is happening as an objective event in objective reality. If, on the other hand, we view these images as distinct from the organism's electrochemical changes, we may consider what is happening as a symbolic event in symbolic reality. Here we appear, at this moment in the development of the science of human behavior, to have a choice of constructs. Until such time as the identity of images and the electrochemical changes which accompany them has been clearly established by neurological investigation, we shall tentatively but arbitrarily designate images—both cognitive and affective—as symbolic behavior being performed in symbolic reality.

Our preference here is based upon the utility of such a construct. By allocating images to the symbolic domain we are able to consider more readily some concepts of unreality, fantasy, and insanity. The adequacy of symbolic reality depends upon two essential ingredients: (1) the degree to which the signs used are meaningful symbols for the events which take place in the objective domain, and (2) the degree to which the structural relationships of events in symbolic reality coincide with the structural relationships found among these symbolized events in objective reality.

As indicated earlier, some signs may not be symbols; that is, they may be unrelated to events in objective reality, or they may present so restricted a picture of the objective domain as to be meaningless. This state of affairs is poignantly illustrated by the case of a small boy, no more than two years old, who wandered from his own back yard to a hammock next door where a new neighbor was reading, and stood there expectantly awaiting some recognition and an exchange of pleasantries. Being no more adept at conversation with small children than the average adult, the neighbor opened the colloquy with the usual "Hello, young man. What's your name?" to which the boy replied, "No! No! Johnny."

After assuring himself that the child actually thought that his name was No! No! Johnny, the neighbor dealt with more pressing matters such as what Johnny was going to do with the large stick he held in his hand (he was planning to break it over the man's head) and had he been to the nearby seashore that summer (he had not). This social exchange came to an abrupt close on the strident notes of a mother's voice calling, "No! No! Johnny, don't hit the man with that stick. Come here this instant!" It was, of course, immediately evident why the sign *No! No! Johnny* had become associated in the child's mind as a symbol representing himself. Further inquiry revealed that almost every conversational exchange between the boy and his mother began with the phrase *No! No! Johnny*, until the child thought that this was his name. Thus the sign *No! No! Johnny* became, for the child, a symbol for himself. Yet this sign symbolized only a highly restricted aspect of the child, namely his relationships with his mother under certain highly specific—if frequent—circumstances. The sign, then, was an inappropriate symbol for the boy as a whole. It was a sign representing almost nothing, hence not a symbol. As long as the boy continued to use the sign as a symbol for himself, and as long as the sign symbolized at best only a highly specific aspect of objective reality, there would be little relationship between the sign and the total reality it was intended to epitomize. Thus the symbolic reality of this child, in very crucial ways for him, had flagrant inadequacies.

5. Unreality

Human beings are so brought up in the use of language symbols that they frequently deal with them in unrealistic ways. Currently (1964) there appears to be an ideological death struggle in progress between *communism* and *democracy*. These signs, embodying many emotional as well as intellectual elements, are intended to symbolize some events occurring in objective reality. One of these signs symbolizes independence, freedom, social values, personal satisfactions, and the like; in short, the good life. But which one? The reader, of course, is pretty certain of his answer depending upon the ardor with which he holds one or another set of beliefs. Essentially, however, there is no entity, no event in the objective domain, that can adequately be symbolized by the signs *democracy* or *communism*. Only by specifying a carefully selected and defined set of circumstances can we label the event *communistic* or *democratic*. Unless we are prepared to detail these specifications, any manipulation of the sign *democracy* or the sign *communism* in thought becomes an exercise in fantasy, unreality, and perhaps unsanity or even insanity. Here the unmodified sign is an inadequate symbol for the objective event.

In order that symbolic reality may become an adequate representation of objective reality it is essential not only that the signs used be symbols for events actually existing in the objective domain, but also that the structural interrelationships of the symbols preserve the structural interrelationships of events in objective reality. Let us consider, for example, the concept of *free elections*. In the U.S.A. (1964) most citizens still have a pretty clear notion of what is meant by the term *free election*. If several individuals are seeking office, they present their cases to the qualified electorate, who judge the candidates' relative desirability on the basis of their arguments, their observed personalities, their party affiliations, and so on. Then, in the privacy of a polling booth that has been surrounded with legal and traditional safeguards, the members of the electorate cast their votes. These votes are counted under rigid conditions to insure honesty and accuracy, and this count becomes the voice of the people of a democratic society expressed in a free election. All of these events and more are encompassed in the symbol *free election* when used by an American. Each of these events is related to every other in objective reality, forming an objective structure. The symbol *free elections* also encompasses a symbolic structure which includes all the symbols for all the events catalogued above.

Notice, however, that the term *free elections* is a highly generalized or, as Korzybski (1948) puts it, a multiordinal, ∞-valued symbol. We may express the general idea of free elections in mathematical-like terms as follows: $E = f(X_i, X_j, X_k \ldots X_n)$ in which E represents the general concept of free elections, f is read *is a function of,* and X is any election-like event. Now if X_i represents a qualified member of the electorate, and if X_{i_1} represents, in Situation 1, individuals of voting age who have paid their poll tax, and who are able to interpret passages from the federal Constitution, and who have hides with very little dark pigmentation, we have one kind of E. If, on the other hand, X_{i_2} represents Situation 2 in which individuals are qualified as voters only by reason of their carrying membership cards in the Communist Party or by reason of having declared themselves members of the Democratic Party in Mississippi, we get another kind of E.

This suggests that the symbols must not only stand for something and for something highly specific, but that they must also be related to each other in the same way that the events which they symbolize are related in the objective domain. Only in this way can the symbolic reality become an adequate representation of the objective reality. When the meaning or the structure of the symbols fails to represent objects and events adequately, the resulting entity is one of several kinds of unreality. When unreality is created intentionally, when the meaning or structure of the symbols is distorted to achieve some purpose, we have what might be called *fantasy.* When the meaning or structure is distorted unintentionally by a fairly substantial part of a social group, as it often is in the case of custom, tradition, and ritualistic observance, we have what might be called *unsanity.* When an individual unintentionally distorts reality in his own idiosyncratic way without reference to the symbolic usages of his society, and when he attempts to act upon the distorted symbols he has created, we have what might be called *insanity.*

Reality, then, is a specifiable relationship between symbolic and objective events wherein the meaning and structure of the symbols are congruent with the meaning and structure of events in the objective domain. And sanity is the process of acting in objective reality upon the conclusions reached through the manipulation of realistic symbols.

6. *The reactional biography*

Let us turn now from the consideration of objects and events in general to those events which constitute psychological behavior. As suggested earlier in this chapter, human behavior may be viewed as a continuous stream of events. The events in which an individual participates may be either objective or symbolic events. As behavior is performed, the symbolic and objective acts interact with each other. Furthermore, proximate objective events may interact with each other, but the interaction of distant objective events will ordinarily require the mediation of symbolic events. Except where the immediate physical or electrochemical energy of a stimulus evokes a physical response on the part of an organism, it is doubtful that objective events occur without the intervention of some symbolic stimuli.

Symbolic events, on the other hand, appear to interact with one another directly. The interaction, as the term suggests, is a two-way situation. Thus, events in the past can change the meaning and nature of present events, but it is possible also for events in the present to change the meaning of past events. In the first instance, where past events shape the meaning of present behavior, we are simply dealing with what we commonly know as learning. A child who through past familiarity with the situation has learned to produce the symbol *6* when confronted with the symbolic stimulus $2 \times 3 =$, will, when confronted with the same stimulus, produce the same symbolic response instead of the infinite number of other responses which might be produced. The reversal of the process, the case where present experience changes the meaning and hence the stimulus value of a past event, is illustrated by the college student who all through her college career found fault with her college experiences and strongly expressed the view that she couldn't wait to graduate and get away from the place. On the day of her graduation, she informed her counselor that aside from her encounters with him and a few of her professors and friends the events of her college experiences had been drab and disappointing indeed. Several years later, at her wedding, she separated herself from the festivities of the reception to seek out the counselor, who was a guest, and urge him to talk to her younger sister and convince her to go to the same college instead of the one the younger girl was planning to attend. When the counselor confronted the girl with all the difficulties and dissatisfactions she seemed to have experienced, the bride expressed amazement that the counselor had viewed it in this way. The events in her college experience as she now viewed them appeared to be quite different from the evaluation she had placed on these events as they were happening. And she was now prepared to act on the basis of this new view of these past events to the extent of trying to get her sister to attend the very school she had once found so distasteful. This suggests the way in which present events may interact with symbolic events of the past and change the nature of those past events.

All these events of the past, both objective and symbolic, as well as the events in the immediate present we will call the *reactional biography*. The reactional biography, then, is the total experience of an individual up to and including the momentary present events in which the individual is participating. It includes events in both the objective and symbolic domain. This concept of the reactional biography, originally suggested by Kantor (1933), is central to an understanding of psychological behavior. We shall have occasion to consider the role of the reactional biography more fully in Chapter Two, as the discussion of the nature of psychological behavior is expanded.

Let us turn now to a discussion of the interaction between events occurring at the present moment and future events. Consider the case of a high school junior who, for one reason or another, decides that he wishes to become a physician. Here he produces, in the symbolic reality of the present, an event *wishing to be a physician* which can occur OBJECTIVELY only in the future. The present event, *wishing to be a physician*, produces at this present moment a future symbolic event, *being a physician*. Now, symbolically, the student backs up in time from the future symbolic event. To be a medical practitioner, he will need to go to medical school; to go to medical school, he will need to go to college; to go to college, he will need to receive high grades in his courses in high school. This brings him, symbolically, to the chemistry homework he is now doing. Now, in objective reality, he attacks the mastery of the periodic tables with new vigor.

Here we have what may well be one of the most significant factors in guidance: the impact of future events on present behavior. The mechanism by which this impact comes about is anticipation. The reactional biography of an individual consists not only of events in which he has participated directly but also of events in which others have participated and which have been communicated to him. These vicarious experiences include not only a knowledge of the overt behavior which was performed but also a sense of the emotional component of the behavior. In his own personal experience the individual learns that certain acts have certain consequences and that these consequences are accompanied by certain satisfying or disturbing feelings. From these personal experiences he is able to generalize the kinds of acts that lead to satisfying consequences and those that lead to disturbing consequences. He knows what it is to be satisfied or disturbed. He can and does apply these generalizations to the vicarious experiences gleaned from the behavior of others and establishes some behavior classifications that become, in a sense, an internal probability table. From these he is able to derive some notions of the likelihood of this behavior's or that's leading to satisfying or disturbing consequences. In this way the individual can anticipate the consequences of his current actions. The anticipation of future consequences serves as a standard against which present behavior can be evaluated. Anticipation, then, is the mechanism by which future behavior (symbolic) determines present behavior.

Figure 1 graphically depicts the interactions of past, present, and future events—both objective and symbolic—that make up the behavioral flow we know as life. The first portion of this, that portion encompassing the past and the present, is called the reactional biography. Proximate objective events in the past and present, shown as O in the figure, interact with each other and are shown as overlapping solid circles. Symbolic events, shown in Figure 1 as broken circles

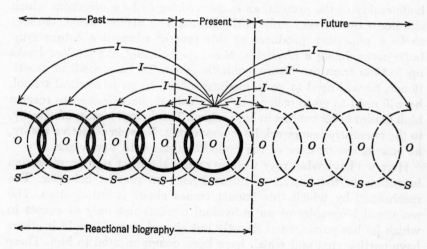

Figure 1. The Interaction of Events in Psychological Behavior. In the present, at any given moment, immediate objective events (O) interact with concurrent symbolic events (S). Objective events can also interact with proximate objective events in the immediate past. Symbolic events in the present interact not only with concurrent and proximate symbolic and objective events, shown by overlapping broken circles, but also with distant symbolic and objective events in the past and the future (I).

labeled S, interact with concurrent objective events and with proximate and distant events both objective and symbolic. This is shown
by the overlapping of the concurrent symbolic and objective events
and by the interaction lines which join each symbolic event with
related elements. The impact of the future events upon some present
activity is represented by the interaction lines joining the present
objective-symbolic event with the future symbolic events.

We see, then, that events in the past and in the present, both
symbolic and objective, interact to form the individual's reactional
biography. The individual's present behavior interacts with symbolic
events in the future by means of anticipation of the most probable
consequences, thus modifying present symbolic and objective events
and hence modifying the individual's reactional biography. This reactional biography may, therefore, be viewed as a stream of events
flowing from the individual's past into his future. Changes in the flow
can be achieved by the external intervention of a guidance practitioner, say, only through the modification of present behavior, since
this is the only behavior accessible at any given instant in time. This
intervention, however, operating as it does on both the symbolic and
objective events of the present, can influence the individual's future
as well as his interactions with past events. Any intervention must
take place, from moment to moment, on the accessible ongoing behavior. It is this present behavior as it is performed, this immediate event,
that we must next examine.

7. *The behavior product*

Every behavioral event in which an individual participates is made
up of two primary elements and a secondary element derived from
the interaction of these two. The interaction of these elements may
be represented by the term *behavior product*. This term is designed
to convey the notion of a dynamic process involving the interaction
among the basic and derived components. It encompasses in its meaning the manifold relationships among all experienced events of the
past and future reacting with present circumstances. It includes the
individual behaving organism and the environmental context within
which he functions. The behavior product represents an amalgam of
symbolic and objective reality.

The two basic elements in the behavior product are the individual's
reactional biography and the environmental context within which
behavior takes place. The reactional biography has already been described as the total objective and symbolic experience of the individ-

ual, up to and including the present events in which he is participating. The *context element* of the behavior product represents all environmental circumstances within which the behavior takes place. These will include the physical surroundings made up of interrelated physical objects and events; they include the meteorological and psychological climate, the persons and events in the environment, and the societal history. In short, the context element of the behavior product encompasses the total behavioral environment, including the individual himself, for the individual is a significant factor in his own environment.

Out of this context there emerge, from time to time and from moment to moment, objects and events that are capable of stimulating the individual to action. These we shall call *stimulus objects* or *stimulus events*. Stimulus objects and events may, of course, be physical objects or events involving physical objects. They may also be symbolic events such as words uttered by another person. These stimulus events, however, do not need to come from out there, outside the individual's skin. Stimulus events may be thoughts or feelings, symbolic events, occurring inside the performer. (This suggests that the context element, the environment so to speak, is as much a part of the individual as he is a part of it. There can be no clear line of demarcation—as will be shown later—that, even at a given instant, clearly differentiates the environment from the nature of the individual.)

Which objects and events in the context element will emerge as stimulus objects and events is determined in part by the characteristics of the objects and events themselves, in part by the individual's experience with these classes of objects and events, and in part by the momentary structural relationships of all the components of the behavior product. These factors are considered in more detail in Chapter Two.

Let us turn from the context element for a moment and reexamine the reactional biography. The reactional biography of an individual is composed, among other things, of a complex of *physiological mechanisms:* organs and systems operating to receive stimuli and to perform acts (both objective and symbolic) and to store the consequences of these activities. At any given moment, these physiological mechanisms are prepared to receive certain messages and to produce certain responses. These momentarily available reactions may be called the *response repertory.*

These two primary elements, the reactional biography and the context element, interact to form the derived element, the *stimulus function* (Kantor, 1933, p. 21). The stimulus function thus produced by the interaction of stimulus objects and events from the environmental context with the response repertory of the reactional biography may be viewed in two ways: the stimulus function may be considered as the way in which an object or event acts upon an individual, or it may be viewed as the essential meaning attributed to the object or event by the individual. A combination of both views operating simultaneously gives us a workable grasp of this derived element and suggests the notion that the stimulus function emerges from the interaction of components of both the reactional biography and the environmental context.

This concept of the stimulus function carries with it the notion that psychological behavior is not performed in response to stimulus objects and events but rather in response to the stimulus functions generated by the interactions of the available response repertory and the events. This may be illustrated by the fact that a dish of strawberries does not evoke the same kinds of behavior from all individuals or even from the same individual at different times. If hunger is a part of the individual's available response repertory, this hunger interacting with the dish of strawberries will give this delicacy the stimulus function *something to be eaten,* and the individual will respond accordingly. If, however, the individual has just finished a rich dessert after a heavy meal, or if he has learned to dislike strawberries, or if he has false teeth which collect the seeds to his discomfort, or if he is subject to strawberry rash, the interaction between his response repertory and the berries will yield the stimulus function *something to be avoided;* again, he will act accordingly. Psychological behavior, then, is an interaction between the available response repertory and the *stimulus function* rather than the stimulus object or event. This interaction we call the *behavior product.*

Figure 2 presents a schematic representation of the behavior product. The basic elements, the reactional biography and the environmental context, are shown as E_1 and E_2 while the derived element, the stimulus function, is shown as E' and is formed by the interactions I_S between response repertory and stimuli. Interactions between the behavior repertory and the stimulus functions, I_B, represent the behavior product as we have conceived it here.

It should become clear from the above discussion that several of the components of the basic elements of behavior enter into the behavior product at several different levels. The response repertory, for example, interacts with the stimulus events to generate a stimulus function. Subsequently, the response repertory again interacts, this time with the stimulus function, to produce the behavior product. As

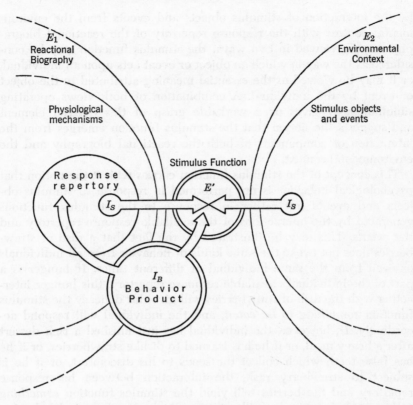

Figure 2. The Behavior Product (first model). The reactional biography of the individual, the first element (E_1) of the behavior product, provides the physiological mechanisms in which is embedded the response repertory. The environmental context, the second primary element (E_2), provides stimulus objects and events. The derived element (E'), the stimulus function, is formed by the interaction (I_S) of the response repertory and the stimulus objects and events. The subsequent interaction (I_B) between the response repertory and the stimulus function yields the behavior product.

these interactions take place, the stimulus functions operate upon the response repertory in ways that modify it, and these modifications reorganize the physiological mechanisms and, in turn, the reactional biography. Since the reactional biography is, itself, a component of the environmental context, changes in it result in changes in the context element, and so on. The entire picture of the behavior product must be seen as a dynamic, interrelated, interacting structure, changing from instant to instant, in constant flux, yet retaining a general orderly structure which moves forward in a steady stream through time.

Changes may be introduced into the general structure and flow by external intervention such as guidance. In order to accomplish this it is necessary to modify an event in one of the elements or to change the relationships established among the components of the basic elements. This requires that guidance practitioners have an intimate understanding of the components of the basic elements which make up the behavior product. Chapter Two considers these components in greater detail.

TWO

Components of the behavior product [1]

◆◆

Human behavior appears to be composed of two primary elements and a secondary element derived from the interaction of the first two. According to the behavior model being described here, the primary elements are the reactional biography and the environmental context; the third element in the process, the stimulus function, comes into being through the interaction of these primary elements. The behavior product, which is the unit of behavior used in this model, is formed through the reciprocal action of the reactional biography and the stimulus function.

1. *Uniqueness of the primary elements*

One of the major difficulties in this formulation is the apparent lack of stable, static units. Even the two primary elements are only modderately distinctive. When, for example, we consider the context element as being composed of all aspects of the environmental context within which the behavior product is performed, we can not exclude the individual performer himself. As an illustration of this, we may consider two children at play. Let us say that we wish to observe the behavior of $child_1$. We shall consider him the performer and the subject of our observations. Now both children mount a seesaw. We wish to investigate what $child_1$ does in this context to make the toy operate. In this behavior product, the physical entity of $child_1$ is, of course, a part of the environmental context. His weight relative to the weight of $child_2$ determines, in part, what the see-saw

[1] This chapter is an expansion and modification of a behavior model published earlier by the present author (Weitz, 1961).

22

and he will do. Similarly, his reactional biography becomes a part of the context element insofar as it includes previous experience with see-saws. The question then becomes: Where does the child leave off and his environment begin?

The air about us may appear to be an aspect of our environment. As it enters our lungs when we inhale, does it continue to be part of our environment or is it a part of us? Does it continue as a part of the environment when we extract the oxygen and transport it through our systems, or when we combine it with carbon to provide our heat and energy? At some point the environmental air becomes us. What happens when we exhale the carbon dioxide? Do we become our environment? And at precisely what point does this happen? When the carbon dioxide is formed? when it enters the bloodstream? the lungs? the nasal passages? or exactly at the point where it leaves our bodies and enters the general atmosphere? What happens when a plant absorbs the carbon dioxide which we exhaled? Do we become a part of the plant? Is there a part of the reader in that petunia? Are you the petunia or is the petunia you?

The difficulty here, of course, is that we are trying to label a dynamic process with static symbols. In the events described, these things do occur. Our language, shifty as it is, is incapable at this stage in its development of coping with these dynamic transformation processes. Some branches of mathematical language give promise of providing a symbolic system which may be able to differentiate between the reader and a petunia or between a $child_1$ and the see-saw event while still retaining evidence of their individual identities. Perhaps some mathematically sophisticated psychologist will make the necessary translations without, it is to be hoped, the self-conscious mathematical affectations one finds in so many behavior models.

It is enough to suggest here that the reader can differentiate between himself and a petunia, even if only in unspecific terms. He can recognize, in a general sort of way, where his environment leaves off and where he, as a psychological individual, begins, although he retains all the while the notion that he is a part of the environmental context in which he performs and that it is a part of him. An understanding of this dynamic state of affairs is essential to the argument that follows; the demarcation of clearer boundaries, although desirable, is not essential at this stage in our thinking.

2. *Limits of behavior products*

In the study of psychology and especially in that area of the science which we call guidance, we are concerned with the observation, understanding, and control of behavior products. The practice of guidance would, therefore, seem to require that we be able to distinguish one behavior product from another. It would seem to be highly desirable that we be able to set limits and boundaries on behavior products.

Psychologists focusing their attentions on highly specialized reactions have used the model $S \to R$ for a unit of behavior in which S represents a highly specific stimulus and R represents a highly specific response. This model suggests that in any unit of behavior the stimulus acts upon or evokes the response. Later the interaction $S \longleftrightarrow R$ suggested the two-way action involved in a unit of behavior: the stimulus (S) acts on the response (R) while it, in turn, acts on the stimulus. So long as we confine ourselves to the observation of minute bits of behavior such as the rapid withdrawal of the hand when it comes in contact with a hot object, say a steam radiator, we can use this model and almost see the beginning and end of the piece of behavior. Such minute units of behavior can appear to have boundaries and limits. Other formulations, which appear to provide for more elaborate behavior, involve the organism (O) in the model thus: $S \longleftrightarrow O \longleftrightarrow R$.

One of the more interesting models of behavior is the too often neglected notion of the *behavior segment* suggested by Kantor (1933), who has this to say about it:

> The behavior life of an organism is absolutely continuous as long as the individual is alive. There is never a moment that it is not interacting with things. . . . This fact brings to the psychologist a serious problem, since rigor of scientific description always demands the isolation of a distinct unit of observational fact.
>
> To meet the demand we bring to our aid the conception of a behavior segment. If we think of the continuous activity of the organism as a line, then we may cut it into parts or segments. Each of the segments represents one of the simplest analyzable units of an interactional event. It consists of a single stimulus and its correlated response. (Kantor, 1933, p. 21.)

Kantor then specifies that the responses in the behavior segment need to be further analyzed into *reaction systems* (*rs*). These he identifies as the simplest action unit comprising a response. He states, "As the very term implies, the reaction system is a complex behavior act,

SIMPLE RESPONSE

STIMULUS ◄―――――――――――――――――► RESPONSE
(Hot Object)   (Simple Jerk rs)

COMPLEX RESPONSE

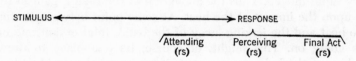

STIMULUS ◄―――――――――――――――――► RESPONSE

                    Attending   Perceiving   Final Act
                      (rs)   (rs)   (rs)

Figure 3. Kantor's Models of Simple and Complex Responses. In the simple response, a single reaction system (rs) comprises the response; in a complex response, multiple reaction systems are involved.

but it is the lowest analyzable integral action that the organism performs." (Kantor, 1933, pp. 22–23.) Kantor diagrams simple and complex response patterns in the behavior segment as shown in Figure 3.

Having established the reaction system as the simplest analyzable unit comprising a response, Kantor then elaborates this model by differentiating between precurrent and final response patterns. He classifies his behavior segments in several dimensions: process-operation, protracted-momentary, witting-unwitting. This elaboration suggests that the behavior segment which started out as the irreducible unit is itself made up of subparticles and that it is not easy to draw boundaries around them in such a way as to isolate one from the other.

Take even the "simple" behavior segment involving the interaction between the organism and a hot object. As the organism approaches the hot object, quanta of energy from the object impinge upon the submicroscopic elements of the receptor cells of the organism's extremities. The impact of this energy excites the cells. (This, of course, leaves out certain electrochemical-physical steps in the process.) Here we have a "first" response. The excitement of the cells immediately stimulated by the heat is transmitted in a decreasing gradient to adjacent cells. A chain of stimuli and responses is thus generated. At the appropriate nerve ganglia, the energy is transferred from the receptor system to effector-transmission and later to effector-operation systems (nerves and muscles, etc.). This involves further chained series of stimulus and response interactions. Now it may be argued that so long as these interactions represent the activities of a single cell and not the organism as a whole, this is not psychological behavior but rather a sequence of physiological responses. At some point, however, the total organism is involved, and the response is psychological—even as Kantor would describe it. But at what point? Surely Kantor would not wish to push the analysis back to the point where the unit of heat energy activated the submicroscopic bit of neural tissue. The speed with which neural transmission takes place, while not instantaneous, is very rapid indeed. Thus the activation of the total organism follows close upon the impact of the heat. At some point between the impact of the heat and the jerking away of the hand, total organismic behavior is going on. This might, of course, be one place to draw the boundary of the behavior segment, if we could clearly identify it. In terms of our present knowledge of behavior, however, the locus for this boundary is not clear, although it must be clear that it is some place below the level of the heat ⟷ jerk interaction.

Now consider the other boundary. Does the behavior segment end —do we take our snip, so to speak—at the point where the withdrawal jerk begins or where it ends? Or do we wait until the organism is aware of the action it has taken? Perhaps we need to wait until the organism says to itself, "Yipe! I'd better keep my fingers away from that hot stove in the future!" That is, do we wait until after awareness of learning has occurred? In short, we find it difficult, if not impossible, to describe this "simplest analyzable unit of an interactional event" in terms of its limits and boundaries, for it seems to have no clearly identifiable beginning or end.

Were it not for the fact that Kantor seems to suggest that there ARE boundaries for his behavior segment, this term would be a happy label for one of the central concepts of the present behavior model. Because of these implied limits and boundaries, however, it became necessary to utilize another term, *behavior product*, which is intended to imply much of what Kantor had in mind but, additionally, to include the notions of limitlessness as well as the notion of amalgamation with and participation in the next sequential act and even in distant acts.

The behavior product, then, is not an entity but a process having no static boundaries. It may, however, be subjected to analysis, as are other processes, by giving it symbolic boundaries, provided we remind ourselves constantly that it is not the objective behavior product itself which has limits, but only the symbolic conception of it. This exists only in the realm of symbolic reality. Thus as we talk about the order and structure of behavior products, we must remember that this is a dynamic, not static, structure. Both the relationships and the functions of the parts change with respect to each other over time. Order in this dynamic structure means not a sequence of bounded segments, but orderly interaction.

3. *The context element*

An essential aspect of every behavior product is the external state of affairs which we have designated the *context element* or the environmental context. This context element is composed of a number of substructures, of which the most important are: (1) the physical world, (2) the cultural matrix, (3) the psycho-social climate, and (4) the behaving organism itself. Let us examine these components of the context element in greater detail.

The PHYSICAL WORLD is made up of the time-space continuum and the objects and events which fill it. This component of the context element is governed by such physical laws as gravity, entropy, relativity, and the like. In psychological behavior, objects and events interact with the response repertory and with each other to produce, for example, such phenomena as recency, frequency, speed, and sequence of events. The order in which objects are arrayed relative to the observer places this one nearer and hence more recent than that one. As one walks past a line of trees, the last one passed is nearer to the observer at the moment of temporal ordering and hence most recent. If, in two lanes of automobiles passing an observer, stream A has three examples of makes X, Y, and Z for each example of make P, whereas stream B has six examples of makes X, Y, and Z for each one of make P, the observer would say that make P showed up more frequently in line A than in line B; if line B moved twice as fast as line A, the observer might conclude that the frequency, with respect to time, of make P was the same in both lanes. These illustrations suggest the ways in which the ordering of events with respect to an observer produce the specialized physical phenomena of recency and frequency.

The physical world produces other phenomena as well. Climate may interact with the organism to produce readily observable psycho-biological states. Continued warm, humid climate induces lassitude; cool, dry climate appears to induce vigorous activity. Extended, stable weather conditions induce boredom; changing seasons induce interest. The density of physical objects in an area determines not only possible movement and direction, but also psychological mood. The densely packed city slum and the overgrown jungle evoke different attitudinal behavior from that called forth by the spacious suburb or the open glade. Thus the physical world contributes to the determination not only of our physical interactions with the objects about us, but also of our physiological and psychological interactions as well.

The CULTURAL MATRIX is a second important component of the environmental context within which behavior is performed. The cultural matrix is composed of societal history and is governed by laws of custom, tradition, and group behavior. In the behavior product the cultural matrix interacts with responses to produce such phenomena as language, value judgments, and institutionalized behavior. Culture influences behavior in at least two major ways. Through the historical refinement of certain general types of activity, the culture provides a catalogue of normative behavior suitable for performance on specialized occasions. Customs, values, and language are among the more obvious examples of behavior which have been refined and modified by history and made available to the individual by his culture. The culture also determines what behavior will be performed at a given instant, crystallizing the psychological climate in such a way as to make one stimulus vivid and evocative and another pale and inoperative. Kantor makes this concept of cultural influences a central theme in his formulation:

Anthropological conditions not only play a great part in the development of actions, but they also influence their later performance. In other words, to understand why individuals believe, speak, create and destroy things one must know the kinds of anthropological or civilizational conditions under which they perform their behavior. These conditions constitute the inevitable auspices of all human conduct. (Kantor, 1933, p. 52.)

Language represents a good illustration of the influence of culture upon psychological behavior. *Homo sapiens* probably originated some 50,000 years ago, around the close of the Mousterian cultural period. It is probable that his early language behavior consisted principally of gestures and uncodified grunts. He required some 40,000 years for the development of a definite written language (Cohn, 1961, p. 504). During this extended period of time, man was not only learning to form the coded signs and symbols that comprise a language, but also discovering that these signs and symbols could serve as stimuli to the actions of others as well as to his own behavior.

Language behavior is designed to communicate information that will evoke some responsive gesture on the part of the receiver of the message. This process of transmitting and receiving information and responding to messages has the effect of conditioning the receiver to modes of behavior that are common to the transmitter.

As we know from the deafferentation experiments in animals and sensory deprivation experiments in humans, the living brain can not function adequately without an input and the living human brain can not function to produce characteristically human behavior without having received coded inputs from other persons. Persons are programmed, controlled, and stabilized by experiences with other persons. (Colby, 1961, p. 367.)

The kind of responses that a person produces in a given set of circumstances, then, are, in part at least, controlled, stabilized, and programmed by the input, principally in the form of language, provided by other persons. But the language itself is the product of the interactions of persons over a long historical succession of events. In the process of development, the refinements placed upon language that make it an appropriate medium for communicating certain types of information simultaneously limit its stimulus value.

Insidiously, man's invented verbal communication modalities exerted restricted forces through their formality and because of the relative paucity of expression forms in equating sense impressions with physical change. The divergence of sense-data from language results from the fact that even under optimum conditions the organism samples only segments of the impinging energy spectrum generated by the environment; that is, vision, hearing, and so on represent only punctuate bands of energy in the continuous energy spectrum. Moreover under conditions of existence as goal-directed systems, the organism does not respond with maximal efficiency to any *single modality* of stimulation. The living organism responds to that which, through past experience, is immediately significant. (Cohn, 1961, pp. 505–506.)

As a manifestation of the culture, then, language plays a role in determining certain large areas of psychological behavior. Moreover, it can determine a specific behavioral act at a given moment, as when it serves as an immediate stimulus. Because of its limitations in conveying the full range of energy stimulating an individual at a given instant, it serves to limit the kinds of responses that can be made to it. Other aspects of language and the roles they play in psychological behavior will be considered later. Here we are concerned only with language as an example of the impact of culture on psychological phenomena.

Behavior is also influenced by other cultural manifestations than language. Custom, for example, plays a significant role both in the kinds of behavior available to be performed and in the specific act at a particular instant. From a biological point of view, the feeding behavior of the human organism is susceptible to great variation as far as the time of eating is concerned. It matters very little to the physical health and development of the human animal whether he feeds seldom or frequently in the course of a day, as long as the nutritional intake is adequate to provide fuel for his labors and the substances essential to his proper functioning and development. In middle-class United States, however, feeding the human animal has been subdivided into a three-meal-a-day operation; in cultures presided over by the British Crown, a fourth meal, tea, is part of the tribal ritual of feeding. A Britisher in the United States at the magic hour of tea time becomes uneasy if he is not fed, although he may have learned to accept the local customary substitute of cocktails. The American abroad, on the other hand, finds the British feeding sequence disconcerting.

Custom has established a reservoir of feeding responses appropriate to certain time-sequence stimuli although unrelated to basic biological needs. Under the proper circumstances, the responses are elicited with machine-like precision. When circumstances change, however, when the custom no longer operates, behavior becomes disorganized. The individual becomes uneasy. New responses which are appropriate to the new culture need to be found and learned.

When two or more incompatible modes of response are available to an individual, he needs to make a choice of performing one or the other. Under such circumstances his choices are more often than not determined by that aspect of the cultural matrix which we refer to as cultural values. The young athlete, running a race which he can win by calling upon his reserve of energy or lose by continuing his same steady pace, will make a choice depending on the value system imposed on him by his culture. The American high school athlete will call on his reserve energy and try to win. He does this spontaneously, with no observable evidence and certainly no awareness of having made a choice. The value system of his culture that honors victory in a competitive society has, in a sense, made the choice for him. There are, however, primitive societies in which cooperation is valued over competition. The young athletes here see to it that all runners cross the finish line together. Any excessive display of competitive superiority, such as winning a race, is placed low on the value scale. Thus the primitive runner, just as his American counterpart, has his actions determined for him by the values of his culture. This is not to say that, from time to time, highly individualistic members of a society may not violate the values of their culture or interpret them in highly idiosyncratic ways and still survive within the society or even be honored by reason of their individuality. This merely suggests that, in the main, cultural values govern many of the choices that are made.

Culture, then, is the womb in which behavior is nourished. From the matrix of language, customs, values, and other cultural products, human behavior emerges. The kinds of behavior that can be performed are manufactured and made available by the sweep of cultural history; the particular response which is evoked at any instant in time is limited, to a marked degree, by the momentary state of affairs in the cultural component of the environmental context.

The PSYCHO-SOCIAL CLIMATE, the third factor in the environmental context, is composed of the relationships of individuals with each other and with the cultural matrix. It is characterized by such interactions as love, affection, aggression, affiliation, nurturance, cooperation, competition, and the like. In combination with the cultural matrix, the psycho-social climate determines the meaning of a stimulus and the appropriateness of a response. Hence, this combination of the psycho-social climate and the cultural matrix determines the probability that a given response will occur. The supplications one offers up to the officials at a football game on a Saturday afternoon are inappropriate and hence unlikely to occur in church the next day.

The psycho-social climate created by the interactions with other persons in the environmental context depends not so much on their physical presence as it does upon what they represent. The children's room of a city library may be a hubbub of disorganized horseplay under the direction of one children's librarian, but becomes the model of quiet childish literary adventure under the watchful eye of another. To be sure, the differences in psycho-social climate induced by the two librarians have their sources in the historical interrelationships between the children and the two librarians. Yet this, it must be remembered, is the way in which psycho-social climate, as well as all other psychological states, is created.

The INDIVIDUAL himself represents the fourth factor in the context element. He is, most obviously, a physical event in the environmental context, and hence subject to the laws which govern physical phenomena. More important, however, is the fact that the individual brings his reactional biography into the environmental context. This reactional biography is governed by the laws of learning insofar as psychological reactions are concerned, but also by physical and physiological principles as they relate to physical and physiological behavior. The reactional biography determines the individual's behavior repertory and hence the availability of a response at a given moment. The behavior of an individual at any given moment determines his readiness to respond in certain ways to various classes of stimuli. Thus the behavior that is current at the moment of making a new response determines not only the availability of a particular response but also the probability that particular stimulus objects and events will take on particular stimulus functions. The student who is currently preoccupied with the charms of the redhead two seats away is likely to perform

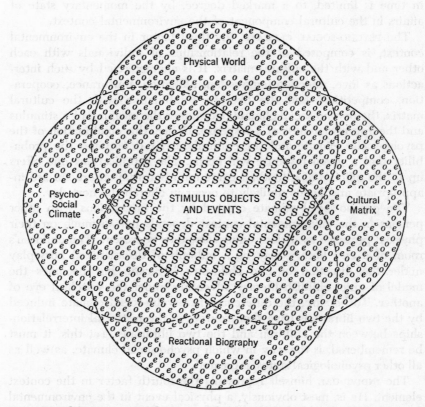

Figure 4. The Environmental Context Element. The physical world, the cultural matrix, the psycho-social climate, and the individual's reactional biography represent the overlapping components of the environmental context. Each is composed of a wide variety of objects and events (*o* and *e*). From time to time, by reason of their special characteristics, the imprint of the culture upon them, and their special relationships with the individual, certain objects take on the properties of stimuli (*S*).

a different response to the stimulus *What are the factors of $a^2 + 2ab + b^2$?* from the one performed by the student whose current attention is innocently focused upon the peculiar effects a buzzing fly has on the eccentric mannerisms of the teacher.

These four components, the physical world, the cultural matrix, the psycho-social climate, and the individual himself, then, are the four factors of major significance in the context element. They may be viewed schematically in Figure 4. The overlapping of these components suggests that, from moment to moment, a component may be first one then another kind of event, depending upon how the observer views the total complex.

From time to time, certain events in one of the components of the environmental context emerge with sufficient force to become stimuli to behavior. The central interactions in Figure 4 represent these stimulus objects and events. The stimulus power that adheres to some objects and events at a given moment and not to others derives from their physical properties, the imprint of the culture upon them, and their historical relationship to the individual. These characteristics that convert some events into stimuli will be considered in Section 6 of the present chapter, where the discussion fits more naturally.

4. The reaction system

Operating within the context element is the individual himself. As suggested in Section 3, the individual is a part of the context element in terms of his physical entity, his reactional biography, and his immediate, current behavior. However, from the point of view of the behavior model being presented here, we may consider the individual as having an existence separate from, although simultaneously a part of, the environmental context. Parenthetically it should be mentioned that this separation of the individual from his context can be accomplished only in symbolic reality; since the structure does not exist in objective reality, we must accept what follows as a piece of intentional fantasy promulgated in an effort to make more vivid the relationships and structures that do exist. We shall replace the individual in the context that gives him his individuality at that point in the discussion where the reunion will support the argument. Here, however, let us examine the individual as an entity separate from his surroundings.

The individual psychological reacting system is what it is by reason of the physiological mechanisms operating within the structure of the reactional biography. Thus the responses performed at any instant in time reflect a physiological potential modified by historical experience. The individual, then, is the product of his interacting experiences including his past and the current ones. We may, therefore, consider the terms *reactional biography* and *indiviaual* to be essentially synonymous.

Within the framework of the reactional biography there exists a structure capable of performing certain functions. This operating structure we have called the physiological mechanisms. Among the many agents that influence man's behavior, his physical structure and physiological functions are fundamental. Man's more obvious structural features are sufficient to suggest the point. Man is upright, standing several feet above the surface of the earth. His view of the world about him and the nature of the stimuli which can energize him thus differ from those, say, of a snake. He is rigidly bilaterally symmetrical; thus his responses are directionally controlled in contrast, say, to those of an octopus or an amoeba. He is mobile, but his mobility is different from the mobility of a bird or a fish. His body may be viewed as a series of rigid segments held together by hinges of limited radius, thus permitting him some flexibility but not the flexibility of an earthworm, for example.

Man's organs and biological systems function in highly specialized ways: the eyes focus and trap light, the ears vibrate to sound waves, the heart circulates fluids about the system delivering nourishment to hungry parts and carrying off their waste products. The nervous system, the skin, the skeletal frame, the glandular structure, and so on, each functions in its own peculiar way. To be sure, the functions of some organs and systems can, when the necessity arises, be taken over by others, as when, for example, the removal of a diseased gall bladder requires that other segments of the system take over its storage function. In the main, however, each organ and system has its own specialized role to play. This is to say that it can be made to operate only in a certain way with only a limited degree of variability. Thus the eye can operate on light of rather limited wavelength: colors beyond the wavelength of violet are not seen; light intensities beyond certain limits are felt as pain. Similarly the range of sound that can be heard is limited in pitch and volume. Psychological behavior is confined within the limits of the range of stimuli the receiving mechanisms are able to admit.

Behavior is limited not only by the stimuli man can receive but also by the range of activities he is capable of performing. The weight he can lift is limited by the force he can introduce into the lever systems of his arms, legs, and back. The sounds he can utter are limited by the size and structure of his lungs, throat, mouth, and so forth. The speed with which he can perform ideational activities is limited by the electrochemical composition of his nervous structure.

Thus the reception of stimuli and the performance of responses depend on the physical and biological nature of man. While he can do many things which are impossible to other creatures, his behavior repertory is less than theirs in many respects. To make up for his limitations in structure and function, man has created machine extensions of himself that permit him to receive more and a greater variety of stimuli and that permit him to perform feats which once seemed so foreign to his nature as to be considered sinful by many.

The simple biological functioning of man's organs is not enough, however, to produce the variety of activity we call psychological behavior. In human behavior we do not have mere performance of physiological function in a structured environment. Each act is performed as a consequence of some previous act. Each act repeats those elements of preceding acts which appear to be appropriate to the new configuration of stimuli. Psychological behavior depends upon experience. Kantor puts it this way:

. . . All psychological interactions are historical; that is, they originate in an individual's contact with things. It is this historical interconnection with objects which distinguishes psychological from biological and physical phenomena. . . . The specific character of a psychological interaction is determined by an individual's prior reactional experience. . . . It is through the behavior details of this reactional biography that the individual develops all of the responses he ever performs. Whatever he can do, his capacities, knowledge, skills, and behavior powers, are engendered in his reactional biography. (Kantor, 1933, p. 44.)

The reactional biography may be seen by an outside observer as the operation of the physiological mechanism within the environmental context. The repetitive nature of these interactions suggests an ordering or regularizing of the functions of the physiological mechanisms. This means that when an operation has been performed once in a given way under a given set of circumstances, it is highly probable that the same or similar operation will be performed again under a similar set of circumstances. The operations are stamped or programmed into the physiological mechanisms as a result of encountered experience. This programming of responses is viewed by Guthrie (1952), for example, as learning. This view of learning holds that when a response is performed in close temporal contiguity with some configuration of stimuli, the repetition of the configuration will again evoke the response.

In this view of learning, motivation, need, drive, and the like simply play the role of developing a state of excitation of the organism sufficient to insure that response energy is available. The excitation must, of course, be relevant to the behavior to be performed. The analogy of the computer is suggestive of this point. The computer is programmed to perform certain operations by means of feeding in certain instruction cards or by prewiring the control board. This may be viewed as previous experience which stamps in the relationships between the stimuli (data cards) and responses (operations). When we now introduce new data by means of cards or tape into the machine, nothing happens until we turn on the switch that provides it with the electrical energy to perform its programmed operations. Note, however, that it is not just any energy that will cause the machine to work, that is, "motivate" it, but only relevant energy. If we build a fire under the machine or drop it from a high building, we transmit energy to it, but this sort of energy is irrelevant energy—irrelevant, that is, to the behavior to be performed. Similarly, in psychological behavior the motivation must produce the appropriate state of excitation to insure that the energy transmitted is appropriate to the behavior to be performed. When the energy is appropriate to the behavior to be performed, the physiological mechanisms, operating within the historical context of the reactional biography, will produce a response repertory that is highly systematized and ordered.

5. *Categories of responses*

A response may be viewed as any interaction between the individual and his environment that brings the individual into a new relationship with one or more of his environmental components. The response repertory, then, is that portion of the collection of responses that may be available at any given instant. It is convenient to our discussion to consider responses as belonging to four reasonably differentiable categories: (1) awareness responses, (2) manipulative responses, (3) communication responses, and (4) feeling responses.

In performing AWARENESS RESPONSES, the organism senses stimulus objects and events, focuses attention upon them, perceives them, identifies them, catalogues their characteristics, and abstracts their general nature. Awareness responses provide meaning, knowledge, and understanding. Out of these interactions between awareness responses and stimulus objects and events the stimulus functions arise.

As will be seen, the remaining categories of responses are discussed in terms of their interactions with stimulus functions, not stimulus objects and events. At this point in our discussion, the reader needs to form the concept of responses interacting with the meaning of an object or event rather than with the object or event itself. This meaning is called, in the present formulation, the *stimulus function*. The ways in which it is formed through the interaction of the awareness responses with objects and events in the environmental context and the manner in which it acts with other categories of responses to create behavior products are considered later (Section 6) in the present chapter.

In performing MANIPULATIVE RESPONSES, the organism orients itself with respect to stimulus functions. This orientation involves both psychological and motor responses. Manipulative responses involve such acts as approaching, withdrawing, submitting, mastering, moving, retaining, exploring, organizing, and reorganizing. The individual learns, reasons, controls, abstracts, imagines, and dreams.

In performing FEELING RESPONSES the organism produces feedback data which inform the organism how his relationships with his environment are progressing. Feeling responses answer such questions as: How am I doing? Was my last response a good one? Do my present actions frighten me? Will that future act I am planning be soothing? Feeling responses include that special kind of awareness that we call emotional or affective, and include a heavy loading of visceral biological behavior that precedes, accompanies, and follows every behavior act. These responses form an internal system of communication informing an individual about the degree to which his manipulative responses are serving to maintain and support his system of values, his concept of himself. The feedback information provided by the feeling responses becomes a stimulus function for subsequent behavior.

In performing COMMUNICATION RESPONSES, the organism conveys information about his activities to another individual or to himself. Communication responses involve both direct and symbolic information transmission; direct as in the case of pushing someone out of the path of an onrushing automobile and symbolic as in the case of language, gesture, nonlanguage noises, and other symbolic media.

All four categories of responses interact not only with internal and external stimulus functions, but also with each other. It is possible, for example, to be aware of manipulation, or feeling, or communication; to manipulate awareness, feeling, and communication; to perform feeling responses to awareness, communication, and manipulation stimuli; and to communicate about awareness, feeling, and manipulation. Moreover, each category of response may interact with behavior of the same category: it is possible to be aware of awareness, to manipulate manipulation responses, to feel about feeling, and to communicate about communication. These components merge from time to time and become indistinguishable from one another, as one category of response becomes another. This merging of the response categories has its counterpart in the merging of the components of the context element.

6. *The stimulus function*

Interactions between awareness responses and stimulus objects and events produce stimulus functions. Out of the buzzing, whirling confusion of objects and events that fills the world of every living organism every moment, some objects and events, from time to time, take on the special quality of being capable of participating in a psychological interaction. This quality may be labeled the stimulus function. The STIMULUS FUNCTION of an object or event is the specialized meaning it has for the organism as revealed in the organism's responses to it.

The stimulus function of an object or event is derived from three sources: (1) the inherent characteristics of the object or event, (2) the conditions under which it emerges from the context element, and (3) the dynamic structure that is generated by the interaction of the object or event with the individual's response repertory.

The kinds of stimulus functions that may be formed are determined, first, by the characteristics of the objects and events from which they emerge. Such characteristics as size, color, movement, number, order, physical state, loudness, pitch, temperature, constancy, change, and the like play major roles in determining the stimulus function of an object or event. The stimulus function of an omelet is *something to be eaten;* the stimulus function of a lecture in abnormal psychology is *words to be noted.* Both stimulus functions result, in part, from the special characteristics of the objects and events in question as these characteristics reach the receptor mechanisms of the individual. The student in abnormal psychology does not swallow the instructor's words with the same relish he shows for the omelet.

In addition to the characteristics of the objects and events, the conditions under which these characteristics reach the organism contribute to the meaning assigned to the object or event and hence to its stimulus function. The conditions in question here involve principally the state of the organism, the psycho-social climate at the moment when the stimuli reach the organism, and the organism's historical relationships with this class of objects and events. The stimulus function of a piece of nude calendar art is different for a sixteen-year-old male and his three-year-old brother. The object has a different stimulus function for the "same" male at different stages of his psycho-biological development or in different settings, as, for example, in his own room or in the office of a prospective employer who is interviewing the boy.

Finally, the stimulus function of an object or event is modified by the dynamic structure of the relationships generated by the interaction of the objects or events with the responses of the organism. The very act of responding changes the relationships of the individual to the world around him. A book, for example, that initially had the stimulus function *something to be read with enjoyment* emerges in the process of being read as having the stimulus function *dull, boring, drivel to be avoided.*

Zener and Gaffron (1962) describe the perceptual process in a schema that helps to clarify the relationship between the events out there and the awareness responses being made by the individual. They clearly differentiate between the objective events and the electromagnetic, chemical, thermal, and mechanical energies that emanate from them and mediate relationships between the individual and his environment. The kinds of energy generated by an object or event are codetermined by the characteristics of the event, as indicated above, and its interactions with other events in the field. Thus an apple hanging on a tree gives off energy in the form of red light rays by reason of its interaction with the light from the sun. It is these reflected rays of light energy that, in part, mediate the relationship between a hungry boy and the apple. This energy generated by the natural characteristics of the event is designated by Zener and Gaffron (1962, p. 526) as the "medium world." Brunswick (1944) views this energy factor as "proximal" stimulus as distinct from the "distant" stimulus of the object in the external world.

It should be pointed out that the hungry boy is not made aware simply of the surface characteristics of the apple that are brought to him by the light rays stimulating the nerve tissues of his eyes, but he also becomes aware of the apple as a whole, its size, shape, ripeness, accessibility, and so on. Some of this information is, of course, operationally inferred, but much of it is direct awareness codetermined by the energy input of the reflected light rays and the boy's previous experience with stimulation of this sort.

These considerations of the energy impact of the physical characteristics of an object upon the response mechanism of an individual must be modified, however, by what we know about the state of the individual at the moment of responding and by the imprint of the culture upon the whole system. The hungry boy's awareness of the apple—what it means to him—is modified, for example, by the fact that in certain subcultures stealing the farmer's apples is fair game, whereas in others it is frowned upon. Thus, the characteristics of an object or event, the kinds and amounts of energy they generate or reflect, the conditions under which they leap into focus from the environmental context and the dynamic stimulus-response interaction that is momentarily generated all contribute to the meaning and hence to the stimulus function of an object or event.

Interactions between awareness responses and stimulus objects and events generate a pattern of symbolic events that we have called the stimulus function. Figure 2 (page 20) includes a schematic representation of this interaction. These stimulus functions are now capable of interacting with manipulation, communication, and feeling responses as well as further awareness responses. Interactions between the stimulus functions and the response repertory may be viewed as the behavior product.

7. The dynamic structure of the behavior elements

The components of the context element interacting with the response repertory create new dynamic forms. For example, in the process of responding to the stimulus $5 + 7 = ?$ on an arithmetic examination, a student writes the symbol 12 on his paper. The context element has now changed: time has passed; the students nearby are working more diligently; the teacher has started to relax after seeing her charges begin the test; and so on. The stimulus component of the context element, the test itself, has changed most: it is, for example, shorter than it was a moment ago. Similarly, changes have occurred in the response repertory: awareness responses originally directed toward the test as a whole are now directed at details of test items; manipulative responses, remembering, reasoning, learning, etc., are made more easily as each answer is recorded; a sense of accomplishment spreads through the reactional biography; communication responses are facilitated because the student now knows where to record his responses to the questions. And then, at about the fifth problem, a feeling of anxiety begins to set in, for the student is not certain that he can finish the test in the time available to him. Thus, the entire structure of the relationships among the behavioral elements changes.

A change in any of the components of psychological behavior can have a profound influence on all other elements and especially on the structure of their relationships. A student drops a pencil and the whole context element changes, providing new stimulus functions demanding responses. One of the problems is difficult to read because of a faulty inking of the mimeograph machine, and the whole test becomes different as a stimulus object, with a resulting change in the psycho-social climate and in the kinds of responses the student makes. The student inadvertently records *21* instead of *12* for his answer and recognizes his error. The other end of the pencil now emerges from the context element and takes on a stimulus function. And so it goes.

The term *behavior product* suggests the essential unity of the inter-relationships among the elements of psychological behavior. The term is designed to convey the resulting structure of the relationships among the components of behavior at any point in a behavior segment or sequence. This term takes into account the fact that each element is changing in the time-space continuum and that the relationships among the elements and among their components is also changing.

The behavior product will be used throughout this book to denote the structure of behavioral components at a fleeting instant of time. No two behavior products can ever be exactly alike. You cannot step in the same river twice, for not only does the river change from instant to instant, but the wader himself is changed by his first encounter with the cold water. Despite this fact of the non-identity of two events, two behavior products, it is possible to abstract, over a large range of behavior products, a sufficient degree of consistency, similarity, and homogeneity to provide the basis for the formulation of some kind of order and lawfulness.

The apparent similarity—but not identity—of certain classes of behavior products of an individual and of groups of individuals results from the relatively slow rate of change of certain of the components of the behavior elements. Cultural factors, for example, which make up so large a share of the context element, are subject to change only over long periods of time. Thus behavior products in which language, custom, or values form an essential aspect of the structure appear to have a strong resemblance to each other. The biological structure and the physiological function of an individual change slowly, and these structures and functions remain fairly consistent across a large sample of individuals of the same species. These slow change rates and the apparent homogeneity of many behavioral components for large numbers of individuals give their behavior products enough of an

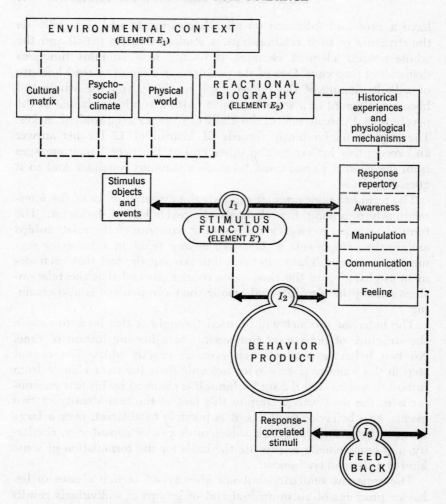

Figure 5. The Behavior Product (second model). In the first interaction (I_1), stimulus objects and events emerging from the environmental context (E_1) interact with the awareness responses, which emerge from the response of the reactional biography (E_2), and form the derived element, the stimulus function (E'). The second interaction (I_2) involves the stimulus function and one or more of the responses from the response repertory to form the behavior product. The behavior product produces response-correlated stimuli that interact with feeling responses (I_3) to produce feedback. Feedback, in turn, becomes a part of the next behavior product by interacting with awareness responses to form new stimulus functions.

appearance of uniformity, or at least repetition, to permit us to abstract certain principles that will identify certain kinds of behavior products and differentiate them from others and to predict and control future behavior products.

8. *Summary of the behavior product*

This model of human psychological behavior, which will serve as a frame of reference for our investigations of guidance principles and practices, may be summarized in the following way: The behavior product emerges as a dynamic process of interactions between the response repertory and stimulus functions. The response repertory is a reservoir of reactions that is available at a given instant, developed through the historical interactions of the individual's physiological mechanisms with his experiential encounters. Stimulus functions emerge from the context element when objects and events in the environment interact—through energy media—with the available awareness responses of the response repertory. Objects and events of the context element emerge as stimulus objects and events as a function of their special characteristics, the imprint of the culture upon them, and the historical relationships established between the individual and these objects and events. Thus the behavior product represents a dynamic structure of interrelated and interacting processes. Figure 5 restates, in a somewhat different and more detailed form, the structure previously sketched in Figure 2.

In considering behavior products, it is of utmost significance that no single product may be viewed in isolation—except in the symbolic reality of language. All behavior products are related to all previous behavior products and each projects its energy into the future. This stream of behavior is the flow of life. It is this flow which the guidance practitioner seeks to direct into more productive channels.

Three

Modification of behavior [1]

◆◆◆

B ehavior products created in a lifetime of interactions between an individual's response repertory and the objects and events in his world do not happen by chance. Certain kinds of behavior products have a higher probability of occurrence than others. If, at the moment of an individual's birth, we were to attempt to predict that a given behavior product would be formed in his lifetime, we could find only one which, under present conditions, could be predicted with absolute certainty, namely the individual's death. All other behavior products have a probability of less than one.

Even as recently as the 1940's most people would have been reluctant to predict that the probability of a given individual's visiting the moon or a nearby planet was any greater than zero. Yet today, some twenty years later, scientists, engineers, and the chauffeurs who pilot their contrivances are planning expeditions to the geography of outer space. This suggests that the probability that an individual born today will visit one of the earth's companions in space some time during his lifetime is some amount greater than zero. The probability, although small, still does exist. Moreover, as time goes on, this probability is changing and, in all likelihood, increasing. Thus, the grandchild of an inhabitant of Brooklyn, New York, may be more likely to perform behavior products essential to a lunar visit than he would be to interact with the necessary elements in his world to accomplish a visit to the oilfields of Texas as an oil rigger. Similarly, a male child born in the United States, with no more than the normal limitations, can be expected with a fairly high degree of certainty to be-

[1] This chapter is an expansion and modification of previously published essays (Weitz, 1955, and Weitz, 1956).

come literate; to train for, enter, and pursue some occupation; to court, marry, and raise a family; to participate in some ritualistic activities of a religious or political nature; to perform appropriate aesthetic responses to artistic, literary, musical, or athletic stimuli; and to espouse, with ardor, some public or private cause. On the other hand, such a child from a similar setting could become an illiterate, unemployed, vagrant bachelor, untouched by ritual, aesthetics, or the demands of "good works." The probability of the latter's occurring under these conditions, in these times, is markedly less than that of the former's occurring.

1. *Society's control of behavior products*

Why is this the case? In general, we may say that the most probable behavior to be performed by an individual is the behavior being performed by the comembers of his culture. The acts we perform, the ways in which we perform them, and the kinds of satisfactions or dissatisfactions we experience as a consequence of our performance are, in major ways, given direction by our society. To be sure, individuals within a society may and often do develop whole systems of behavior that are so different from those common to the society as to be highly improbable. These, however, are rare and, in the main, represent only minor variations on the common behavioral mode. The society sees to it that when variations occur, they are acceptable variations on a common theme.

The survival and growth of any society depends on the condition that a certain structure of behavior products has a high probability of occurrence. This is a kind of circular definition of a society. When a fairly systematic pattern of behavior products does occur at a high level of probability among a group of persons closely associated in time and space, this systematic pattern may be viewed as a society. Survival of a society and hence of its members requires that many behavior products be formalized and institutionalized, thus giving them a high probability value. This high probability of certain crucial behavior products makes it possible for an individual to predict the consequences of his own interactions with his comembers. In this way, the individual is guided in performing acts that have high biological and psychological survival value. A society, then, is an artifact created by individuals to insure their own psychological and physical maintenance and development.

Acting in concert, comembers of a society construct and utilize a variety of institutions to insure a high probability of occurrence of those behavior products having high survival value. Illustrative of these institutions are: government and laws, religion and ritual, familial associations, and customs. Among the institutions used by a society to insure its survival and thus the survival of its comembers is one in which we are most interested here: education.

2. Learning and education

Education may be thought of as a kind of institutionalized learning process. Learning, in general, is the process of behavior acquisition through experience. It involves, as suggested earlier, the formation of stimulus functions and the attachment of certain response patterns to them in such a way as to form highly probable links. The approximate repetition of the context element, then, including a similar configuration of stimulus objects and events as well as organismic states, should produce—if learning is effective—a behavior product that is specifiable at a high order of probability.

It is important to keep in mind, however, that much of the behavior acquired in a lifetime is acquired fortuitously and incidentally to the performance of behavior products in which the focus is elsewhere. Many of our attitudes, interests, and prejudices were acquired under circumstances which were not specifically designed to produce the acquired behavior. The graduate student who is required to demonstrate his fluency in one or more foreign languages, which have previously been matters of complete indifference to him, acquires attitudinal behavior toward foreign language study, in particular, and toward the tribal ritual of graduate study, in general, which is remote from the original intent of the foreign language requirement (Weitz, Ballantyne, and Colver, 1963). The child who learns that other children often have the same name as his own acquires a new response pattern to the sound of his own name. This kind of learning, which contributes in major ways to our reservoir of behavior products, is accidental or incidental to contrived learning.

3. Contrived learning

Contrived learning is that aspect of experientially acquired behavior in which the behavior to be acquired and the method of acquisition are both predetermined by someone. In this kind of learning, the behavior products are specified by the person managing the learning process, whether this is the instructor or the learner himself. In general, the end products are specified in terms of the kinds of responses to be linked with specified stimulus functions derived from selected objects and events. In contrived learning, also, the instructor and the learner have a plan for attacking the learning problem that is intended to insure the acquisition and fixation of the desired behavior. This involves the systematic manipulation of objects and events in the context element in such a way as to increase the probability of occurrence of certain specified stimulus functions with which only certain responses can be expected to interact. This planned or contrived learning may be called *education*. It is exemplified in such diverse behavior acquisition as toilet protocol and the mathematical manipulations involved in the analysis of covariance. In both instances, the goals and methods of behavior acquisition are contrived and predetermined. Education, then, is a special case of the more general process of learning. It is an institutionalized process utilized by a society and its subdivisions to insure survival.

4. *Education and the school*

Viewed in this light, education becomes a part of the whole fabric of the culture rather than being the exclusive property of the school, as some enthusiasts would have us believe. Major contributions to education in the form of contrived learning experiences are made by such institutions as the home, the church, and industry; by the press and its more or less legitimate offspring, radio and television; and by social, professional, and civic clubs and other ganglike associations. Each contributes, in its own small way, to the acquisition of predetermined behavior products by its members.

The melancholy facts of the matter appear to be that most of what we know as education, most contrived learning, takes place outside the schools. This general education involving the selection of fairly clearly defined methods to achieve fairly clearly defined goals produces, outside the classroom, highly predictable behavior products which are essential to individual and cultural survival. Basic motor skills such as walking, running, balancing, self-feeding, and the like are taught in the home. These essential behavioral patterns are taught by parents and agemates using extremely simple contrived learning situations requiring the manipulation of a minimum of the behavior product components. Basic language skills, quantitative concepts, fundamental behavior patterns involving cooperation and competition, and the attitudes appropriate to each of these, for example, are all established as a part of a child's response repertory before he comes in contact with the formal instructional systems of the school.

Relatively few entirely new modes of behavior are acquired by the child through the educational efforts of the school. Literature and grammar are merely refinements of the language behavior already a part of the child's behavioral equipment. Mathematical education would be an impossibility if the child did not come to school already well trained in the concepts of *oneness* and *manyness*. History is merely an extension of the child's understanding, acquired outside the school, of the sequence of events in time and of the interrelationships of these events. Thus, education in each instructional area is dependent upon the behavior products that the child has already acquired outside the classroom.

This general busyness with the problems of teaching and learning by all of the instrumentalities of a society would seem to leave little of education to the schools. This, however, is not strictly true. The school's major contribution to education is in the area of symbolic learning. With the few minor exceptions of the relative newcomers to the school's curricula such as art, music, physical education, manual arts, and the like, schools are concerned principally with training students in verbal and other symbolic behavior. Most of the school's time is devoted to teaching the students the labels for objects and events—most of which the student has never experienced directly and never will—and in developing students' skills in the manipulation of these symbols in formal and ritualistic ways. This state of affairs is, of course, more characteristic of the humanities than it is of the sciences or arts, but the total instructional effort appears to be focused primarily on the learning of symbolic behavior.

This use of the school's time, facilities, and personnel to provide symbolic education is probably an efficient use of the resources, for symbolic behavior can be translated into objective interactions under the proper circumstances. In terms of the time and resources available, it may be that secondary school teachers of "social studies" and their collegiate counterparts in departments of history, economics, political science, and sociology are better qualified to educate their students in the use of the correct words with which to talk about citizenship than they are to plan experiences for the students which will facilitate their exercise of democratic control over the organizations in which they hold membership. It may be that teachers of mathematics are better able to train their students in the manipulation of number symbols in computational situations than they are to organize real experiences requiring the rigidly disciplined behavior demanded by mathematical logic. And it may be that instructors in literature and the language arts find it more socially efficient to educate their charges to link a piece of dead literature to the corpse of its author than to help them acquire behavior products involving the expression of ideas in semantically sound, as well as grammatically sound, language or involving the evaluation of the semantic and philosophical vigor of a piece of verse or prose as well as its formal structure.

These may be the most desirable as well as the most efficiently attainable educational functions of the school, but if they are, educators should rest content with the excellence of their performance and their product. This is not the case, however. Most educators persist in the fiction that their purpose and their achievement extend beyond the acquisition of symbolic behavior into the realm of behavior that participates in almost every aspect of human life. In 1918, the Commission on the Reorganization of Secondary Education enunciated the "seven cardinal principles of education" (U.S. Office of Education, 1918). These included: health, command of fundamental processes, vocational efficiency, worthy home membership, citizenship, worthy use of leisure time, and ethical character. This was not the first such pronouncement, nor is it likely to be the last. The point being emphasized here is the fact that education in the schools pretends to be one kind of activity when, in fact, it is another. It purports to assume responsibility for contrived learning experiences related to a broad range of human behavior, although it provides only academic experiences concerned almost exclusively with facilitating the acquisition of symbolic behavior. This seeking of goals by inappropriate means and, at the same time, pretending that the means are achieving or even can achieve these goals serves as a barrier not only to the achievement of the stated goals, but also to the achievement of goals for which the means ARE appropriate.

Perhaps this picture of education as it takes place in the schools is too somber. There are bright spots. There are, of course, instances where the experiences provided appear to be relevant to the acquisition of the desired behavior. Students in home economics courses do not spend all their time learning the names of exotic foods they will never taste. They learn to bake a cake by baking a cake. Engineering students in a few colleges do take time out from solving higher-order abstract equations to lay an occasional brick or to test the strength of an I-beam. The chemistry student occasionally lays aside his cookbook to find out what this peculiar substance is that fills his flask. The classroom occasionally does provide living experiences appropriate to the acquisition of behavior related to living.

5. *Contrived learning in the extracurriculum*

More often, however, these kinds of living experiences are provided in that educational limbo called the extracurriculum. Student councils and other school clubs do provide their participants with limited experiences appropriate to the acquisition of democratic behavior. Athletics provide opportunities for the acquisition of behavior involving team effort and health improvement, as well as other behavior so esteemed in our society such as striving for eminence on the basis of inconsequential accomplishments and taking physical punishment to achieve transitory goals.

6. *Noncurricular experiences in the school*

Among the noncurricular experiences provided by the schools, some are directed toward the acquisition of behavior that might be effective in the solution of the student's problems of personal adjustment. The total student personnel program, for example, is directed toward this end. More particularly, that aspect of the student personnel program called *guidance* has the objective of assisting students in acquiring behavior that can be effective in resolving the student's choice frustrations.

The youngster who must choose between preparing for college or preparing to learn a trade is likely to find little assistance in the classroom for making this choice. The youth whose early religious training appears to be in conflict with the new values he encounters at the university can not resolve his conflict by faithful attendance in a course in comparative religion. The youngster who has learned about sex and has learned about love but who has found no way to integrate these concepts will gain scant solace from a course in physiology or hygiene. The student who believes that he is putting forth his best effort and is still failing a course and the student who "just doesn't give a damn" are both experiencing academic frustrations which go unrelieved through their next classroom encounter. The student seeking unique outlets for his unusual talents, the student with no special talent at all, and the student with the single special talent of being at cross-purposes with his family and teachers, all require educational experiences that will bring them into some harmonious relationship with their society. These experiences would be rare occurrences indeed within the instructional framework of the school, but they are made available in that aspect of schooling called guidance.

7. *Functions of education*

This suggests that education as it takes place in the school is composed of two functions: instruction and guidance. The school performs its educational role through these two closely interrelated activities. Guidance, like instruction, represents contrived learning experiences that are provided through many agencies of society. Counseling, one of the techniques of guidance, is practiced by clergymen, psychotherapists, physicians, club leaders, industrial personnel workers, social workers, parents, and just plain do-gooders. The goals and means used in counseling by all these practitioners appear, on the surface, to have much in common, namely behavior change appropriate to the resolution of choice conflicts accomplished by means of the manipulation of symbolic behavior. It is in the guidance program of schools, however, that this approach to behavior change has become most highly institutionalized—psychiatry, social work, and religion notwithstanding.

Instruction and guidance are highly institutionalized means for providing contrived learning experiences to individuals with a view to effecting some change in their behavior. While these two major functions of the schools have much in common, they differ in certain fundamental ways. Tiedeman and Field (1962) view these differences in the following way.

It now becomes possible to establish a basis for differentiating the two complementary functions. In terms of our argument, teaching involves a communication of *others'* experiences—data and conclusions. Guidance, on the other hand, involves primarily an examination of the individual student's experiences—data and the *process* of forming conclusions about them. Teaching continually creates useful discontinuity by saying, "Here are things you do not know, or know how to do." Guidance, on the other hand, deals with the individualized reduction of discontinuity:

(1) by pointing out where discontinuity has (or has not yet!) come to exist;
(2) by making it *not* seem undesirable or overwhelming, but useful; and,
(3) by making it more possible for the individual to choose actions designed to reduce (or establish and *then* reduce) such discontinuity. (Tiedeman and Field, 1962, p. 495.)

The discontinuity of which these authors speak is the change in circumstances that confronts individuals from time to time as they pass through life and that imposes upon them the necessity for making choices.

Both guidance and instruction have as their central goal redirecting the flow of behavior into more productive channels. This goal of installing more effective behavior products in the behavior repertory of individuals is an expression of society's drive for survival and growth. Both guidance and instruction utilize contrived learning experiences as a means of influencing behavior change. By manipulation of components of the context element, stimulus functions are revised to evoke new response patterns. This manipulation of the context-element components is designed to produce new behavior products that the society deems to be more effective.

8. *Control of goals and methods*

When one examines the goals and methods of both instruction and guidance more closely, however, one becomes aware of the striking differences in these two functions of education. To realize the scope of these differences it is necessary to reexamine the notion of education as a contrived learning experience. We generally consider that in education learning experiences are contrived by an instructor, that is, by some one other than the learner himself. We are likely to feel that the goals of learning as well as the methods by which these goals are achieved are the province of the teacher. This, of course, is not the entire story. Exclusive control of the learning process is not exercised by the teacher even in instruction. There is, here, a sharing of the control.

The goals of learning and the methods by which they are achieved may be determined, and frequently are, by the learner himself. Although the education of young children is usually carried on under the direction of adults, as the individual matures, he assumes more and more responsibility for the establishment of the goals and methods of his learning. Adults in our society have considerable freedom in selecting what they will learn and the ways they will learn it. Children, too, have considerable latitude in the matter of their own education. The child decides that he would like to learn how to swim. He consequently follows a rigorous learning program in order to acquire this behavior. Although he may enlist the aid of a swimming coach, the outcome and most of the essential methods for achieving it are established by the learner himself. Here education appears to be under the almost complete control of the child himself.

Mastery of the multiplication tables, on the other hand, presents a markedly different structure. In most instances, the child who is to learn the table of products has little understanding of what multiplication is at the time he is expected to learn it. The good teacher will make adequate preparation for this piece of instruction by filling in enough background material, in terms of meaningful illustration, to make the child feel that this whole enterprise is worthwhile. In this way he comes to accept the teacher's outcomes of learning as his own. In this illustration, the teacher assumes central responsibility for manipulating objects and events in the student's environment in such a way as to establish new stimulus functions for the child. The feed-back from the child's response-stimulus function interactions provides him with feeling responses which he interprets as satisfying. Thus the teacher, in a secondary way, manipulates the child's responses by means of manipulating objects and events in his universe. As a consequence, the child has some notion, if only a vague one at first, of where the learning process is taking him. No matter how skilful the teacher is in enlisting the child's interest and participation in the learning of the multiplication tables, however, this educational enterprise may be said to be contrived, in the main, by the teacher.

Educational experiences, then, are of two kinds with respect to the agent contriving them. On the one hand, there are learning activities in which the goals and methods are contrived by the learner himself; on the other, there are those contrived by agents other than the learner. Few learning experiences can be catalogued as belonging exclusively to one or the other of these categories. Most learning experiences are made up of complex interrelationships between external and self-direction.

Nor does the directing agent necessarily have to be an individual. A state of affairs may be the agent that contrives certain aspects of a learning exercise. The adult who decides to learn a foreign language is externally limited, among other things, by the foreign languages available to be learned, the form and structure of the language he selects, the learning materials at hand, and the attitude of his social group toward foreign-language study. His acquisition of this foreign-language behavior is modified by the total social framework in which he finds himself. Although the major emphasis here is upon self-direction, the educational experience in this illustration is not entirely a learner-contrived activity; it is modified by an external state of affairs rather than a personal agent.

In some educational experiences, the learner appears to exercise greater control over goals and methods than do external agents. In others, the external agent exercises the greater control. In both types of event there is a strong central core of shared involvement.

In both, also, there is a strong overlay of social and environmental determination of the goals and methods.

This difference in emphasis on control provides us with one basis for differentiating between guidance and instruction. Instruction is viewed here as contrived learning experiences that are managed primarily by the teacher. In guidance, however, the individual exercises the primary control over what he will learn and the ways he will go about learning it. This is not to say that the learner concedes all control in instruction or that the guidance practitioner is a passive reflection of the learner in guidance. It is simply a matter of emphasis.

9. *Nature of educational goals*

Degree of control over educational objectives and methods is not the only basis on which one can differentiate between guidance and instruction. The very natures of the goals differ in these two very important educational functions.

Educational goals become most meaningful when they are stated in behavioral terms. They become more meaningful and useful when they are stated in terms of behavior products which are observable by someone other than the learner. We may say, for example, that one of the objectives of a literature course is to "develop in the student an appreciation of literature." Statements of this sort are found in many outlines of goals and objectives for courses taught in the schools. Yet such a statement has very little meaning to the learner himself and even less to an outside observer. The student can, of course, observe his own reactions to a piece of writing and note that he finds it easy to read; the plot carries him along from one episode to another; the characters resemble people he has known or can imagine; and he feels "good" as he reads the story. He can report to the instructor that he enjoyed the story and hence appreciated it. Another student reading the same story may find the phrasing of the ideas surprisingly new, the symbolism provocative, the style dynamic, and the philosophy expressed by the author thought-provoking. He, too, can report to the instructor that he enjoyed the story and thus appreciated it. It may even be that the enjoyment of both these students was enhanced by their participation in the literature course. Yet what do we know about the behavior change which took place as a consequence of the instruction? If we wish to attach meaning of this kind to an instructional objective, we must be prepared to say (1) that whatever feeling feedback a student gets as a result of reading a piece of literature—including distaste, boredom, or irritation—it represents appreciation; (2) that as long as this feedback is different from what it might have been before instruction began, it may be considered an instructional outcome; and (3) that the student's report of his feeling responses represents accurate communication responses clearly depicting the internal events of the behavior product. We can see that, on at least these three counts, such an educational objective as "the appreciation of literature" lacks the precision necessary for an instructor to organize the learning experience in any meaningful way.

As a consequence of the almost meaningless goals that have been established for so many educational activities, education in the schools tends to founder in a morass of traditional and ritualistic procedures. Curricula appear to have developed not by rational plans based on an understanding of the contrived learning situation, but by accumulation. They remind one of the Mississippi delta, except that they are not so rich nor are the channels ever cleared out. New content appears to be deposited upon the old, traditional offerings in response to the whimsical interests of a few taxpayers given voice by educational faddists. Of course, some of what has been added may be good. The laws of chance operate indiscriminately.

Guidance as well as instruction has been the victim of the inadequate clarification of its goals. Early in its development, guidance had as its central goal assisting young people to select, train for, enter, and progress in an occupation. While this was a highly restricted kind of goal, it had the virtue of being meaningful. Most early guidance practitioners were able to plan programs of educational experiences that seemed to have a high probability of leading to goals of this sort. As time has moved forward from the early events of guidance, we find this essential function of education operating in a broader arena. Vocational selection, training, placement, and progress are no longer enough. These have been subsumed under the more general and, unfortunately, less meaningful objective of adjustment. Guidance these days appears directed toward the goal of student adjustment. The precise meaning attributed to this concept depends on whether it is uttered by a school administrator, a teacher of mathematics, a school cafeteria director, a physical education specialist, a school nurse, an attendance officer, a school dentist, or a counseling psychologist. Each conceives of adjustment in terms of his own central concerns. The child has achieved adjustment and hence "been guided" when (1) he has a schedule of courses which fits the instructional timetable of the school; (2) he turns in neatly written homework papers on time; (3) he moves through the school feeding line with quiet dispatch, selecting a balanced diet from the fare provided; (4) he stands quietly in the calisthenic line while the roll is called; (5) he misses school only when he is ill and always brings a note from home to explain his illness; (6) he brushes his teeth the appropriate number of times each day; and (7) he performs well on psychological tests. To the child's own mind, if he ever thinks about it at all, adjustment probably means being able to get along with the school functionaries, other adults, and his agemates. Adjustment to him is relief from demands and stresses he views as unpleasant. Organizing learning experience to achieve all of these goals—and many others as well—which may be subsumed under the general notion of adjustment becomes, on the face of it, an impossibility.

How, then, may we form our objectives for both instruction and guidance so that they may make some semantic sense? Goals that are stated in such a way as to represent observable behavior change can have meaning. Objectives stated in terms of observable behavior change have a high probability of forming similar stimulus functions for a large number of persons charged with responsibilities for instruction or guidance. Such objectives will evoke in the teacher or guidance practitioner systems of behavior products related to the management of the learning process that are consistent with the objectives and that, at the same time, have a certain consistency from teacher to teacher and from practitioner to practitioner.

As we consider the notion of educational objectives' being stated in terms of observable changes in behavior products, we are immediately confronted with the problem of what kind of behavior products represent fit subjects for education as it takes place in the schools. Some behavior is clearly observable. It is susceptible to change through the processes of contrived learning. Estimates of the rates and the direction of the change can be made. Yet these behavior products may be so trivial or so irrelevant to the general goals of the school as to require exclusion from the objectives of education. For example: A child may be able to spit some distance. With proper instruction, he may become able to increase the distance and accuracy of this behavior to the point where he may even achieve some local notoriety. (A watermelon seed spitting contest was held in North Carolina in 1961 in which a number of dignitaries of local and statewide political stature participated.) This behavior, however, seems too trivial—even by North Carolina standards—to be introduced into the curricula of the schools. Examples of behavior that are irrelevant to the aims of the schools yet are not trivial are more difficult to describe, for some school some place is bound to offer training in the behavior that may seem to some people to be irrelevant to the purposes of education in the schools. (A course in fly casting was once offered for college credit at the State University of Iowa.) Formal religious behavior is one activity that is specifically excluded as irrelevant to the purposes of many public schools, and the 1962 Supreme Court decision made it legally irrelevant.

Some behavior is susceptible to change, and the change is observable, but the behavior is incompatible with the purposes of the school. These behavior products include those activities we call delinquent or criminal. An individual may develop a high degree of skill as a counterfeiter through a rigorous program of education. This accomplishment, however, not only does not fit into the school's usual configuration of goals, but actually runs counter to it.

Educational goals of the school must, then, be stated in terms of observable behavior change and must also involve behavior that is significant to and compatible with the general purposes of the school as a social institution. Thus the goals of education in the schools are strongly rooted in the values of the society that created the school as its agent.

10. *Values in education*

Values may be defined as the goals toward which the activities of an individual or a society are directed. Values differ from society to society, from subgroup to subgroup, and from individual to individual. Each society requires of its members that they have a pattern of values that will contribute to the maintenance and development of the society. Furthermore, each society insures that its members hold to the general structure of values by providing rewards for adherents and sanctions, even including death, for defectors.

In order that a society may progress toward the achievement of its goals, it is necessary that members of the association acquire a body of skills and hold a system of beliefs and attitudes that contribute to the attainment of that society's values. In a democratic society, such as that found in the United States, the system of values toward which the society strives would include "perfect states" of some of the following: individual freedom coupled with individual responsibility, majority welfare with the protection of minority rights, material and intellectual honesty, the reward of individual effort limited by a code of "accepted practice," and so forth. Individual and group behavior that facilitates the achievement of these goals is valued highly, whereas behavior that does not contribute to their achievement is, in general, disapproved and insofar as possible thwarted.

Members of a society need, furthermore, to develop certain behavioral patterns that will facilitate their striving toward the goals established by their society. Included among the essential behavioral patterns in a democratic society are (1) the ability to communicate ideas and feelings through a variety of media including verbal, quantitative, graphic, plastic, tonal, and gestural language; (2) the ability to analyze problems and situations by means of induction, deduction, intuition, and similar processes; (3) the ability to organize ideas, events, and circumstances into meaningful and manageable configurations; and (4) the ability to perform a body of formal, ritualistic conduct deemed appropriate by the society. These basic skills—communication, analysis, synthesis, and ritualistic performance—are the essential ingredients of the behavior products required for the attainment of the goals of a democratic society. With few exceptions, they represent the basic human capabilities essential in any society.

These basic skills form the content of education; the values form the goals. The subjects that are taught—English, mathematics, science, history, and the like—are simply media for presenting the socially essential course content. Instruction is a means of facilitating the clarification of values and engendering of skills appropriate to the attainment of the values.

The values of a society are, in general, fairly clearly discernible and identifiable. They are, at the same time, especially in a democracy, sufficiently flexible to permit individuals to interpret them in terms of their own behavioral history and to select as their own those that appear to be most meaningful. The implementation of society's goals may take a variety of forms in actual practice. As long as an individual's values are not markedly incompatible with those of his society, he is permitted by the society to act in idiosyncratic ways and to find his own kind of harmony with his environment.

An example of this kind of personalized value system may be seen in the case of the young army veteran who came to a Veterans Administration counseling center for assistance in reestablishing himself in some civilian vocation. After the usual preliminaries of vocational appraisal, an inquiry was undertaken to determine the young man's long-term goals. He indicated that one of his major vocational objectives was to have a high standard of living as measured in monetary terms. He wished to be very wealthy. However, he saw little hope of earning large sums of money with his present limited financial backing and limited professional training. He had concluded, therefore, that since he was a reasonably charming young man—and he seemed to be—his best chance for getting ahead in the financial world was to marry a wealthy young woman. In short, he saw his career to be that of a fortune hunter.

Note that the goal *the accumulation and use of great wealth* is a perfectly acceptable value in our society. It is not only acceptable, it is honored by the expenditure of considerable effort at all levels in our society. Furthermore, his means of attaining his goal, although not conspicuously honored in our society, is a means covertly used by many respectable and respected members of the community. Hence, although the counselor himself had already demonstrated by his choice of a profession and a wife that the young man's values and his means of attaining them were not consistent with his own, he aided him in selecting, training for, and entering an occupation that not only was consistent with his patterns of abilities but also would provide him with opportunities to meet wealthy young women. In this way both society's values and the young man's idiosyncratic interpretation of them were satisfied.

We see here another difference between guidance and instruction with respect to goals and the means to attain them. Instruction consists of informing the student about the broadly accepted values of society in such a way as to train the student to cherish these values and to try to attain them. Skills of analysis, synthesis, communication, and ritual performance that are designed as aids in attaining these goals are also taught using conventional subject matter as media of instruction. In guidance, the emphasis is placed upon the highly individualistic interpretation of society's values made by the person seeking guidance. These interpretations are clarified and brought into some kind of harmony with society's values. Training in the skills essential to the solution of the kind of problem faced in guidance involves aiding the individual in finding socially acceptable ways of attaining his goal.

11. *Summary of differences*

The two functions of education, instruction and guidance, have the common purpose of redirecting human behavior into new and more productive channels. Despite this common central purpose, these two functions differ from each other in significant ways. The differences are primarily matters of emphasis, but the emphasis has important consequences in practice.

In guidance the emphasis is placed upon the student's idiosyncratic interpretation of society's values; in instruction the emphasis is placed upon the broad values held in esteem by the society. In instruction, then, the teacher becomes a representative of society, and is invested by the society with the authority to interpret and transmit these values to the young. The guidance practitioner, on the other hand, is only secondarily a representative of the society; he is primarily an agent of the individual, used by him to clarify, through interpretation, his own value system.

In guidance the immediate objectives of learning, that is, the specific behavior products, the skills, the attitudes, the content, and so forth, are determined by the individual seeking guidance, whereas in instruction the teacher determines what these will be. The matter of control of immediate objectives is again a matter of emphasis. Since the acquisition of new behavior products in both guidance and instruction involves an interaction between the learner and some external agent, each exercises control over the immediate end product. In guidance the major control is exercised by the learner; in instruction it is exercised by the teacher.

The same differentiation in emphasis may be made with respect to the control of the methods of learning. The learner exercises major control in guidance, using the practitioner as a device to facilitate his achievement of some learning objective. The teacher exercises major control of the process in instruction, manipulating the environment in such a way as to evoke the responses required by the society.

Thus guidance and instruction differ in their emphasis on the individual and society with respect to values, immediate objectives, and the control of methods used in the educational process.

12. *Significance of the differentiation*

These differences in emphasis between instruction and guidance have considerable importance when we begin to consider the techniques of each function and the organization and staffing of an institution for the performance of the functions. Group methods, authoritarian control, and rote learning of fundamentals are techniques appropriate to instruction. Individual methods, permissiveness, and problem-centered learning are techniques appropriate to guidance.

The organization of the educational structure and the selection of staff to carry out these functions are determined by these differences in emphasis and techniques. Instruction requires a fairly rigid, authoritarian organization to insure a broad interpretation of society's values and an efficient management of the instructional process. Guidance requires a highly flexible organization in order to provide a structure in which an individual seeking guidance can find his own means of control.

These differences in organization and techniques require different kinds of personnel to carry them out. The differences in personnel are necessary not only in terms of their differences in training, which is an obvious and essential difference, but also in terms of their outlook and role perceptions. Good teachers who see themselves primarily as representatives of society may become poor counselors, and good counselors who view themselves as agents of individuals may become indifferent teachers.

Failure to recognize these differences between instruction and guidance has been detrimental to both. School administrators who determine policy in these matters may, and often do, view the educational process as a single homogeneous act (Weitz, 1958). This kind of administrator is certain that the classroom teacher can and should carry on all guidance activities. He claims that a guidance practitioner who is not also a teacher, and especially one who has never been a teacher, is "incapable of understanding the problems of the classroom." What he is saying is that education is primarily the transmittal of society's values, skills, and ideas and that any other practice is alien to its central function. Such a view eliminates the guidance function and at the same time dilutes the effectiveness of the instructional function of education.

For the remainder of this volume, we shall make only casual reference to instruction. The focus from here on will be on guidance. Only as instruction and guidance have common problems will the former be noted. It is sufficient to say here that both guidance and instruction have the common purpose of changing human behavior, hopefully to a more effective, satisfying performance, but that in achieving this purpose each function places the emphasis on a different apparatus.

Four

The guidance function of education

◆◆

E ducation has been defined as a process of contrived behavior acquisition. The immediate objectives of the enterprise and the means by which these objectives are to be achieved are determined before the educational experience is undertaken. Education, then, is one of the means by which an attempt is made to direct an individual's behavior into more effective channels. The degree of effectiveness of this newly acquired behavior can be estimated in terms of the degree to which the individual is able to establish more harmonious relationships with his environment. Society's values play an important role in establishing general goals for education and in determining which of a number of possible immediate objectives are most desirble to achieve.

1. *Overlap of guidance and instruction*

Education, thus defined, consists of two closely related, yet somewhat different, functions—instruction and guidance. These two educational functions have the common purpose of providing contrived learning experiences that will result in more effective behavior. They differ, however, in the emphasis they place on the control of the process. Instructional activities place the emphasis on society's control of the values which govern the process, the immediate objectives to be achieved, and the methods by which they are achieved. Guidance, on the other hand, emphasizes the control by the individual seeking guidance. His idiosyncratic interpretation of society's values govern the process. He decides what changes in behavior he wishes to effect and selects the means for achieving these changes. Although these two functions of education differ in emphasis in these respects,

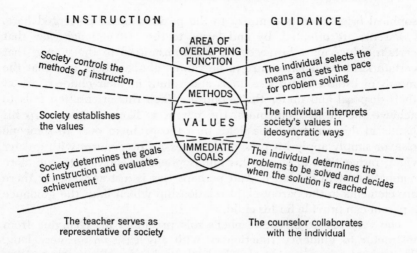

Figure 6. The Relationship between the Instructional and Guidance Functions of Education. Although there is some overlapping of functions, there are major differences in emphasis upon the control of values, methods, and immediate goals.

it is important to note that there is a considerable overlap in the activities performed, in the ways in which they are performed, and in the outcomes. Figure 6 suggests the difference between these functions of education and the common elements. This figure suggests that the guidance practitioner has certain instructional functions and that the instructor has some guidance functions. The overlapping functions represent a relatively limited area of the responsibility of each, however.

2. *The guidance practitioner*

Up to this point in the discussion, we have referred to the individual who has responsibility for guidance functions in education as a guidance practitioner. This use of the term was not accidental. As indicated earlier, many persons perform guidance-like activities who are unqualified by training, temperament, or philosophical orientation to provide professional or technical guidance services. Parents, teachers, school administrators, and clergymen engage in activities which they view as guidance. Leaving aside their limited technical training, which may be assumed to be generally inadequate to the demands of the task, and their temperaments, about which no generally applicable statement can be made, we may say with some certainty that their philosophical orientation is contrary to the position being presented here.

Parents are oriented, by and large, to the instructional view that certain values must be accepted and transmitted to the young, that certain kinds of behavior are to be valued above others, and that the means of establishing these goals and values in their children are at their disposal and under their control. When this orientation fails to achieve the desired outcomes, the parent is likely to throw up his hands in despair, leave the field, turn the problem over to someone else, or simply apply his present unsuccessful procedures with greater vigor, rather than to change his philosophical orientation to one more compatible with guidance. And perhaps this is just as well, for there are elements in the parent-child relationship which limit the guidance a parent can provide for his child.

The very nature of the teacher's role precludes his changing from instructor to guidance functionary with any ease or for very long. The school administrator also finds the role of policy and decision maker (essential to his primary function) incompatible with the role of a guidance functionary. It is interesting to note that the typical administrator not only cannot himself provide the kinds of guidance described here, but he also cannot separate the guidance and instructional functions of education in general administrative practice. A survey (Weitz, 1958) was undertaken to determine whether state guidance supervisors viewed training as a teacher essential to the effective functioning of a guidance worker in the schools or whether they considered training in the special field of guidance enough. The kind of guidance training suggested by the survey included an undergraduate program in psychology or sociology, with graduate training at the master's degree level in the specialties of guidance. (Note that persons trained in this way would not have had the usual education courses required for certification as teachers and may not have had the usual academic courses in customary teaching areas.) Without exception, the state directors of guidance reported that it would not be possible to employ such persons as fully certified guidance workers. A few (six out of forty-eight) indicated that such a person might be conditionally employed on a part-time basis. Only five reported that they would be willing to try out people trained in this way on an experimental basis. The comments of the state supervisors were most revealing in this connection:

People are permitted to counsel in (our) schools without a counselor's certificate, but are not permitted to be employed as teachers of any classification without holding a valid regular teacher's certificate. This simply means that special certification as counselors is considered desirable, but not a requirement for employment as counselors. A classroom teacher's certificate will suffice, leaving the special training necessary for employment to the employer.

At the present time any qualified teacher may be assigned by a school administrator to perform counseling duties. It is recognized that there are persons trained to do counseling work who do not meet teacher requirements or have not had teaching experience, but the philosophy and practice . . . has been that persons who do work in specialized school services should also qualify as a teacher.

The larger high schools and school systems have guidance personnel, but most counseling and guidance is done by the principal and his staff in the other high schools in the state.

More of the states viewed guidance as so intimately related to the other educational services as to be inseparable from them. The following excerpts indicate the feeling that the guidance worker cannot perform adequately without training as a teacher.

We take the position that persons who are to function as counselors should be acquainted with the public school situation, understand the problems and needs of the classroom teacher and the role which the teacher must play in the over-all guidance process.

Due to the fact that these people—that is, the counselors—must work very closely with teachers, it is an established fact from long experience that school administrators are rather hesitant in employing people who do pupil personnel and guidance work who are not cognizant through experience of problems of the classroom teachers.

. . . the guidance program is a part of the total school program, and not a separate entity. (Weitz, 1958, pp. 270–271.)

To be sure, this rigid view of guidance as an adjunct of the instructional program is softening somewhat. Recent investigations of training programs for guidance workers suggest that these functionaries require different training from that needed by the instructional staff. (See the recent reports of the American Psychological Association and American Personnel and Guidance Association committees on training.) There is some hope that even if school administrators cannot see themselves in clearly defined guidance roles, perhaps they may someday recognize the need for specialized personnel to provide specialized guidance services.

The clergyman, however, is in a somewhat different position from that of the school administrator. He must by virtue of his position, accept—with humility, if necessary—his role as an authority, especially in matters where values are concerned. As a participant on a panel concerned with the guidance process, an ordained priest commenting on permissiveness in the counseling relationship made the telling point that in matters involving "right" and "wrong" little latitude of interpretation could be permitted. He, the priest, was expected by his parishioners to know which was which. To deny him this certain knowledge and the obligation to transmit it would be to deny the necessity and perhaps existence of his office. To be sure, clergymen of less formally rigid denominations might not insist so vigorously on the clarity of their moral vision, yet, unless they do accept the responsibility for moral judgment, they forfeit their main claim to their robes. As long, however, as the clergyman does claim moral judgment as his main business, he cannot do much in the way of guidance as it is viewed here.

There are others besides parents, teachers, school administrators, and clergymen who carry on guidance-like activities. Club leaders, industrial personnel workers, social workers, nurses, physicians (including psychiatrists), and clinical psychologists are among the functionaries in our society who may provide guidance services. In general, the guidance provided by these people is highly restricted to a single area of behavior. Nurses, social workers, clinical psychologists, and physicians, in particular, are concerned with that specialized aspect of guidance involving the treatment and redirection of pathological behavior. They are, of course, guidance practitioners of a sort, and often highly skilled ones, but their preoccupation with markedly deviant behavior has frequently caused them to lose sight of the vast reservoir of "normal" behavior products available to all humans, including the mentally ill. Thus the advances in this branch of guidance that deals with the pathological have been few and slow in coming— so few and so slow, in fact, that there is some likelihood that the chemists and the pharmacists will preempt this essentially psychological field by means of their drug therapies.

3. The professional guidance worker

Guidance-like services are provided by many agencies of the society. We are concerned here, however, only with those guidance services that meet the criteria discussed in Chapter Three and that conform to practices described in this and subsequent chapters. The person providing this sort of service who follows some such practices as are outlined here and who is qualified by training, temperament, and philosophical orientation to assume the responsibilities of this service may be viewed as a professional guidance practitioner. We have reserved for this professional worker the label of *counselor* or *counseling psychologist*. The latter term is used to designate those counselors who have completed a program of training and internship in the field of counseling psychology at the doctorate level. Although it might be desirable to have all professional guidance workers trained at the doctorate level, it is not realistic to expect this in the immediate future. Hence the general term *counselor* will be applied to all professional workers in the field of guidance, including those trained as counseling psychologists.

4. *Problem-centered guidance*

What is the nature of the service provided by counselors? We have already noted that guidance involves the interaction of the individual's and society's values, the acquisition of new or modified behavior, and the selection of means that will facilitate this behavior acquisition. The emphasis throughout this process is upon the control of the process by the person seeking help. But how does this work out in practice? Let us examine the operating steps in the guidance experience.

We have, at the outset, an individual going about his everyday business. He performs the tasks required of him with a minimum of stress. He meets his social obligations satisfactorily. His feeling responses return the information that his current behavior is acceptable and that it is satisfying his own criteria for self-maintenance and development. As long as events continue on this even course, there is no need for guidance. At some point in this serene sequence of events, some obstacle to his current behavior intervenes. The impediment may be any of a number of events that interfere with the customary serenity of the behavioral flow or that threaten to cause radical and unknown changes in the flow. An elementary-school student may find that his schoolwork is not going as well as he thought it was when his teacher reports to his parents that he is not working up to his capacity. A junior-high-school student begins to dream of independence from parental and school authority and finds that daily school attendance is an obstruction to his finding the personal freedom he seeks. A high-school student wishes to fulfill his parents' hopes of being the first member of the family to go to college, but is pained to learn that he does not seem to have the talent to earn the grades which will gain him admission to the college of his father's choice. The attractive adolescent miss discovers that holding hands in the movies can lead to other demands which surprise and frighten her. Through courses in comparative religion and philosophy, but especially through dormitory "bull sessions," the college freshman learns that the fundamentalist moral lessons he learned at home are not so widely held as he believed. The college sophomore finds himself the butt of everybody's practical joke. The adult develops an antipathy for his boss and the routine demands of his job, but knows of no other available employer or employment.

The major sorts of obstacles to current behavior include failure to meet the demands of an institution such as school or work; failure to meet the demands of interpersonal relationships with parents, authority figures, friends, or associates; failure to cope adequately with sexual pressures; and inability to act upon the consequences of a consistent system of values. These failures may result from an inadequacy in talent or experience. They may result from some unfortunate or untimely configuration of events in the environmental context. More often than not they are the consequence of the interaction of personal limitations with a capricious environment.

Many of the obstacles encountered in a lifetime are surmounted or circumvented with the behavior repertory already at the disposal of the individual. New combinations of available behavior usually meet the requirements of the situation. From time to time, however, the individual tries one combination of behavior after another only to find that none of his attempts are successful in removing the obstruction to his goals. Repeated failure to overcome the difficulty evokes a sense of fearful urgency out of which emerge more frantic, frequently irrelevant, almost random attempts to come to grips with the situation. This state of random, irrelevant, stressful activity has been labeled by the catchall term *anxiety*.

At this point in the situation the frustrated individual may seek guidance. Such an act may simply be part of the almost random behavior being performed by the individual; or, in a more highly structured situation, seeking professional assistance in the solution of problems may be part of the available behavior repertory. Whatever the factors which determined that the individual shall seek assistance, at some point his role changes. At the point where the frustrated and anxious individual seeks the aid of a counselor, he becomes what Rogers (1942) calls a *client*. This title suggests that he has reached a state where he sees that the solution of his difficulty can only be found in collaboration with another.

Certain preexisting conditions obtain, then, at the time guidance begins. Some obstacle has interfered with ongoing behavior. The individual has attempted to remove, surmount, or circumvent the obstacle but has failed, and anxiety has resulted. In a further attempt to overcome the obstacle the individual seeks the aid of a counselor and becomes a participant in guidance. It should be pointed out here that the client need not be aware of the nature of the obstacle to his goals, nor even of the goals themselves. He does not need to know what is troubling him, only that he is troubled. Many clients approach the counselor with some such statement as, "Things don't seem to be going right. I don't know what's the matter, but I don't seem to be getting any place." Furthermore, even when the client states his goals and the obstacles to these goals as he sees them, his appraisal may turn out to be an unintentionally false or even a deliberately masked estimate of the state of affairs. The important elements in the guidance process BEFORE IT STARTS are an obstacle to current behavior and the anxiety evoked by the client's unsuccessful attempts to remove the obstacle.

These elements represent a problem. Guidance, then, begins with a problem. The solution of the problem should permit the client to achieve serenity and to continue the smooth flow of his behavior as it was before the intervention of the problem. If, however, this were the only objective of guidance, it would scarcely be worth the effort, for there are more efficient methods of solving problems than the elaborate and time-consuming guidance process described here and elsewhere. Although human problems represent the necessary precondition to guidance, their solution is not the ultimate goal. The central purpose of guidance is to engender in the client a set of problem-solving skills and attitudes which will permit him to face new emergencies as they arise. The course of human life is beset on all sides by obstructions to fulfillment. If each obstacle had to be attacked and removed de novo, human existence would become intolerable, if not impossible. In guidance, one not only solves the immediate problem, but uses the solution and the methods by which it was achieved as a model for subsequent problem-solving behavior. In terms of the concept of guidance as client-controlled, we may view the individual seeking guidance as presenting his case not as, "How do I solve this problem?" but rather as, "How do I solve problems like this one?"

5. *The problem-solving process*

This problem-centered approach to guidance suggests the necessarily collaborative nature of the guidance relationship. The client and counselor, TOGETHER, will bring to bear their resources and skills upon the solution of the problem. The client uses the counselor as a device for solving his problem. In doing this, the client controls the process in such a way that he may extract from the collaborative relationship an understanding of how the counselor manipulated events to achieve a solution. Thus, if the counselor is a true collaborator and has been open, revealing, and instructive about what has been going on in the problem-solving process, he is able to facilitate the client's acquisition of new problem-solving behavior.

How, then, does the process operate? The solution of the day-to-day problems of human beings requires, at the outset, a clear, manageable statement of what the problems are. This involves not only the identification of the obstacles but also some clarification of the course which they obstruct. Thus, in securing an accurate and tractable description of the problem, it becomes necessary to know the client's goals, values, and objectives and his capacities for achieving them, as well as the social and personal limitations that serve as obstructions to achievement. This description of behavior products involving goals, means, and limitations constitutes the diagnosis or, as we shall call it here, *problem identification.* The problem-identification step in problem solving includes the observation of behavior, the structured description of it, and the identification of the many interrelated facets of the multiordinal problem.

A second step in the problem-solving process is making some estimate of the kinds of solutions which might be reached. Here the client's values are examined in the light of social values. His long-term goals and immediate behavioral objectives are tested against his values and the values and objectives of his society. The degree of reality of each of these is assessed, and, finally, alternative solutions to the problem are considered, and the probability of their being achieved is estimated. This assessment of possible solutions to the problem is, of course, carried on in a collaborative manner. The counselor, out of his considerable experience and understanding, suggests general courses of action. The client particularizes these to his own situation.

This seeking of possible solutions is, necessarily, carried on at the symbolic level of behavior. As these symbols are manipulated to form possible solutions, they take shape as components of a symbolic context element. The client reacts symbolically to stimulus functions that emerge from this symbolic context and produces, among other things, feeling responses. Some of the feeling reaction to these collaboratively developed solutions will take the form of anxiety reduction. When the possible solution "feels good" to the client, that is, when one of the solutions tends to reduce the anxiety brought on by the problem, that solution becomes one of the alternatives to be given serious consideration in subsequent steps in the guidance process. This procedure of collaboratively describing and selecting alternative solutions to a problem may be called *structural planning*.

The selection of possible alternative outcomes to a problem does not, however, solve the problem. Now comes the difficult and often tedious process of selecting and implementing the means of executing the solution to the problem. Again, the counselor suggests general means by which the alternative solutions may be achieved. Depending on his appraisal of the situation, the counselor may make these as direct suggestions, or he may manipulate the situation in such a way as to call forth the suggestion from the client himself. In carrying on this phase of the guidance process, the counselor may manipulate objects and events symbolically, as in face-to-face counseling; he may manipulate events by providing information, as in group guidance; he may manipulate events by direct personal intervention, as when he writes an employment recommendation or arranges for necessary remedial instruction; or he may manipulate events subtly, as when he reinforces certain client responses by saying merely, "Uh-huh," and extinguishes others by saying nothing. Whatever his method, the counselor, at this stage in the guidance process, assumes a basic responsibility, which he cannot successfully abdicate, for manipulating events either symbolically or directly. This manipulation of objects and events in the client's objective or symbolic environment gives them new structure and clothes them in new meaning, so that they will serve as new stimulus functions for the evocation of new patterns of response. As the client performs some of these new reponses, he finds that the anxiety brought on by the obstacles to his fulfillment is reduced. Since the anxiety provided the energy necessary to the random, irrelevant behavior that was inappropriate to the solution of the problem, its reduction serves to reduce the number and frequency of random behavior products as well as to reduce the probability of their occurrence. Hence, with the number of inappropriate behavior products diminished, the behavior products that are appropriate to the solution of the problem have a higher probability of occurring in the newly structured situation. Goal-seeking energy appropriate to the corrective behavior is installed by the collaborative manipulation of the context element. Thus, when the context-element configuration reappears, the previously performed appropriate responses will be evoked again. If these responses are merely the symbolic responses that occur in the verbal interchange of the guidance situation, they must subsequently be translated into objective behavior. This phase of the guidance process, involving the selection and implementation of means of achieving possible solutions to the problem, may be called therapy or, perhaps more appropriately in the present context, *structural activation*.

Two additional steps are essential to effective guidance as the structural-activation phase is successfully accomplished—generalization and evaluation.

If the entire guidance experience is to take on any meaning beyond that of solving the immediate problem, the counselor must see to it that the client's original question, "How do I solve problems like this?" is answered. The methods by which the immediate problem was solved must be generalized to other similar problems. Depending upon the maturity of the client and hence his ability to abstract principles, this process of *generalization* involves several modes of attack. In almost any general problem presented by the client there are several subordinate problems. As solutions to the latter are reached, the counselor may point out the methods by which they were solved, or he may manipulate the client's behavior in such a way—as is done in the so-called nondirective techniques—as to draw from him the essential generalizations. Often, when a client has received assistance in solving one problem, he will return to the counselor for help with another matter if he has not already learned how to apply the general problem-solving procedures. Under such circumstances, the counselor can use the earlier problem-solving experience as a source from which generalizations can be drawn. Through group situations in which theoretical problems are considered, instruction in problem-solving techniques can be given. These and other procedures to be considered later suggest means by which problem solving can be generalized.

Evaluation of the guidance process is the step which tells the counselor whether or not his goals for guidance were achieved. Evaluation permits him to answer two major questions, "Was the behavior of the client redirected into more productive channels?" and "Did the client acquire the necessary problem-solving behavior that will permit him to meet new emergencies as they arise?" Secondarily, the counselor needs to know which of his approaches and techniques were most effective and which turned out to be inadequate in achieving these goals of guidance. The practice of guidance is a learning process for the counselor as well as for the client. He must, therefore, be able to make some reasonable appraisal of his present effectiveness in order to revise and improve his performance in the future.

Evaluation of guidance requires the careful observation of client behavior during and subsequent to his participation in guidance, as well as a clearly defined value structure against which the observed behavior can be measured. Simply asking the client how he feels about his guidance experience is an inadequate and often misleading measure of its effectiveness. The present writer recalls with some embarrassment just such a faulty appraisal of guidance. A veteran of World War II came to a Veterans Administration guidance center for assistance in securing training and placement in a civilian occupation. Diagnosis and vocational appraisal revealed, among other things, that the seventh-grade education which the client had received prior to entering the military service probably represented close to the limit of his academic capacity. There were, however, considerable space perception, mechanical ingenuity, and manual dexterity and a fairly high measured interest in craft activities. But the client wished to become a preacher. The Veterans Administration would not approve of the vocational objective of clergyman for this veteran because of his obvious lack of the necessary academic abilities and because the length of time that would be required to train this man was unrealistic in terms of the training eligibility available to him. Extended counseling was undertaken to awaken the veteran to the realities of the situation and to help him select a vocational objective more nearly in keeping with the facts of the diagnosis. In time, the client seemed to accept the notion of selecting, training for, and entering one of the semiskilled trades. Arrangements were made for his enrollment in a trade school and for a subsequent apprenticeship. He signed the necessary papers to pursue the supported training for his chosen vocation. In the concluding interview, the counselor asked the client how he felt about the whole procedure. The client expressed not only satisfaction but even gratitude for the help he had received and went on at length to rehearse the steps by which he and the counselor had collaboratively solved his vocational problem. The counselor, confident of a job well done, shook the client's hand warmly and sent him on his merry way.

As the client left the office, he stopped at the secretary's desk and exchanged a few words with her. Noticing this, the counselor expanded with the notion that the fine counseling, already acknowledged by the client, had extended the client's good will to all the members of the staff. And this is as it should be, he thought.

Later, in response to the counselor's inquiry about her conversation with the client, the secretary reported that the client had said that he was leaving on the next day for the Midwest, where he planned to attend a small bible school which specialized in providing elaborate-looking diplomas for such prospective preachers as this one. When she had pointed out to the client that the school in question was not on the approved training list, he stated that he was aware of this, but his mind was made up. He was grateful for the interest taken in him by the Veterans Administration, the counselor, and the center. They had all been most helpful in getting him to make up his mind. He would be on his way tomorrow, thank you.

This painful experience, as well as the unwarranted conclusions drawn from self-report questionnaires used in guidance-evaluation research, has forced one counselor, at least, to view with suspicion and alarm any guidance evaluation which depends exclusively upon the expressed views of the client. Evaluation needs to be carried out in terms of direct observation of behavior. Such direct observations should provide a basis for estimating behavior change measured against some clearly established value system.

6. *Guidance as an interacting process*

The foregoing outline of guidance practice may leave the reader with the false notion that the steps discussed are sequential. To be sure, the problem situation is a precondition to guidance. This is to say that an obstacle to current behavior must intervene and anxiety must result from the unsuccessful attempts to overcome the obstacle. Beyond this, the steps in the guidance process follow no formal sequence. Although problem identification will usually precede structural planning, and it, in turn, will be followed by structural activation, generalization, and evaluation in that order, several of these phases are often carried on simultaneously. As a partial identification of the problem is made, it leads to some hypotheses about possible courses of action and the means for carrying them out. This in turn often forces the process back to further diagnosis, which will help sharpen the structural plan and provide estimates of the client's capabilities for executing the steps leading to the solution. Throughout the processes of identification, structural planning, and structural activation, generalizations will be abstracted as they become evident.

Intermediate evaluations are being made as the whole enterprise proceeds.

Since guidance is a collaborative behavioral effort, each set of responses as they are performed becomes a part of the reactional biographies and hence a component of the context elements in the next behavior products of BOTH counselor and client. The stimulus functions which may arise from these context elements may evoke identification, structural planning, structural activation, generalization, or evaluative responses, depending on the total configuration of the context elements.

To illustrate the dynamic interrelationships of the strategies in guidance consider the case of a high-school junior who comes to the counselor's office to discuss his choice of courses for his senior year. Since this is a routine conference held with all juniors in the spring of the year, the student is not especially concerned about it. The only anxiety he feels is the customary anxiety of a student about to talk with a school official. He is, of course, disturbed about what the counselor may say when he learns that the course card has not been filled out yet, but he shrugs this off with the notion that a great many other students did not know what they wanted to take, and the counselor filled out their cards for them. After all, almost everybody takes English, civics, mathematics, and science or language in his senior year.

The initial exchanges between the student and the counselor go pleasantly enough. The counselor expresses no disapproval and almost no surprise when the student reports that he hasn't the foggiest notion about what he will take next year, except that he'd like to get into Miss Bland's English section because he had heard that she was a good—i.e., easy—teacher. When the counselor raises the question about what he plans to do after he graduates from high school, he supposes that he'll go into the Army if he can't avoid the draft, or perhaps he'll get a job, but he doesn't know what sort. The counselor then suggests that he might be able to make more sensible decisions about his senior-year courses if he had some reason for taking them. The general suggestion is made that if the student has some general idea about where he wants to go, he might have a better chance of picking a suitable route for getting there. This first conference is closed with the suggestion that the student give some thought to the matter, and that he discuss his decisions with his parents, friends, and teachers.

This first encounter between the student and his counselor was devoted to that aspect of problem identification concerned with formulating the problem in some manageable terms. The student appeared to be unaware, at the outset, that there was any relationship between his course choices and his plans after leaving school. (This, of course, is not an unusual state of affairs.) The problem, as the student saw it, was that of satisfying the administrative requirement that he have some courses listed on his schedule card for next year. In these terms, he felt no great anxiety and no need for guidance. The reformulation of the problem by the counselor directs the focus of the process to the student himself, and arouses some mild anxieties which can be used in subsequent guidance interviews.

When the student returns for his second conference, he states that all the things that he has thought of doing after high school require that he go to college, but his family can't afford a college education for him, his grades are not good enough to earn him a scholarship, and besides he's not sure that he wants to go to school for four more years. In response to the counselor's inquiry about the kinds of work he has been considering, he indicates: athletic coach (he is an active participant in school sports), electrical engineer (he has built a home hi-fi set), or a salesman (his father is the assistant manager of a hardware store). These objectives are examined collaboratively by the counselor and the client. Estimates of the student's probable success in each of these areas is made by means of an analytical investigation of his previous school performance, his extracurricular and hobby activities, and his measured abilities and interests. Additional psychometric information is secured if both student and counselor seem to believe that it will contribute to the identification of the problem. Data on the student's social situation, his financial capabilities, and his own and his parents' aspirations are considered. Other possible vocational and educational goals are added to the list: electrician, radio repairman, professional athlete, and so on, as well as trade school, vocational school, and on-the-job training. Information about each of these possible lines of attack is provided either through reference to the vocational literature or directly by the counselor.

Here structural planning and problem identification go hand in hand. As possible courses of action are considered, data on the student and his environment are collected in order to provide a basis for estimating the probability of a particular outcome. Meanwhile, the student is testing each new proposal against his own feelings. In raising the question of relating the immediate choice of the senior year courses to ultimate educational and vocational goals, the counselor aroused some anxiety in the client about his future. If a particular proposal appears to the client to reduce some of this anxiety, it is likely to persist; if, however, the proposal has no anxiety-reducing effect, or if the thought of the proposal heightens his tensions, the client is likely to withdraw from this line of investigation. Furthermore, the expert counselor will take pains throughout this stage of the guidance process to suggest the rationale of the problem-solving process that is taking place, thus clarifying the generalization aspect of the process.

As guidance proceeds and goals are tentatively selected, as the senior year course schedule is established, and as the student undertakes his program of studies—in other words, as the process of structural activation begins to operate—further diagnoses are made, the predictions are sharpened, the effects of the intermediate steps are evaluated, new therapeutic measures are introduced, and, throughout, the general principles of the problem-solving process are emphasized.

All this suggests that the mode of attack in guidance is not a step-by-step, formal approach to problem solving. All strategies are brought to bear at once. The practice of guidance demands a high degree of flexibility on the part of the counselor. Guidance requires of its practitioners that they be highly skilled in the use of these strategies, that they be sensitive to the appropriateness of a particular strategy at each stage in guidance, and that they exercise this sensitivity and skill with a high sense of responsible purpose.

Five

Problem identification

◆◆◆

Guidance is a collaborative process in which the client and the counselor together seek to create new and modified behavior products which will serve to remove, circumvent, or surmount obstructions to the client's productivity and satisfaction. When effectively applied, guidance not only resolves the immediate problem but also engenders in the client a general understanding of the problem-solving process through which he can meet new problem situations more successfully on his own. Central to the problem-solving process is the identification of the obstacles that the client has encountered and the organization of these identified obstructions into some meaningful and manageable form. This structuring of events into configurations that reveal their relationships, expose the order of their significance, and determine those that may be crucial to the immediate problem with which the client is faced is called diagnosis or *problem identification.*

1. *Semantics in problem identification* [1]

The structuring of events into meaningful and manageable configurations occurs during the collaborative interactions between the client and the counselor. For the most part, these interactions take place in the domain of symbolic reality. The client tells the counselor about the objects and events which are obstructing his progress. His report is made up of symbols representing the events. The client takes a test, and his performance is symbolized by a score. The client

[1] This section and those which follow represent a revision and expansion of previously published material (Weitz, 1954).

fails a course, and his failure is represented by a grade on a report card. The client wishes to enter a profession, and his desires are symbolized in the words he uses to tell about them. Rarely does the counselor observe the client's behavior directly. Thus, although problem identification is centrally concerned with the analysis and structuring of behavior observations, the observations and the analysis of their structure take place in the counselor's and client's symbolic reality.

Semantic reactions are responses made to symbolic events (Korzybski, 1948). These reactions form patterns and follow processes which are similar to behavior products in objective reality. In semantic reactions, the symbol—a word or a test score, perhaps—represents some event in the environmental context. This symbol, rather than the objective event, interacts with the awareness responses to produce stimulus functions. These, in turn, react with the total response repertory to form behavior products. Under these circumstances, the entire operation takes place almost exclusively in the realm of symbolic reality. Semantic reactions, as differentiated from responses performed exclusively in the objective domain, have a wider range of flexibility, because the symbolic stimulus events can assume a wider range of meaning than can objects and events in objective reality. At the same time, the meanings or stimulus functions assumed by symbols in semantic reactions may become fanciful, unsane, or even insane, to the extent that their structure departs from the structure of relationships in the objective world they are intended to represent.

2. Abstracting

One of the processes in the semantic reaction that makes the flexibility possible and that at the same time can lead to fanciful, unsane, or insane reactions is the process of abstracting. Abstracting involves focusing upon certain aspects of an object or event and classifying the object or event according to these selected characteristics, then following this with further focusing upon selected aspects of the class of events and placing the class in a more general category of events, and so on. The end product of the abstracting process is a high-order abstraction or generalization. Abstracting permits us to deal with a single event in terms of general principles applicable to the class of events. This is efficient behavior, for it means that we do not have to deal with each new event as a unique encounter, PROVIDED NONE OF THE ESSENTIAL CHARACTERISTICS OF THE ORIGINAL OBJECT OR EVENT IS LOST IN THE PROCESS OF ABSTRACTING.

The lowest order of abstraction, the zero order, is the object or event itself as it exists in objective reality. This is the "unspeakable" level of abstraction. That chair standing there in the corner is a physical event in objective reality. We may now observe its characteristics and respond to them by sitting in the chair. We may also call it *a chair*. Having labeled it we move into symbolic reality. This label may be viewed as a first-order abstraction. Now we may classify this symbol into a more general category, say *furniture*. The symbol *furniture* may be further classified as *household equipment*, and so on. As long as the high-order abstraction *household equipment* retains the idea *something we can sit on*, and we act toward the chair in this manner, our symbolic and objective behavior retain the same structure and hence we are operating in the realm of reality. If, however, we recall that household equipment can be used for cooking, and we attempt to scramble an egg on the chair, we have confused our order of abstraction; we have entered the world of unreality, fancy, unsanity, and perhaps insanity, and besides, we have annoyed our wives.

Problem identification, involving as it does the manipulation of symbols representing objective events and the formation of symbolic structures based upon higher-order abstractions, is a connected series of semantic reactions performed by client and counselor. Problem identification requires that the right (i.e., the realistic) symbols be found to describe events in the client's life and that they be organized into structures which clearly represent the relationship of events as they occur in objective reality.

Just as guidance cannot be segmented from the rest of the life of the client, so problem identification cannot be separated from the rest of the counseling process. We cannot think of problem identification as some discrete segment of the guidance process, for as symbols are manipulated in the total problem-solving process, new symbols and labels are called for to complete new patterns. The new symbols are generated from the application of new diagnostic procedures and techniques—tests, interviews, and the like—or are abstracted from the symbolic configurations already at hand. It is important to note, however, that the identification process is in operation throughout the entire course of the guidance undertaking.

This process of discovering appropriate symbols and realistic structures in the course of helping a client solve a problem takes place in somewhat the following manner:

1. The client participates in some event.
2. Out of all the elements in the event, the client selects some; these he perceives and responds to.
3. Out of all the responses made by the client in the situation, he selects some; these he reports to the counselor.
4. The counselor listens to the client, and while he is listening, he symbolically projects some of his own similar experiences into the client's description.
5. Out of this total description—including the counselor's projections—the counselor selects some elements; these he perceives and responds to by drawing inferences and formulating structures.
6. Out of all of these inferences and structures, the counselor selects some; these he reports. This report by the counselor, involving high-order abstractions in some cases far removed from the original event, is his tentative problem identification or diagnosis.

This description of the identified problem is made up of verbal symbols representing objects, events, conditions, and so on, of which some exist in the objective reality of the client, some in the objective reality of the counselor, and still others only in the symbolic reality of both. This description also represents the symbolic interrelationships of the events. The tentative identification of the problem is composed of the symbols that the counselor and the client will collaboratively manipulate in the problem-solving process. As can be seen from the above description of the problem-identification step in guidance, it is essentially a process of abstraction. As the diagnosis proceeds, the level of abstraction becomes more general and farther removed from the objective events as they occurred. In the process of abstracting from one level to the next in problem identification, there is always the danger of mistaking one level for another; an illustration adapted from Korzybski (1948) may help clarify this point.

Let us say that Charlie Brown participates in an event such as a stone falling on his foot. Charlie Brown's perception of what happens is not the same as the event itself. Charlie Brown's aching foot is not the falling stone. The pain is the perception of the event, not the event itself. When Charlie describes his sore toe to a friend, the description is not Charlie's toe. When the friend listens to the description and draws inferences about how Charlie feels, these inferences are not Charlie's description. And, finally, when the friend labels his inferences *pain* or even *pain₁, the ache in poor Charlie's purple, swollen toe,* this label is not the same as his inferences. This diagnostic label, *pain*₁, is not the inference, is not Charlie's description, is not Charlie's pain, is not the foot, and is not the objective event in nature, the falling stone that landed on Charlie's toe. Each step in the process of abstraction represents the selection of specific aspects of the preceding step, so that the end product, the diagnostic label, is quite different from the original event, even though the selection which takes place is unwitting.

In the guidance situation, when a client, in an effort to justify his present fear of animals, reports a painful experience, let us say, of having been bitten by a dog when he was a child, and the counselor responds to this emotionally delivered report by saying, "You were frightened by that dog," the counselor must not delude himself into thinking that he is, or even can be, reflecting the same fear being described by the client. He is merely providing the diagnostic label *frightened by a dog*, which can subsequently be manipulated in the problem-solving process. This confusion of level of abstraction has led a generation of nondirective counselors to a fanciful view of their counseling behavior, their function, and their responsibility.

Thus far we have been discussing the process of abstracting diagnostic labels from the client's own reports of his experiences. The same semantic principles apply, however, to other diagnostic machinery. For example, counselors find tests extremely helpful as diagnostic tools in observing human behavior. This is especially true in that class of events that has been called educational guidance. Let us suppose that the client is a college sophomore seeking assistance in securing better grades in school. In such a situation the counselor and the client may collaboratively decide that it would be helpful in this problem-solving situation to know something about the client's ability to earn better grades. Thus they decide to make an estimate of the client's academic talents by using a test of ability labeled *scholastic aptitude test*. Just what does this mean on the objective level of behavior?

The client has a repertory of responses, acquired through a great variety of experiences, that makes it possible for him to behave, under certain circumstances, in ways which seem to please college professors. This mode of behavior we may call *scholastic aptitude*. Out of this rather vast store of responses, the client is stimulated by the test to produce a few. This sample taken from the client's response repertory is measured and assigned a numerical label. The counselor knows that this numerical label represents some combination of appropriate and inappropriate responses interacting with the test items. This label, he also knows, is subject to a variety of sampling and administrative errors. The test score, this numerical symbol, represents an error-loaded abstraction from the client's response repertory that the counselor calls *scholastic aptitude of X magnitude*. In terms of what the counselor knows and feels about such a diagnostic label, he is prepared to draw inferences and manipulate the symbol in an attempt to help the student solve his problem and receive better grades. Note, however, that the scholastic aptitude test score is not the student's academic response repertory. Here, then, in using tests as diagnostic tools, we employ the process of abstraction in much the same way as we do when we attempt to generalize from the client's own description of his experiences. Both are symbolic structures representing but not duplicating objective reality. Both are subject to the same errors of confusing the level of abstraction. The counselor must keep constantly in mind that the symbol is not the objective event. The first step that he might take in differentiating between symbolic and objective reality when he uses tests as diagnostic devices for observing behavior is to reject the notion of *objective* tests or even of *objectively derived test scores*. These concepts are figments of intentional fantasy, for the selection of items and the determination of the appropriate responses depend in a large measure on the attitudes of the test maker, while the interpretation of the test score is so deeply embedded in the symbolic reality of the counselor that its contact with objective reality may be a tenuous one.

3. *Non-identity of events*

What has been said about abstraction in problem identification may be summarized in a general principle which holds that EACH OBJECT, EVENT, CONDITION, ETC., OCCURRING IN NATURE OR IN SYMBOLIC REALITY IS UNIQUE, HAVING NO EXACT COUNTERPART. Thus, not only are labels different from the events they symbolize, but no two objects, events, conditions, etc., are the same. Similarly, no object or event is exactly like itself from moment to moment. This principle of non-identity has important implications for problem identification. If we accept the principle that no two objects, events, conditions, etc., are exactly alike and that the diagnostic label is merely a considerably removed abstraction from the event it is intended to symbolize we must employ our diagnostic terms in new ways. Old, familiar terms like anxiety, reinforcement, scholastic aptitude, aggression, rejection, and the like do not have the same operational meanings we used to think they had. This notion may become clearer when we examine the following illustration.

Take the diagnostic statement *25th percentile on a test of scholastic aptitude.* Suppose that it represents part of the problem identification in the case of the college sophomore mentioned above. Even if great care is exercised in manipulating this symbol to insure that it is not mistaken for the event it is intended to symbolize, it does not provide an adequate enough description of the objective event to permit meaningful inferences. In the case of the particular student in question, the diagnostic term may symbolize some of the following: This student performed better than 25 per cent of the students at University *X* on a test involving samples of rather specialized verbal and quantitative reasoning administered on the day he arrived at the University from a small, rural community. This happened after one of the student's friends warned him that if he did too well on the test, he would be assigned to an advanced section of the freshman English course where his chances of earning a grade better than a "C" were mighty slim indeed. All of this is quite different from saying that the student has low scholastic aptitude. The more extended diagnostic description provides more meaningful symbols to manipulate, whereas the shorthand higher-order abstraction may be misleading.

The situation is much the same in dealing with other diagnostic labels. Consider, for example, the notion of the *rejected child.* In the process of seeking guidance on a problem involving interpersonal relationships, a client presents the view that his parents did not want him when he was born and now hate him. If the counselor accepts this statement as given and abstracts from it the diagnostic label *rejected child,* he finds himself with a symbol which can be manipulated in certain ways in the problem solving situation. If, on the other hand, the counselor encourages the client to explore the parent-child relationship further, he may and probably will find that there are situations in which the parents, in fact, did reject him, but there were also situations in which the parents displayed love and affection toward him, and that there were still other situations in which they treated him in a neutral manner. Such extended descriptions of the objective-level relationships in the case provide the counselor and the client with different diagnostic terms which operate in the problem-solving situation quite differently from the symbol *rejected child.*

4. *Extensive description*

This situation suggests an important general principle of problem identification, which may be stated somewhat as follows: PROBLEM

IDENTIFICATION IN GUIDANCE SHOULD AVOID THE USE OF SHORTHAND LABELS INSOFAR AS POSSIBLE AND SHOULD INSTEAD PROVIDE EXTENSIVE DESCRIPTIONS OF THE OBJECTS, EVENTS, CONDITIONS, ETC. Extensive descriptions of life experiences require the identification and labeling of the unique behavior of a unique individual under a unique set of circumstances at a specific time in history. In theory, description by extension requires the identification of all elements in the situation, for only in this way can the uniqueness of a particular object, event, condition, etc., be understood and manipulated realistically within its particular structure. Since the time limitations in a human life make such complete descriptions impossible, it becomes necessary to resort to a notation device that permits us to limit the extent of our diagnostic labeling and simultaneously suggest its extensibility. The device operates as follows: A number of labels are selected for use in describing a situation. There should be a number of such terms, say three or four for each important situation. These terms are then followed by the term *etc.* This suggests that although the description is incomplete, the event is capable of evoking additional symbols. Care must be exercised, however, to insure that the use of the term *etc.* implies additional terms actually known to the client and counselor and does not serve simply as a means of avoiding further consideration of the matter.

Care needs to be exercised also in this extensive approach to problem identification to differentiate between those symbols that represent the client's experience and those that represent the counselor's projections of his own experiences. A certain amount of the counselor's experience will, of necessity, find its way into the diagnosis. Some of the events in the client's life can best be described in terms of normative information known to the counselor. Test performance is one example of this kind of event. Some client experiences having a heavy overlay of feeling can be described by the counselor, in the beginning at least, only in terms of the symbols he has used to describe his own similar emotions. As guidance progresses, however, the symbols provided by the client will be substituted for the counselor's original labels. The greatest danger, of course, occurs when the counselor mistakes his own idiosyncratic labels for those of the client and tries to draw inferences about the structure of the event without being aware of the difference.

5. *Appraisal and problem identification*

This extensive approach to problem identification has much in common SUPERFICIALLY with the current notion in appraisal that the more the counselor knows about the client, the better he is able to help him. The college admissions "counselor" secures voluminous data on each candidate for admission. These data include test scores, grades, surveys of family educational and financial resources, recommendations, and essays by the candidate on why he wants to attend Ol' Siwash. These data are tabulated, weighed, and evaluated to determine the candidate's relative chances of success. Voluminous as these data may be, and conscientious as the admissions officer may be, the interaction of the two does not represent an exercise in problem identification as it has been formulated here. Instead, this represents an appraisal of data, an evaluation of symbols. Little can be done with this mass of information to give a picture of the unique individual seeking a solution to the problem of acquiring an education. Diagnosis by extension seeks to paint a picture of the reactional biography— all of it—and the ramifications of the problem situation that momentarily impede the forward movement of that biography in such a way as to emphasize the unique character of the individual and his problem. Problem identification is a multivalued description. Appraisal is, on the other hand, a two-valued description: acceptable or not acceptable. The effective counselor will employ extensive diagnosis to provide not a mass of data for evaluation but rather a multivalued description of a unique client with a unique problem.

6. *Safeguards in extensive labeling*

This procedure of diagnostic labeling by extension provides certain safeguards in problem identification. In the first place, it provides a safeguard against the counselor's treating the symbol as if it were the event. Thus, if the counselor summarizes a client's description of some behavior as *irrational fear of dogs*, say, he may in the course of guidance try to manipulate the label as if it were the fear itself. He may attempt to "reflect" the fear when he is merely restating a label. If, on the other hand, the counselor summarizes the client's story in a series of specific descriptions of unique events in which the client was frightened by or avoided dogs, he is less likely to treat these extended descriptions as if they were the fear felt by the client. In this way, confusion in the order of abstraction is more likely to be avoided.

This procedure of extensive labeling is likely, also, to provide a safeguard against faulty symbolization. If the labels are extensive enough, if enough terms are used and the conditions of each event are specified, terms that are inconsistent with the major outlines of the pattern will become evident. This will force a reexamination of the pattern and a restatement of the inconsistent terms in symbols which appear to fit the structure of the event and thus represent more closely the objective behavior being described. While this test of the internal consistency of the symbolic structure of a description will not necessarily insure a true picture of the objective event, it is more likely to do so than a single high-order abstraction employed to symbolize a complex behavior pattern.

Illustrative of this is the situation in which a counselor was trying to assist a client in making some decisions about her educational and vocational future. The client indicated that she was considering the possibility of entering the teaching profession, and wished to know if she were temperamentally suited to a teaching career. The discussion with the student indicated that she was presently engaged in satisfying social experiences; her relationships with her teachers, parents, and agemates appeared to involve no more stress and tension than is usually found in these relationships; and she appeared to be meeting her present academic demands adequately in terms of her talents. All seemed to be in order. The student reported, however, that she had taken a personality inventory in one of her classes and that the instructor had raised the question of her temperamental suitability for the teaching profession. She had asked her professor to send a copy of the profile to the counselor for further interpretation. The personality inventory profile described a person so emotionally disturbed as to be not only not suited to teaching but to be in urgent need of extended emotional guidance. This piece of diagnostic information was inconsistent with the rest of the structure. Had the counselor seen only the personality profile, he might well have proceeded very differently by focusing the attention of the guidance process upon a more detailed personality diagnosis leading ultimately to extended psychotherapy. This is, in fact, what happened in the case of the instructor who, upon seeing the profile, had referred her at once for counseling. A collaborative examination of the events described by the personality profile yielded the information that whatever was being described by the profile had little relationship to the structure of real events in the student's life. The inconsistency of the profile with all the rest of the diagnosis, assembled not only from the student's own statements but especially by the extended diagnostic description which had been put together from independent sources, confirmed the necessity for examining the test profile further. An investigation of the student's original personality test answer sheet revealed that the source of the inconsistency lay in the way in which her answers had been recorded. This may seem to be a trivial illustration of the use of extended diagnosis to establish poor test-administration procedure. Any counselor, however, who has had the misfortune to use inaccurate test data in problem identification and has carried through on his diagnosis to the detriment of his client will not find the illustration trivial. It is simply an obvious example of the way in which diagnosis by extension will reveal inconsistencies in the description.

Finally, this process of extensive diagnostic labeling will provide some safeguards against faulty perception of events and faulty labeling of events by THE CLIENT. In such situations as the earlier illustration in which the client perceived and described himself as an unwanted child, it will be found that the client will discover the label to be inconsistent with the extensive description of situations in which he is sometimes loved and sometimes given neutral treatment. The discovery of these inconsistencies in the structure of the symbolic events should cause him to reexamine his own perceptions and his original description. Clarification at this level should hasten therapy and the problem-solving process.

Diagnostic labeling by extension should force the client and his counselor to treat each event as unique, which it is, and provides safeguards against faulty problem identification at several levels of abstraction. This semantic approach to problem identification has the additional virtue of emphasizing the probability nature of events. It is, of course, true that in any approach to diagnosis we are merely saying that the chances are good that the client will act thus and so under a given set of circumstances. When, however, we use one of the customary diagnostic labels, say *aggressive*, without specifying the conditions under which aggressive behavior has and has not been performed, we run the risk of manipulating this term in structural planning and activation as if the client were likely to be aggressive in all or most situations. Stressing the specific conditions under which aggressive behavior is and is not exhibited brings forcibly to the attention of both the client and the counselor the tentative nature of any prediction and frees them to examine the probability that aggression will take place under specified conditions. The probability nature of the symbol is thus emphasized.

7. Problem-identification techniques

Problem identification involves the structuring of events in symbolic reality in such a way as to give a clear and extensive picture of the events in the objective domain. In guidance we are especially interested in depicting the events and their structure that form the problem for the client. We are seeking terms that will describe adequately the obstructions impeding the productive flow of the client's behavior. This identification requires the meticulous observation of the client's behavior as well as means for the coding of these observations.

Guidance workers have developed a variety of means of identifying problem events and of assigning labels to them. Among the techniques most commonly used for observing behavior are the diagnostic interview, the direct observation of the client in natural or contrived problem situations, and the psychometric evaluation of behavior products. In the sections that follow we shall consider the first two of these general observational techniques. The observation of psychological behavior by means of psychometric techniques will be considered in the next chapter. Throughout this discussion of these observational techniques it must be borne in mind that we are interested in the devices considered only because they provide a means of identifying and describing client's problems. The descriptions derived from these observations will subsequently be used as essential ingredients in the problem-solving process and will be utilized especially in the structural-planning and structural-activation phases of guidance.

8. Direct behavior observation

The direct observation of the client's spontaneous behavior can provide diagnostic information of major value in the guidance situation. This involves observing the client as he behaves in situations other than the one in which guidance is carried on. Observations of the student client in the classroom, on the playground, in the cafeteria, etc., observations of an adult client in work or social situations, and similar observations of clients in unstructured situations represent the kind of direct observations we are concerned with here. Unfortunately, the busy counselor rarely has the time or the opportunity to make systematic observations of clients in such natural or spontaneous circumstances. A few such observations on a single client can mislead the counselor as much as they can help him. Some counselors place great store in occasional informal contacts with the client. Although these may serve to develop an effective and warm relationship between the counselor and the client, they are likely to produce little in the way of useful diagnostic data; first of all, the counselor is himself so much a part of the situation that the responses performed by the client are colored by the stimulus functions aroused by the counselor; and secondly, such observations are rarely of sufficient frequency and length to permit systematic observations leading to the kinds of generalizations essential to effective problem identification.

The counselor must, therefore, depend upon others to provide him with this sort of direct observational data. In some situations it is possible to secure systematic direct observations of behavior from teachers in a school system or from supervisors in a work setting. If such direct observations of spontaneous behavior can be made a part of the regular activities of teachers or work supervisors, the counselor can have readily at hand an invaluable body of information when the client comes for help. The counselor who can secure such observations and who wishes to use them in problem identification must insure that his cooperating observers are carrying out their functions adequately.

To be of any value in guidance, observations of spontaneous, natural behavior, will need to have the following characteristics.

1. The observations will need to be made in a systematic manner.
2. The observations will need to be made by several people.
3. The conditions under which each observation is made will need to be specified.
4. The report of the observations will need to be prepared in such a way as to separate the record of the behavior performed from any evaluation of it.

Although these conditions for making diagnostic observations are rarely completely met, it is possible to view them as criteria for examining such observational records as may be available for use.

Consider the situation in which a junior high school counselor, with the concurrence of the administration and the enthusiastic cooperation of the teaching staff, undertakes to institute a program of direct observation of behavior to provide necessary information for problem identification in his guidance program. In order to achieve the criteria indicated above, he might go about setting up the program in the following manner. Each teacher would be asked to make about five observations on each student during the year. Thus, if each teacher had five classes of about thirty students each, he would be expected to prepare some 750 observations per year, or slightly fewer than one per day per class. At the beginning of the year, five Behavior Observation Report Cards (see Fig. 7) would be assigned to each student by filling in the student's name in the card heading. The cards for each class (five for each student) are then shuffled to insure random arrangement. They are then dated in order with the dates of school days. Now each teacher teaching five classes will have five decks of dated cards (one for each class), each containing five cards for each student in the class, with the cards for a given class arranged in random order. The teacher now files these cards by date. As a given date arrives, the teacher makes his observational records for the students whose cards are filed under that date. This arrangement provides a systematic procedure for making random observations.

Since in a departmentalized junior high school each student takes four or five courses, there will be, at the end of the year, some twenty or twenty-five observations on each student made by four or five different observers. By having a number of different observers make several observations on the same student, it is possible not only to avoid the influence of a single observer's biases but also to gain some insight into the ways in which the student responds to different kinds of people.

Space is provided on the Behavior Observation Report Card to record the class, the subject matter, the activities being undertaken, and any special conditions which might influence the behavior of the student. When an observation is made on a student, the teacher simply fills in the data in the upper part of the card and describes what the student did during the period for which he was observed. By insuring that the students selected for observation were chosen at random, the teacher is able to focus upon the natural spontaneous behavior of the child. Unless this is done, teachers are likely to make observational records on students only when something unusual happens to the child. This method of reporting only critical events is likely to give a distorted picture of the normal behavior of the child.

Since many teachers are likely to find it difficult to record only observations of the objective events, and are inclined to wish to evaluate them, space is left on the Report Card for the teacher's comments. All evaluative comments and inferences about the observed behavior can be reserved for this space. Occasionally these comments will illuminate the behavior being reported. More often, however, they provide more information about the teacher's behavior than about the child's.

When all observations are in for a given child, they should be summarized by the counselor in such a way as to give a generalized

BEHAVIOR OBSERVATION REPORT CARD

STUDENT _Mary S._   CLASS _Alg. (grade 9)_   DATE _23 Dec. 19—_

TEACHER _H. E. W._   PERIOD _4_   OBSERVATION TIME _1st 10 min of class_

ACTIVITY: _Solution of linear equations involving fractions. Students put homework on the board and describe what they did to secure the answer._

SPECIAL CONDITIONS: _students had just come from the assembly where they had seen a Christmas play and sung carols. Vacation begins tomorrow._

OBSERVATION: _Mary came into the room about a minute late with her friend Sally. They were singing a carol as they entered the room. They continued to sing softly as they took their seats and until the teacher called for the attention of the class. Mary was sent to the board to put up one of her homework problems. She did this quietly and took her seat. While the other students explained their problems, Mary addressed Christmas cards behind her book. When her turn came, she went to the board and started to explain her problem. About half way through the explanation, she discovered that she had made an error which resulted from her lack of understanding of fractions. The teacher led her through a series of questions designed to explain the point she had missed. Mary became more and more agitated as the discussion continued. The teacher drew a circle on the board and divided it into thirds. He asked Mary how many people could be served from a pie divided into thirds. Mary said, "Three. But we don't get pieces of pie that big at my house!" She went to her seat in tears. The teacher asked her if she would not like to go to the rest room to calm down. She left the room and returned just as the class bell rang._

COMMENT: _Mary is generally highly emotional. Today she reached the crying stage earlier than she usually does. When demands are placed upon her, she is inclined to cry and leave the room._

Figure 7. Sample Behavior Observation Report Card.

but extended description of the child's classroom behavior. This summary can serve as a valuable diagnostic tool when employed in subsequent guidance. Unfortunately, both the record keeping by the teachers and the summarizing by the counselor are time-consuming activities. The results, however, have been found to be worth the effort, for not only is the information highly useful in guidance, but the process of gathering it has served to sensitize teachers to the general activities of their students beyond their responses to the mere content of the course.

9. *The cumulative record*

The school's cumulative records and the personnel records of industry represent a kind of summary of observations and can be helpful in diagnosis in many kinds of problems. Furthermore, these records are less demanding in time and energy than the direct observational records. The identification data provided by the cumulative record (name, age, sex, place of birth, family structure, etc.), the physical data (height, weight, vision, hearing, etc.), the social data (extracurricular participation, socio-economic level of the family, etc.), all provide diagnostic information especially relevant to the reactional biography and the environmental context elements of the behavior products performed by a client. These, of course, are not the same sort of things as the direct observational report discussed above, but data of this kind, if properly analyzed and evaluated, can make important contributions to the process of problem identification.

Of special interest in the cumulative record of the school is the report of the student's academic performance over a period of time. In general, academic performance is fairly consistent. Records of several thousand college students examined over a period of time revealed that the correlation between grades earned in the freshman year and those earned in the senior year exceeded .85. Easley (1937), in a more formal investigation of the same behavior, found that academic performance from year to year had a high consistency. Although the relationships found were not perfect, they were sufficiently high to conclude that under ordinary conditions a student's academic performance remains fairly constant from year to year. Although this consistency is not as great for younger children, it is still sufficiently high to make suspect any record that deviates from it. Here again we see that by examining a series of events, we can identify difficulties by inconsistencies in the structure. Marked variations in academic performance from year to year, from marking period to marking period, or from subject to subject will provide significant diagnostic information about the client's behavior. While cumulative records of this sort are not the same as direct observations of behavior, they can be employed in much the same way. By applying the principles of non-identity and description by extension, discussed earlier in this chapter, these records, both direct observations and cumulative, can supply the counselor with the necessary symbols for manipulation in the problem-solving process.

10. *The diagnostic interview*

Problem identification in guidance involves the cataloguing of events that comprise the problem situation, the discovery of appropriate symbols to represent these events, and the formulation of a symbolic structure that is a faithful map of the structure of the problem events occurring in objective reality. Some of these events can be identified by means of psychometric techniques and some by means of direct observation of natural, spontaneous behavior, but many can be identified only by means of the diagnostic interview. Furthermore, the selection of the appropriate symbols to represent the events and the structuring of these symbols into a realistic representation of the objective world require the collaborative efforts of both the client and the counselor. It is within the exchange of the diagnostic interview that this collaboration can achieve its most telling effect.

Earlier it was suggested that many if not all of the guidance strategies are carried out simultaneously or at least concurrently. Problem identification, structural planning, structural activation, generalization, and evaluation are functioning at about the same time in guidance. To speak, then, of the diagnostic interview may be misleading, for guidance interviews involve all five processes concurrently. We can, however, examine one facet of the guidance interview at a time if we continually remind ourselves that, in the domain of objective reality, problem identification or diagnosis is only one component of the total interview. For convenience we shall speak of the diagnostic interview when, in reality, we mean the problem-identification aspect of the guidance interview.

The diagnostic interview is usually initiated by the counselor, who makes some such statement as, "Would you like to tell me what brings you to see us today?" In diagnosis, this is the first of many questions, either stated directly or implied, that the counselor will address to the client. In response to this and other questions, the client will produce symbols, mostly verbal but frequently in terms of bodily movements or expressions, that are designed to represent his internal and external state of affairs. These symbols will stand for the objects and events in the external world and the actions taken by the client and other persons toward them, but they will also stand for the client's thoughts, feelings, attitudes, and value systems. They will depict the client's images, intent, and plans (Miller, Galanter, and Pribram, 1960), as well as the obstructions to these plans.

As these symbols are produced by the client, the counselor examines each one to determine, first, whether or not the significance of it is the same for the client and for himself and, second, whether the symbol is a faithful representation of the client's objective reality. The first of these evaluations may be illustrated by the case of a student who reports to the counselor that he is seeking help to keep from failing some of his courses. Failure to the counselor means, among other things, receiving grades so low that the student may be required to drop a course or repeat it. The student, on the other hand, may view failure as receiving grades of C in courses required for admission to the college of his choice; or he may view failure as receiving grades of B in courses in which his father believes him capable of earning A's. This latter notion of failure is not uncommon among bright college freshmen who received top grades in their high schools and who find that the same kind of study effort will earn them only C's or B's in college. The counselor must, therefore, make certain that his symbols mean the same thing to the client as they do to him. They must be talking the same language in the same conversation. This may be accomplished by extensive exploration of the terms provided by the client.

Evaluation of the symbols as representations of objective reality is also accomplished by means of extensive description. This may be illustrated by the case of a student who reports that he is failing Miss X's course because "She's out to get me." Extensive examination of the term *failure* leads to the conclusion that the student has correctly appraised and labeled the situation. His grade of F on the last several tests verifies his symbol. The term *she's out to get me* is supposed to represent something like the following, which the student supplies as explanation. "She always seems to know what I don't know and asks questions about it on the tests. She does this to all the students. Practically everyone in the class is failing."

Now the accuracy of this symbol needs to be explored further. Miss X, of course, may be a disturbed woman who overcomes her own sense of inadequacy by demonstrating the hopeless inadequacy of her students. She may do this all in the name of education, explaining to herself and anyone else who cares to listen that students must achieve a high degree of mastery before she will pass them on to the next teacher or to the cruel, demanding world. If this is the case, the structure of the student's symbols faithfully represents the nature of the events in objective reality. If it is not the case, however—and it rarely is—then the structure of the client's symbols is not a veridical representation of reality.

When the symbols and their structure are unreal, fanciful, unsane, or insane, the disjunction between them and reality can frequently be demonstrated by the applications of the principle of extensive description. As more events in the structure are symbolized, the inconsistency of *she's out to get me* with the rest of the structure will become apparent to both the counselor and the client. The fact that the client knows other students—if only a few—who do well on the tests, the fact that the teacher uses a scaling system for assigning grades, etc., will suggest that Miss X is not against students in general. The fact that Miss X offered to help the client before his last test, the fact that she assigned him to a special remedial class, etc., suggests that she has no personal antagonism toward him. The fact that the client had not studied for the last few tests, that he sees the course as irrelevant to his future plans, etc., all suggest a different, more realistic structuring of the state of affairs.

The correction of faulty symbolic structure cannot always be accomplished by having the client provide the proper symbols and reorganize the structure. The client may not have the necessary facts at his disposal. In some instances, the facts may be available to the counselor but not to the client. Under such circumstances, and especially if these new facts are detrimental to the client's preconceived notions about the situation, he may not wish to examine them or accept them as an integral part of the realistic structure. In such a case it becomes necessary to establish a state of affairs in which the corrective information can be fed into the structure. The counselor will manipulate symbolic stimuli in such a way as to force the client to see the need for the new information and to suggest the kinds of diagnostic information required as well as the means for securing it. The term *force* is used intentionally in the preceding sentence. Tact, ingenuity, and understanding are used to manipulate events in the situation and to aid the client in achieving the clarification he requires to move forward in the problem-solving situation. These, however, are merely devices, just as "permissiveness" is a device for forcing the client to put himself on the right track. Froehlich (1956) once pointed out that it made little difference whether the counselor told the client what to do or merely said, "Uh-huh," at an appropriate moment. The client, as client, was still being treated as a bouncing ball responding to stimuli manipulated by the counselor. The facts of the case are that the client in seeking out the collaboration of the counselor in the solution of his problem anticipates some assumption of responsibility by the counselor. The issue is not whether or not the counselor applies force in assuming his responsibilities, but rather whether he applies the force in ways that will facilitate the client's generalization of the problem-solving process or in ways that will engender resistance or dependency in the client. We are concerned in this instance of using force with techniques and not with the central problem-solving process.

The diagnostic interview, or that portion of the guidance interview which is concerned with problem identification, is designed to provide appropriate and accurate symbols to represent objects and events in the behavior products being performed by the client and to provide a symbolic structure for these events that characterizes the configuration of events in the client's problem. Through the joint participation of the client and his counselor, behavior observations derived from a variety of sources, including the diagnostic interview, are given structure and meaning. They thus become significant elements in the problem-identification and subsequent phases of the problem-solving undertaking.

11. *Summary*

Direct observation of spontaneous behavior and observation of symbolic behavior by means of the diagnostic interview are means by which essential data can be assembled for inclusion in the identification of the problem. Observational records, cumulative records, and interview techniques are useful devices for assembling such data, but, despite the contributions they can make to the process of problem identification, they are at this stage in their development extremely time-consuming to use and often quite unreliable in the information they provide. These devices have not been sufficiently standardized and formalized to insure that their users can treat their product with confidence. While the uncertainty that one has about the product of direct observation, secondary observation, and observations based upon the interview has the disadvantage of causing the conscientious counselor to be somewhat more cautious than the urgencies of some problems might seem to demand, it has the advantage of being congruent with the uncertainty of human behavior, which is fluid, flexible, and susceptible to many interpretations.

Six

Measurement in guidance

◆◆◆

Measurement of psychological behavior is perhaps the most formalized of the techniques for making behavior observations. Personality and interest inventory scores, flicker-fusion rates, galvanic skin response recordings, inkblot protocols, achievement and aptitude test scores, and the like are symbols representing the ways in which organisms respond to stimuli under highly specific conditions. Psychometric data are a major source of the information used in the problem-identification phase of guidance. Psychometric devices are, of course, used in many other ways as well. Research in the behavioral sciences depends heavily on psychometry to supply data on the ways in which humans act. Therapy, education, management, and similar activities involving the understanding, prediction, and control of psychological behavior look to measurement for basic information.

It is not surprising, therefore, that the creation and perfection of psychometric devices has absorbed the interests, energies, and talents of numerous psychologists and workers in related fields for almost three-quarters of a century. As a result of these efforts, observers of psychological behavior have at their disposal a few instruments, perhaps not more than a dozen or so, which will permit them to examine some behavioral elements and their interrelationships. There may be as many as two dozen more instruments which are capable of providing adequate information about isolated aspects of behavior. But the majority of psychometric instruments appear to give the user the impression that he is observing behavior when he is seeing only the fluttering of his own eyelashes in the viewpiece. Ample evidence for this unflattering appraisal of our inventory of alleged psychometric paraphernalia will be found in those monumental catalogues of testing indiscretions, *The Mental Measurements Yearbooks* (Buros, 1941, 1949, 1953, and 1959). It may also be found in the lack of resemblance

98

between behavior performed in test and nontest situations and in the awe with which validity coefficients in excess of .70 are viewed.

The question of why half a century or more of talented effort has produced so little of real value needs to be raised—and once raised, insistently demands a reply. One answer which may be given is that the professional psychometrist and his far more numerous amateur imitators have focused their attention on the instruments rather than on the behavior they are intended to observe. It is as if a carpenter using a machinist's depth gauge to measure the length of a piece of window trim devoted his energies to attempting to make more reliable and valid settings of the gauge instead of noticing that the characteristic of the molding of greatest concern to him, namely its length, cannot be observed by the instrument he is trying to perfect.

In this section of the discussion we wish to focus our attention on the behavior to be observed and only secondarily upon the observation instrument. We should recall from Chapter Two that the unit of behavior we wish to investigate is the behavior product. In essence, this behavior product is the interaction of stimulus functions and the response repertory. Stimulus functions emerge from the interactions of the awareness responses with objects and events in the environmental context.

When an observation of behavior is made, we are, in effect, looking at a behavior product. Because of the complexity of the event being observed and because of the limitations of the available instruments of observation, observers have tended to focus upon a single component or a few aspects of the behavior under investigation. Psychologists, sociologists, and educators—members of the professions most intimately concerned with behavior observation—have tended to focus their attention on the response repertory and frequently on the communication aspect of the response repertory. Meanwhile they have been inclined to overlook other aspects of the behavior product. Most important, however, is the tendency to overlook, in a very damaging way, almost the entire environmental context of which the test, as a potential stimulus object, is an important part.

1. *Independence of instrument and product* [1]

In general, psychometric instruments—tests, inventories, rating scales, biographical information blanks, or what have you—are, first, a

---

[1] This section and several which follow represent an expansion and revision of previously published material (Weitz, 1961).

part of the context element of the behavior product. The introduction of a psychometric device into a clinical, educational, employment, or experimental situation immediately changes the conditions of the setting. This is perhaps most evident in the climate aspect of the context element. As the context element of a behavior product crystalizes, the test emerges from the general environmental context and becomes a specialized stimulus event capable of interacting with specific responses. As this occurs, however, the psychological climate of the environmental context changes. Even students who a moment before the presentation of the test were expecting to be tested develop new stress responses as the test is placed before them. The whole atmosphere of the testing room changes as soon as the test itself appears as an effective stimulus.

Psychometrists place the greatest emphasis upon the stimulus characteristics of the test, but not as one of the stimuli making up the psychological climate of the context element. A test is more generally viewed as a group of highly refined and specialized stimuli capable of evoking a specified range of responses that can subsequently be quantified and evaluated. But the test is not only a part of the environmental context and the stimulus situation; it also becomes a part of the response component of the behavior product. The examinee, by having learned something in a class, brought his problem to a clinic, agreed to submit to a psychological experiment, or applied for a job, produces the test as a part of his behavior product as surely as if he had written the items himself.

Thus we see that the observing tool itself becomes an intimate part of each constituent of the very behavior product it is intended to observe. Now this may be a general characteristic of observation instruments, but it is unlikely that the telescope contributes much to the behavior of the moon or that the foot rule or transit contributes much to the height of Pike's Peak. Yet most of the psychometric instruments now in use contribute very actively to the behavior products they are designed to observe. The consequences of this are far reaching. In general, we use tests as a source of information about behavior so that we may make predictions about that behavior when the test is not there. We give history tests, for example, not to find out how a student will respond to specific stimuli presented on the test—although some social studies teachers appear to find this a sufficient reason for the test—but to be able to predict the behavior products of the students when confronted with historical stimuli outside the classroom, as, for example, when he is faced with a referendum ballot. Since the test is so intimate a part of classroom behavior products and is completely absent from nonschoolroom products, it is not surprising that there is such a wide discrepancy between one kind of product and the other.

This suggests one reason we find such limited relationships when test scores are compared with external nontest behavior criteria and greater, but still limited, relationships when test performance is checked against performance on another test as an external criterion. This further suggests at least one step that might be taken to remedy the situation. That step is to make the behavior product we wish to observe, insofar as possible, independent of the psychometric device used to observe it, or at least introduce some correction mechanism to compensate for the fact that the test is a part of the behavior product. Some feeble steps have been taken in this direction. The correction scores on the MMPI and the malingering scores being developed by Kuder for his interest inventories are examples of this effort. But we need to look at psychometrics in an entirely new way if we are to achieve the necessary independence of observation instrument and behavior product. Some steps which may be taken in this connection are discussed in Section 12 of this chapter.

2. *Sampling in psychometric observation*

It is impractical, if not impossible, to observe all behavior products related to a given type of context, stimulus function, and response situation. Take, for example, the relatively simple matter of attempting to observe the arithmetic computational behavior products involved in adding all numbers taken two at a time between 0 and 99, thus: $0 + 0$, $0 + 1$, $0 + 2 \ldots 99 + 99$. If we consider this situation only from the point of view of the stimulus objects, we note that there are some 10,000 possible stimuli. The number is doubled if we consider the form in which the stimuli may be presented—$1 + 1 =$ or $\frac{1}{+1}$ —and is made infinite, for all practical purposes, when we take into account the kinds and size of print, the color of the ink, the kinds of paper, and so on which might be used in conveying these stimuli. When we consider this situation from the point of view of the environmental context, in general, we begin to develop some understanding of the magnitude of the number of behavior products which may be produced in such a situation. Simply considering the number of sequences in which 10,000 stimuli can be presented staggers the imagination, yet to this must be added the variety of situations in which the student is called upon to add numbers together in this way. The classroom represents only an insignificant aspect of such circumstances. Furthermore, the responses which the stimulus $57 + 38 =$ can evoke is overwhelming, ranging from 95 to *I don't know* to almost anything.

This suggests that if we wish to observe the behavior products generated in this situation—or any other, for that matter—we must take a sample. But how is the sample taken in the typical arithmetic computation test? In the first place, the sample is determined not in terms of all possible behavior products, but almost exclusively in terms of the stimulus objects. In the second place, even in the area of the stimulus objects there is no evidence to lead one to believe that the sample selected is representative of the totality of stimuli which can contribute to behavior products in this kind of situation.

3. *Test reliability*

This state of affairs gives us some insight into the nature of test reliability and some clues as to why it is generally so low. The reliability of a test, as we all know, provides us with an estimate of the degree to which repeated observations of the same sort of behavior will be in agreement. Thus, if a sample of stimuli are presented today and again tomorrow, we would expect a group of examinees to fall in substantially the same order when ranked in terms of the appropriateness of their responses, PROVIDED THE SAMPLE OF STIMULI PRESENTED AND THE SAMPLE OF RESPONSES PERFORMED ARE REPRESENTATIVE OF ALL STIMULI AND RESPONSES IN ALL BEHAVIOR PRODUCTS APPLICABLE TO THE SITUATION. But why do we never get perfect reliability?

There are, of course, many reasons. Principal among them, however, is the fact that no psychometric device as presently constructed can ever be representative of the total behavior product. Emphasis upon one aspect of one dimension of behavior precludes its being representative. The inadequacies in our sampling techniques also make perfect reliability impossible to achieve. The major factor, however, that precludes the construction of a perfectly reliable test—that is, one based upon an adequate sampling of all the components of the behavior product—is the fact that the total context element varies from test to test, even from moment to moment. These variations in the context element, interacting as they do with all other components, are an inherent condition of psychological behavior. Any method of observing behavior that excludes or ignores this variability will produce observations of something, but not of psychological behavior products.

4. Methods of estimating reliability

A test which one day estimates that Student A is first in his class in performing arithmetic computations and on the next day estimates that he can perform no better than the poorest student in the class would not be a very useful instrument for observing computational behavior, because the observations appear to lack consistency. Such a test would, of course, have a low reliability coefficient. On the other hand, a test which placed Student A and all other students in the class in the same relative position with respect to their arithmetic skill each time it was administered would be a highly consistent, highly reliable, and hence highly useful instrument for anyone wishing to observe arithmetic computational behavior. If we know the reliability of a test, and if the reliability is sufficiently high to suit our purpose, then we do not need to take repeated test observations in order to estimate the efficiency of the observed behavior. Highly reliable tests save the examiner time and energy by providing consistent measures of behavior, thus avoiding the necessity for inefficient, extended, or repeated observations.

In actual practice, the reliability of a test may be determined in any one of a number of ways. Although each method for determining the reliability of a test provides us with slightly different information, all are based upon essentially the same rationale. This rationale holds that if it is possible to differentiate among individuals with respect to the way in which they perform certain kinds of behavior, it is then possible to rank individuals in a group according to some aspect of that performance. For example, it is possible to rank a group of elementary school children in the order of the number of "right" answers they record on a piece of paper to questions of the sort: $a + b = ?$ in which a and b are one- or two-digit numbers. "Right" answers are those predetermined to be right by the examiner. It is further possible to repeat the ranking process; that is, by using either the same questions or others like them to rank the same students with respect to their computational skill a second time. If the two sets of questions are the same or highly similar, and the conditions under which they are asked—including the student's attitudes—remain reasonably constant, we would expect that the relative positions of the students, their ranks, would remain substantially the same from one administration to the next. If the positions of a large num-

ber of the students change from one administration to the next, and
especially if some of the high ones fall markedly while some of the
low ones showed marked improvement, we would be inclined to suspect that there was something wrong either with the questions that
were asked or with the way in which they were presented to the
students. If test conditions are carefully controlled, including the opportunity for learning, so that the two administrations of the sample
of items have as much in common as possible, then the degree of
consistency with which the sample stimuli rank the students is a
measure of the reliability of the test.

Six procedures for estimating test reliability are easily identifiable
(Thorndike and Hagen, 1962): (1) immediate retest with the same
sample of questions, (2) retest with the same sample of questions
after a time interval, (3) immediate retest with a second sample of
questions—a parallel form of the test, (4) retest with a parallel form
of the test after an intervening interval of time, (5) analysis of split-
halves of a single sample of items, and (6) statistical analysis of scores
derived from a single administration of a set of questions. In each of
the first five of these methods for estimating reliability two separate
scores are obtained for each student. Each score represents an estimate
of the efficiency of the behavior being observed. A correlation coefficient is now computed for the two sets of scores. This correlation
is the reliability coefficient and represents the degree of correspondence in rank of a group of students on repeated observations of two
samples of behavior. In the split-half method of estimating test reliability a correction of the coefficient is required, because it is found
that the reliability of a test is intimately related to the number of
items the test contains. Since the split-half method gives us a reliability
coefficient which measures the correlation between two scores on tests
having only half the number of items we will want to use in the final
form of the test, it is necessary to apply a correction in order to estimate the reliability of the total test. (See the Spearman-Brown formula in, for example, Cronbach, 1960, p. 131.)

Among the purely statistical procedures for estimating the reliability
of a test perhaps the most widely used is the Kuder-Richardson (1937).
In this method, the assumption is made that items within one form
of a test have as much in common with each other as they do with
corresponding items on another form of the test. What is done, in
effect, when the Kuder-Richardson method for estimating reliability
is applied, is to divide the test into all possible subtests and to determine the intercorrelations of these subtest scores. The interactions of
these subtest scores are then summarized in one or another of the

Kuder-Richardson formulae. Here we have the split-half technique, so to speak, except that we split the test into all possible combinations of items.

5. *Behavior products and reliability*

Consider, now, the relationship between behavior products and test reliability. If we examine what is done when a test is constructed, we can secure a better idea of how test reliability is related to the behavior of human beings. Earlier we discussed the problem of taking a sample of computational behavior. Let us review this problem in somewhat greater detail and see what the behavior products look like and examine the sampling problem involved in testing. Below we have summarized some of the components of the complex computational behavior involved in adding all one- and two-digit numbers from 0 to 99:

A = the symbolic representation of an addition problem, such as $1 + 1 = 2$, etc.

F = the form in which the symbols are presented, such as $1 + 1 =$, $\frac{1}{+1}$, etc.

P = the method of presentation, such as blackboard, mimeograph, etc.

C = the conditions under which the symbols are presented, such as homework, quiz, group competition game, final examination, etc.

E = previous experiences of the individual with computational exercises of this kind.

G = the feelings the student has about the exercise at the moment.

S = the situations in which this kind of behavior might be performed, such as making change, counting marbles, etc.

O = the ongoing, current behavior of the individual at the time the exercise is presented.

H = the health and physical condition of the individual at the time the exercise is presented.

These represent only a few of the conditions under which computational behavior may be performed. Thus the behavior product involved in arithmetic computation (B) is a function of the interactions of all the factors given. This state of affairs may be symbolized thus: $B_i = f(A_i \longleftrightarrow F_i \longleftrightarrow P_i \longleftrightarrow C_i \longleftrightarrow E_i \longleftrightarrow G_i \longleftrightarrow S_i \longleftrightarrow O_i \longleftrightarrow H_i \longleftrightarrow \ldots Z)$. Then B_1 represents one possible configuration of these subconditions, and B_2 another, and so on. Each of

these behavior products, B_1, B_2, B_3, ..., B_n, represents some configuration of computational components. All the behavior products
combined may be thought of as a complex pattern of behavior which
we call *arithmetic computation*. To test this behavior pattern, it
is necessary to take samples from it, for it would be impractical if
not impossible to observe all the possible combinations. Figure 8
represents all possible combinations of B_i in the computational pattern and shows two samples taken from the configuration in the form
of tests.

Figure 8 illustrates what is done when we administer two tests of a
behavior pattern. Test I includes B_{12}, B_{13}, and B_{14}, and Test II includes
B_{101}, B_{102}, and B_{103}. In no case can two tests have common behavior
products, for even when the "same" test is administered twice, the
time of the presentation of the items, and hence the reactional biography, is different. The symbols, the form of the test, and other physical
aspects of the exercise may remain unchanged, however, thus giving

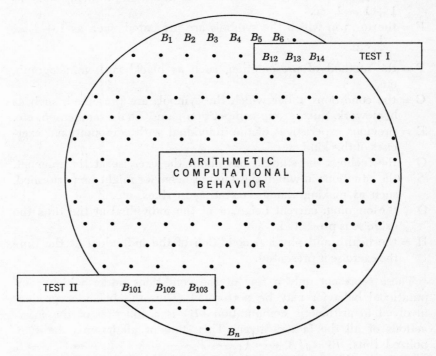

*Figure 8. Test Samples Taken from a Configuration of Arithmetic Computational
Behavior.*

the two samples a superficial appearance of similarity. If we now assign numerical values—test scores—to the two samples and compute correlation coefficient for these values over a group of students whose behavior has been sampled, we have a coefficient of reliability for the test.

Note, however, that the samples of behavior we observe represent only a small part of the total pattern of computational behavior products, and note, further, that only with respect to a limited number of behavior components may two samples overlap. Thus, we would expect to find that there were many sources of variation in performance from sample to sample. For this reason it is impossible to secure a perfect reliability coefficient. The remarkable thing is that some coefficients of reliability are as high as they are.

6. *Test validity*

While reliability estimates give us some notion of the consistency with which a test observes behavior products from one sample to the next, they appear, on the surface at least, to tell us little about what it is that we are observing. Conventionally, the term *validity* has been assigned to the estimate of the degree to which a test measures what it purports to measure. Thus, if we have a sample of test items which we are told will permit us to observe computational behavior, we would like to have some estimate of the degree to which the test, in fact, does measure computational skill and not musical talent or reading ability. Validity coefficients provide us with such estimates.

Validity, then, is the degree to which the sample of behavior observed by the test represents the total pattern of specific kinds of behavior products we wish to observe. Several methods of estimating test validity have been developed. Perhaps the most obvious method of estimating the validity of a test is what has been variously called *empirical* or *statistical* validity. Estimating the validity of a test by empirical methods involves correlating the scores earned on the test in question with scores earned on some criterion measure of known validity. If we already know that one test measures what we wish to measure, then we can administer it as well as our new test to some group of examinees and compute the coefficient of correlation for the two sets of scores. The relationship thus obtained gives an estimate of the degree to which our new test measures the same thing as our criterion test; hence, it represents an estimate of the validity of the new test. It is not necessary, of course, to use a test in the usual sense as our criterion measure. If we wish to estimate the validity of a reading test we may administer the test to a group of examinees whose reading skill can be rated by their teachers, for example, and the test score may then be correlated with these teacher ratings. If we wished to estimate the validity of a test of salesmanship, we might use as the criterion the volume of sales of a group of salesmen.

These statistical or empirical methods of estimating the validity of a test all depend on the correlation between the scores on two observed samples of the behavior in question. The criterion sample is known to be a valid observation either by definition or by some previous determination of its validity. The degree to which the two observations correspond, then, is the estimate of the validity of the new test. Other methods of estimating the validity of a test depend on the logical rather than the statistical relationship between the new test and its criterion. In content or process validity, the nature of the questions on the test is evaluated in terms of the content or processes involved in the behavior segment under investigation. In construct validity, we are concerned with the degree to which the test appears to be able to observe characteristics related to some theoretical construct of the nature of human behavior. In content, process, and construct validity, the nature of the behavior to be observed is described by persons considered to be expert in these matters. Thus no actual scores are obtained for these criterion observations. The relationships between the test and the criteria are established logically.

7. *Behavior products and validity*

When we estimate the validity of a test by empirical or statistical methods, it is clear that what we are doing is observing two quantifiable samples of behavior and computing the relationship between them. We have the test score representing one sample of behavior and the criterion score—another test score, teachers' grades, sales volume, or what have you—representing the other sample. The situation is similar to that represented in Figure 8 for estimating reliability.

But what of logical validity? In estimating the logical validity of a test, a specialist of some sort examines the criterion—content, process, or construct—and creates a symbolic pattern of behavior which might be expected from a person having the knowledge, skill, or trait in question. He then examines the test and creates from it the sample of behavior it is likely to evoke. Here, again, we have two samples of behavior similar to that shown in Figure 8. In the case of logical validity, however, we are dealing not with objective behavior but with behavior samples that exist only in the symbolic domain of the expert. If it were possible to assign numerical values to both symbolic samples, it would be possible to determine the coefficient of logical validity by computation. In practice, this is the general sort of thing the expert himself does. He determines the amount of agreement which might be expected between the sample of symbolic behavior drawn from the criterion and the sample likely to be drawn from the test.

8. *Reliability and validity*

Since both reliability and validity depend upon the correlation between two samples of behavior drawn from the same behavior pattern, they represent substantially the same kind of information. The only reason for retaining the two terms *reliability* and *validity* is that we select our samples in slightly different ways for each of these estimates, and psychometrists use the results in slightly different—not always legitimately different—ways. From the point of view of the behavior product being observed, however, there is little difference between test reliability and test validity. Both are measures of the degree to which one sample of behavior is like another sample drawn from the same general pool of behavior products. In drawing samples of behavior to estimate reliability, care is exercised to insure that the stimulus objects—the test items—remain fairly constant. Either the same test or a parallel form is used. In drawing samples of behavior products to estimate validity, however, care is exercised to insure that the stimulus objects and as much of the environmental context as possible in the criterion is different from that employed in the test. This is done, of course, to insure that the sample being observed by the test has as broad an application as possible. These methods of drawing behavior samples for estimating reliability and validity may help to explain why reliability coefficients almost universally exceed validity coefficients, although theoretically the validity coefficient could be as high as the square root of the reliability coefficient (Cronbach, 1949, p. 75).

9. *Reliability, validity, and behavior*

The foregoing discussion of reliability and validity applies to the consistency with which observations can be made and to the degree to which the observer is looking at what he wants to see. These estimates relate primarily to the instruments of observation and only secondarily to the behavior itself. Tests may or may not be reliable and valid instruments for observing behavior, but the behavior products themselves, those occurring outside the test situation, cannot be categorized by terms like reliability and validity. The application of reliability and validity techniques can help the test technician improve his instruments for observing behavior, but they should have very little influence upon the behavior observed, for if they do influence the sample of the behavior of which they are a part, they obscure the very thing we wish to investigate.

Tests used as instruments of observation, as indicated earlier in this chapter, may play a role in many components of the behavior product. They may be a part of the response repertory in the sense that the individual brings them into being by seeking guidance. Experience with tests of one kind or another is part of the reactional biography of most human beings. They are also a part of the civilized environmental context. As the test technician views them, however, their dominant role is that of stimulus objects designed to evoke stimulus functions which will interact with the response repertory to produce observable, measurable behavior products. In perfecting them for this central role, the test technician tries to see to it that they will evoke consistent—reliable—stimulus functions and that they will interact in such a way as to give realistic—valid—samples of the behavior he wishes to examine. By constructing reliable and valid tests, the test technician is able to provide a set of psychometric behavior samples from which the counselor can make some realistic estimates of the state of affairs of the client and from which he can estimate the probability of future behavior. Thus, although the counselor wishes to focus on the behavior products themselves, the test technician focuses his attention upon the perfection of the stimulus objects that participate in the behavior products the counselor seeks to observe.

10. *Psychometry and the response repertory*

Once a test is administered, we shift our focus from the perfection of the stimulus objects in the behavior product to the response repertory. Even when the test represents a highly valid and reliable instrument of observation, how clear is the focus likely to be when we concentrate on the responses? Let us return, in seeking an answer to this question, to the hypothetical test mentioned earlier in this chapter (the addition of numbers 0–99 taken two at a time), which purports to measure arithmetic computation responses. In this test, situation, the stimulus such as $57 + 29 = ?$ must activate some receptor. The examinee must become aware of the stimulation and attend. This attention must be translated into a perception that gives meaning—stimulus function—to the squiggles on the page. This meaning must be classified with respect to the examinee's reactional biography and available response repertory. Now a breakdown in any one of these steps in the awareness process will result in some response other than 86 being written after the equals sign. The examiner is concerned with the evaluation of arithmetic computation behavior, but the behavior may never be performed simply because of the breakdown in the awareness aspect of the response element.

The examinee may, of course, perform all the appropriate awareness responses and still come up with the wrong manipulative response. He may arrive at the answer 76 because he forgot "to carry one." Or he may perform the awareness and manipulative responses correctly, but he may record his answer as 68 instead of 86, or he might write his answer so carelessly as to cause the examiner to read the answer as 88. Here we have a deficiency in communication responses.

If the examinee's father happens to be a bookeeper whose preoccupation with arithmetic precision causes him to be a threat to the examinee each time he does his homework, then we may expect that the examinee's feeling responses that accompany each awareness, manipulation, and communication response will be so negative and so violent as to obscure any computational skill he may possess.

It may, of course, be argued that all these responses make up computational behavior. If the correct answer is recorded, computational skill is present; if the wrong answer appears on the test, it is not. When we consider the purposes for which we make behavior observations, however, this argument falls of its own weight. Aside from some idle or even busy curiosity, we observe human behavior in order to understand, predict, and control it. If these, then, are our purposes, we need to look beyond the immediate observation. In the case of an examinee who records an "incorrect" response to the test item for any of the reasons suggested above, the following are some of the courses of action open to us. If we should conclude that the examinee is lacking in computational skill, we may send him to a remedial arithmetic course. He may need to be taught only "to carry one," but the total remedial instruction may be so degrading to him as to suppress any arithmetic skill he already has. It may be that he requires remedial reading instruction to improve his awareness responses. Or he may require remedial writing instruction to improve his communication responses or psychotherapy to improve his relationships with his father. Or perhaps this behavior sample suggests that the father requires psychotherapy or that the examiner requires eyeglasses or cryptographic instruction.

This is to suggest that even when the attention is focused upon the response element, most present instruments do not provide sufficiently precise observations to permit subsequent meaningful action. There has been in recent years a commendable effort to design instruments which will give more precise observations of responses. Tests like the Yale Educational Aptitude Tests, the Differential Aptitude Tests, and the like are examples of instruments which permit views of a variety of aspect of the response element. They are steps in the right direction, even if they do not go far enough. Factor-analysis approaches to the design of psychometric instruments may be promising, provided the elements fed into the technique are sufficiently precise from the outset.

11. *Approaches to improving psychometric observations*

The question might well be raised as to whether psychometric devices do not obscure at least as much as they reveal. Yet even if we accept all of the criticisms of psychometry as presented here and elsewhere, tests still tell us more about some aspects of psychological behavior than we can learn in any other way. The answer to the imperfection of psychometric devices is not to discard them entirely, but to improve this approach to behavior observation. The following discussion will suggest the broad outline of some steps that might be taken to improve our present instruments and precautions that might be observed to safeguard against faulty observations resulting from the misuse of these instruments.

Improvement of psychometric instruments will need to be sought in at least three directions. First, steps will need to be taken to insure that the observing instrument is as independent as possible of the behavior to be observed. Second, it will be necessary to insure that the behavior observed is an adequate sample of the pattern of behavior products we wish to examine. Third, the instruments need to be constructed in such a way as to provide a higher degree of precision than is now available.

12. *Making the test independent of the behavior*

As demonstrated earlier, most psychometric devices now in use participate actively in the behavior they are intended to observe. This participation is principally noticeable when the test is the central stimulus object in the behavior product. If it is, observations of test behavior can be related to other behavior products of the same pattern only if the other behavior products also include test-like stimulus objects. Although they often do in testing carried out for the purpose of educational appraisal, and to a lesser degree in vocational appraisal, this state of affairs rarely obtains in other kinds of observations, as for example in personal interactions, attitudinal behavior, and the performance of a variety of "creative" activities. To the extent that the test participates in the behavioral interaction being observed, it contaminates and confounds the observation. Problem identification in guidance, under these circumstances, becomes a highly imaginative business insofar as the test data are concerned.

In order, therefore, to separate the test from the behavior to be observed, it may become necessary to keep the examinee temporarily in the dark about the fact that an observation is being made or at least to keep him uninformed about the kinds of observations which are being taken. Maintaining the independence of the instrument and the behavior may require that psychometrists and counselors reexamine their own value systems as they relate to the notion of an individual's "right" to know when he is revealing his ignorance or knowledge and his "right" to control these revelations. During World War II, testing procedures were set up for the selection of highly specialized personnel in such a way as to keep the purpose of the testing more or less unknown to the candidates, although they knew that some observations were being made. Psychogalvanometers have been used to observe the physiological components of emotional reactions from which inferential observations can be made about the feeling responses of examinees. The examinee, of course, knows that he is being observed by means of the psychogalvanometer, but he has only limited control over the responses he makes in the test situation. Electroencephalographic measures of neural activity in the brain have been used to identify pathological conditions, and recent studies of normal brainwave behavior have suggested the possibility of fairly localized isomorphic neural activity representative of events outside the individual (Kohler, 1958). Development of these procedures could supply observations of neural activity that, because it appears to be differentially patterned as analogs of objective reality, could give the observer some bases for shrewd inferences about the examinee's objective behavior, and the examinee would be unable to produce false or confusing modifications in the activity being observed.

This is not to suggest that the administration of tests in which the examinee is unaware of what is being observed or at least unable to control it is "right," but merely to suggest that it is possible. Psychotherapists, and especially psychoanalysts, base much of their procedure upon the observation of patients who are urged not to try to control the behavior being observed. It would appear then that in some quarters making covert observations of behavior is viewed as "right," provided the observations contribute somehow to national survival, the correction of a psychopathological condition, or the body of knowledge we call science. (The status of the psychogalvanometer in crime detection is still fairly ambiguous.) Covert observations made for the purpose of aiding normal individuals to achieve a higher level of productivity have not yet achieved this state of approval. All that can be said on this score, then, is that the psychometrist or counselor who wishes to insure some independence between behavior and test by making covert observations will need to make his own peace with his conscience.

Even if the counselor could make the decisions necessary to maintain the separation of the instrument and the behavior, however, he would find few adequate techniques available to him. Those which might be available are expensive and time-consuming. Perhaps the most promising approach would be variations on the situational test, behavioral miniatures, so to speak, with sound and action recorded on film and tape. Contrived problems could be presented to members of a class that would provide behavior observations useful in both guidance and instruction. For example, it would be possible to measure the outcomes of instruction in a civics class and the interpersonal interactions of the students at the same time by presenting the task of organizing a classroom library to a group of students. Their efforts to perform the democratic behavior which presumably is supposed to be one of the major outcomes of civics instruction could be recorded. The behavior of each student interacting with the other members of the group and with the task could be observed. His knowledge of the facts and principles taught in the class could be evaluated as they are applied to the problem. His attitudes could be inferred from the ways in which he communicates his ideas and from his interactions with the other children in the class. If similar recordings of group behavior in a task situation made before instruction began were available to the teacher and counselor, they could observe the changes and consistencies in the behavior products of each of the children from the first observation to the second. They might even be able to make some guesses about the influence of the intervening instruction in civics.

What would be required here would be some standardized procedure for evaluating the task situation behavior. Only occasionally would there be bits of behavior that could be marked right or wrong. Machine scoring of observations of this sort would be out. The translation of such observations into the quantitative language of a test score is difficult, if not impossible. Yet this too might turn out to be an advantage, for it is highly probable that our attempts to embed the mysteries of behavior products in test scores have made them even more mysterious while giving the false impression of removing the veil. Rather than a quantitative test score, this sort of evaluation requires the description of the behavior by extension. An extensive description of the behavior permits the observer to apply the principle of consistency to what is observed. At least two kinds of consistency need to be evaluated: the internal consistency of the behavior of an individual student and the consistency with the task of each student. Two kinds of structure are involved in the task situation: the structure of each individual's behavior and the structure of the behavior of all individuals about the task. A third derived structure is formed within this system from the interaction of the individual behavioral structure with the task structure.

"Correct" answers on this sort of test are those behavior products which maintain a consistent individual structure, contribute to the consistent task structure, and participate in consistent structural interaction. Structural consistency may be defined as the degree to which the behavior performed enhances the available energy of the system being observed. In the illustration of the task situation civics test, the student who comes into the situation with an understanding of what is required by the task, who contributes ideas and effort in moving the solution of the task forward, who takes his turn in contributing to the discussion, who assumes leadership as it is thrust upon him but follows when others lead, who strengthens his bonds of friendship and affiliation with comembers, who focuses his own attention and actions on the task and helps others focus theirs, and who derives a sense of accomplishment from the experience is a student whose behavior represents individual and task structural consistency. His behavior enhances the energy available not only for his own performance, but also for the accomplishment of the task. On the other hand, the student who enters the situation with no clear understanding of the task and with little taste for what he does understand, who sulks in his corner, who participates by throwing spitballs and making sarcastic remarks, who refuses to follow others and rejects the responsibilities of relevant leadership, and who, as soon as practical, removes himself from the situation is performing behavior which has structural consistency for the individual, for it enhances the energy available for his ongoing behavior, but it lacks structural consistency with the task, for it increases entropy and disorganization in the task system. Furthermore, this last lad contributes to the structural disorganization of the task–individual structure interaction.

Task-situation tests lend themselves admirably to evaluation by means of extensive description and consistency analysis. The very fact that they are not standardized, not exactly reproducible, gives them a lifelike verisimilitude lacking in other test procedures. Task situation tests as well as situational observations which can be made through such devices as psychodrama combined with the use of psychogalvanometers, electroencephalographs, and similar instruments for observing the operation of physiological mechanisms may go a long way toward removing the instrument from the behavior to be observed. As such a replacement of our present tests begins to happen, the psychometrist and the counselor will need to find new language for the communication of their observations. This new language, however, is likely to have a structure more similar to objective reality than our present vocabulary of percentiles, t-scores, standard errors of estimate, reliability and validity coefficients, and norm groups.

13. *Considerations in sampling behavior*

When we make psychometric behavior observations, we are looking at samples of behavior products which represent some pattern of behavior. From this sample we attempt to evaluate the effectiveness of the total pattern. On the surface this seems to be a straightforward procedure. The fruit grader is able to evaluate a carload of oranges by selecting a sample of the fruit and describing its size, weight, texture, sweetness, etc. He can then draw some pretty accurate inferences about the quality of the whole carload of oranges. Certain procedures and statistical techniques can be applied to fruit grading to insure that the sample selected is not biased in some way and that the evaluation finally arrived at can be applied to the total lot with a known degree of error. In evaluating oranges, the fruit grader knows what an orange is; he knows the limits of the total group of oranges he is supposed to evaluate on the basis of his sample findings; and he has some fairly specific standards for the qualities he is looking for. This happy state of affairs, however, does not exist in the case of attempting to evaluate a pattern of behavior products from a sample.

When we think of a pattern of behavior products, we think of a group of human activities which are related to each other in some way. Computational behavior, complex as it is, seems to be clearly enough identifiable to differentiate it from, say, musical behavior. Computational behavior, to most people, would mean that behavior involved in the manipulation of literal and numerical quantities according to some formal procedure set down in the operational symbols which are associated with the quantities. This description of computational activities appears to "hang together" in a sort of pattern. But does it? In this description of computational behavior we appear to be focusing our attention upon manipulation and communication responses interacting with literal and numerical quantities operating as stimulus objects. This appears to be different from the musical behavior involved in playing a piano. As we examine piano playing further, however, we discover that it too involves a considerable amount of formal manipulation of quantitative material, for each note represents a quantity of time, each bar represents a unit of phrasing, the positions of the notes on the scale represent quantitative units of pitch, and so on. Thus we see that two patterns of behavior which superficially appear to belong to different categories become, on closer investigation, parts of a larger category. Since it becomes difficult if not impossible to differentiate among patterns of behavior on this molar scale, it becomes even more difficult and probably impossible to select samples of the behavior to evaluate. We must therefore look for smaller units to observe.

Behavior products are made up first of stimulus functions which result from the interaction of awareness responses with stimulus objects and events. Awareness responses are, however, made up of physiological mechanisms operating within the framework of the reactional biography. If we could observe the stimulus functions directly, we would be able to draw inferences about the meanings which certain configurations of objects and events have for an individual and hence about the operations of his physiological mechanisms and the nature of his reactional biography. Stimulus functions, however, cannot be observed directly at the present stage of our psychological knowledge. It may be possible at some time in the future to examine the operation of the physiological mechanisms in greater detail and to observe the electrochemical, mechanical, magnetic, etc., energy discharge patterns. If these patterns have an isomorphic relationship to events "out there," we may wish to label this energy pattern the stimulus function. Until our understanding of neural isomorphism is extended, however, we shall need to infer stimulus functions from the way in which the individual responds to stimulus objects and events. Manipulation and communication responses are presently the most likely sources for these inferences. Awareness responses are made known to an outside observer only when the responder communicates his awareness to the observer either by telling him about it or by reacting with the stimulus event in some observable way. Feeling responses are of the same internal sort. The observer cannot tell what feeling response, if any, is being performed unless the performer informs him in some way. This information may be communicated symbolically in language or it may show up in externally visible responses such as muscle tensing, sweating, blushing, and so forth. It must be kept in mind, however, that the blush is not the embarrassment nor the smile the pleasure felt by the individual.

From the point of view of the outside observer, then, the only portions of the reactional biography element of the behavior product that are observable are the manipulation and communication responses. Therefore, the outside observer may think of behavior products as falling into patterns of manipulation and communication. Response type thus becomes one dimension of a behavior product pattern. It will be recalled that direct manipulation of objects and events has been previously discussed as objective behavior, and the manipulation of symbols has been viewed as symbolic behavior. This differentiation is, of course, an essential aspect of the response type dimension.

The other principle dimension of a behavior product pattern is the kinds of stimulus objects and events which are involved in the interaction. Here we must recall that stimulus objects and events emerge from the total context element, which is itself made up of the cultural matrix, the physical environment, the psycho-social climate, and the individual himself. Here we also need to be aware that some of these components have objective and some symbolic existence.

In terms of these dimensions, the observer can classify behavior products according to the larger categories of which they are members. Behavior that involves a particular type of manipulation of a specified group of objects under conditions that can be defined represents a pattern of behavior. Thus addition, subtraction, multiplication, and division of number symbols under classroom conditions may represent one behavior pattern. It is different from the same manipulation of the same symbols on the baseball field when the individual is computing batting averages. These two behavior patterns appear to have much in common, since the stimulus objects, the number symbols, are similar in both. The context in which the behavior takes place, however, appears to be an important variable, as teachers of arithmetic and parents of small boys will readily attest. It becomes necessary, then, to define the behavior pattern in enough detail to differentiate it from other similar but significantly different patterns. Here again we can apply the principle of description by extension.

Once we have defined our behavior pattern in sufficient detail with respect to the response type and the context element components and have specified whether we are concerned with objective or symbolic behavior, we are prepared to select a sample for observation. This sample must represent both the context element components and the typical responses. In practice, the psychometrist samples the context element by selecting representative stimulus objects and events and by attempting to insure standard test administration conditions. He samples the responses by instructing the examinee in what he is expected to do. In the objectively scorable test the number of communication responses that can be made is limited. In this way the psychometrist attempts to get a more specifiable set of manipulation responses. Since the only communication response available in this sort of a test is an X in a box or a black mark between a pair of dotted lines, the observer is liable to infer that the position of the X or the black line represents important symbolic manipulations performed by the examinee. This, of course, may well be true, but in not infrequent instances the manipulation responses consist of "mental" or physical coin tossing instead of an operation directed at the manipulation of the stimuli provided by the examiner.

In the main, the samples of behavior taken by most of our present psychometric methods represent only small, biased samples of objects and events in the context element and of responses available in the response repertory. Psychometric observations of behavior must, therefore, clearly specify the composition of the sample. The test score is not enough. We need a description of the behavior sample in enough detail to indicate the pattern it is intended to represent. If we can specify in sufficient detail the pattern of behavior we wish to sample, and if we can sample the pattern in such a way as to insure representativeness, there is no reason to believe that reliability and validity coefficients for such samples, if we still wish to compute them, would not begin to approach 1.00.

14. *Precision of observations*

With respect to the response repertory in particular, but also with respect to all components of the behavior product, it will be necessary to observe each aspect independently and in terms of its interactions with the other aspects so that some differentiation as to the dominant source of the behavior may be made. We need to be able to say that such and such a behavior product emerges because reasoning, imagining, feeling, awareness, or communication responses dominate, or because time, space, or climate conditions dominate, or because some peculiar aspect of the stimulus dominates the behavior. One aspect of the behavior that we will need to observe with great precision if we wish to see the full picture is its variability. Experience tells us that from behavior product to behavior product, even when many of the characteristics remain constant, variation will be a central theme. It is this variation, according to Lepley (1954), that distinguishes living organisms from inanimate objects. We need, then, to inquire into the laws, if any, that variability in behavior follows and to observe this variability with great precision.

15. *Measurement in problem identification*

With all its limitations, measurement can contribute in several important ways to the problem-identification phase of the guidance process. Its main contribution is providing data that will help confirm or reject the client's own views of his state of affairs. By feeding measurement data into the extended description of the client's problem, it is possible to expose inconsistencies in the description more readily than if we accepted our data from a single source. Exposure of the inconsistencies will provide a basis for identifying some of the obstacles to the client's progress. This is especially true in educational and vocational guidance, when the client's appraisal of his skills and talents may not be consistent with the reality revealed in the test scores.

A second contribution that measurement can make to guidance is that of providing clues as to where further exploration may be desirable. This is especially true of interest inventories and personality inventories. Although neither of these types of instruments gives very accurate pictures of the client's feeling responses, they do suggest the possibilities of certain structures of feelings that, in many instances, the client is unable or unwilling to give spontaneously. The inventory, then, can point to areas that the counselor might find it profitable to examine in more detail with the client.

Finally, instruments of the sort we have been considering here may contribute to problem identification by serving as a communication bridge between the client and the counselor. There are many instances where the client is willing and able to discuss aspects of his problem, but is incapable of communicating his ideas to the counselor. This may be because the terms used by the client to describe a state of affairs have different meanings to him and to the counselor. Psychometric devices can often help the counselor see in terms that he can understand what it is that the client is trying to communicate.

By themselves, psychometric devices are likely to contribute little or nothing to the guidance process. Used in conjunction with other techniques such as direct behavioral observation and the diagnostic interview, they can serve the purposes indicated above. Their utility can be markedly enhanced, of course, if the psychometrist develops effective techniques for separating the instrument from the behavior to be observed, taking adequate samples of the pattern of behavior to be observed, and improving the precision of his observations, especially those related to the variability of human behavior.

Seven

Structural planning

◆◆◆

Problem identification provides the client and the counselor with an understanding of the behavioral events in the problem situation. The general nature of the difficulty and its sources are disclosed through extensive description. Inconsistencies, disorder, and overgeneralizations in the client's behavior are uncovered. Effective problem identification can lead to insight.

1. Insight in guidance

But insight is not enough. To know that behavior is ineffective and leads to confusion, frustration, and anxiety, even to know why it is so, does not lead inevitably to remediation. To be sure, in many if not most of life's day-to-day problem situations, the detection of behavior deviations from certain prescribed limits is usually adequate stimulation for the initiation of the necessary corrective action. The student who becomes aware of the fact that he is about to fail a course because he is not studying enough prepares a study schedule and follows it until he achieves the level of proficiency he has set for himself. This student is able to undertake corrective behavior because it is already an intimate element of his behavior repertory, having been learned previously.

A client seeking guidance, however, has generally tried those behavior products at his disposal, only to find them ineffective. Often, before he seeks help, he knows what his problem is, and frequently he is aware of many of the sources of his difficulty. These insights do not automatically evoke corrective behavior, because the behavior just is not available to him. Similarly, it would appear to be unreasonable to expect any additional insights derived from the process of problem identification to activate corrective behavior for the same reason. The troubled individual can not be expected to initiate corrective action if the required behavior products are not a part of his immediate operating behavior repertory. INSIGHT INTO THE NATURE AND CAUSES OF NOXIOUS BEHAVIORAL EVENTS CAN ACTIVATE CORRECTIVE BEHAVIOR ONLY WHEN THE APPROPRIATE BEHAVIOR HAS PREVIOUSLY BEEN ACQUIRED AND IS AVAILABLE FOR RELEASE.

This suggests that there may be several possible impediments to the activation of corrective behavior in the face of some obstruction to ongoing activity. On the one hand, the individual may never have acquired the behavior, so that no amount of insight, however derived, can release it. On the other hand, appropriate corrective behavior may be a part of the client's behavior repertory, but it may be momentarily inoperative because it has not been sufficiently well mastered to be effective on call, or because it was learned in a context different from the present one and hence does not seem appropriate to the present problem; or it may be made ineffective (suppressed or repressed) because of some special conditions in the present environmental context. If the necessary behavior products have been acquired previously but are not immediately available for one of the above reasons, it is possible that the insights acquired through problem identification may be adequate to activate them.

Since most individuals have developed a fairly extensive behavior repertory by the time they have reached adolescence, and since most studies of guidance, counseling, and psychotherapy have been conducted with adolescents and adults, it is not surprising that practitioners and students of these processes have given so much emphasis to the role of insight in problem solving. To be sure, insight is frequently followed by corrective action with little apparent further intervention by the counselor. More often, however, the behavior that has been ineffective in coping with the problem seems resistant to change even when both cognitive and affective insight appear to have been achieved.

The reasons for this seem quite obvious when the needed behavior has never been acquired by the client. They are less obvious when the behavior seems to be available or ought to be available but does not seem to be evoked by the insights. The case of inadequately mastered behavior can be explained and treated in much the same way as behavior that has never been acquired. Some form of remediation training or reconditioning seems called for, rather than simple insight. When insight fails to evoke previously acquired behavior in situations in which the environmental context differs from that in which the responses were previously learned, or when events in the present situation acquire stimulus functions that are repressive rather than facilitative to the previously learned responses, it becomes necessary to provide a new set of structural relationships between stimulus functions and responses within which the previously acquired corrective behavior can be performed.

Since the new behavior or the new structural relationships for previously acquired behavior are not already available to the client in guidance, the counselor must intervene. This intervention will take the form of collaborating with the client, first in structural planning and later in structural activation. These guidance strategies are actually two phases of a continuing process leading to the goal of behavior change. The first, structural planning, creates the new behavior in symbolic reality; the second translates the symbols into events that take place in objective reality. This first phase is the subject to be pursued in the present chapter.

2. The general process of structural planning

The counselor is an active and responsible participant in structural planning. Although it is theoretically possible to rely heavily on the client's understanding of his culture, from which he may draw the necessary plans, the exclusive reliance upon the client's own resources limits the variety and richness of the plans that may be made. This suggests that even if it were possible for the counselor to be wholly nondirective—an extremely remote possibility in the light of the interactive nature of the events in guidance—the guidance process would become a time-consuming and wasteful enterprise resulting in structural plans restricted by the client's limited understanding of the wealth of behavioral alternatives made available to him by a rich environment. The counselor, then, must actively intervene and assume the reponsibilities that the client has every right to expect of him.

It will be recalled that in the process of problem identification, the counselor permits his own experience to intrude in the client's description of his situation. The counselor could not avoid this even if he wished to do so, for only by relating the client's reports and the data derived from psychometry and other observational devices to his own direct and vicarious experiences and professional training can he understand the diagnostic descriptions that emerge. Thus the basic data from which the structural plan is to be created are an amalgam of the experience of both the client and the counselor. As the structure of new behavior is developed, the counselor plays a more dominant role in the collaboration.

In essence, structural planning involves generalizing from the behavior performed in the problem situation to new behavior that is likely to resolve the problem. The structural-planning process produces a set of alternative courses of action that give promise of providing relief in the client's present situation. These are given symbolic reality and are projected into the client's future. The client responds symbolically to these future events. Some seem to "feel right"; others do not; and some evoke ambiguous feeling responses. As possible solutions to the problem are collaboratively developed, the client projects them into the future and "tries each one on for size." From what he knows about his own past satisfactions and frustrations, he is able to make some estimates of the kinds of feeling responses that are likely to be evoked by these events projected into the future. This anticipation of future reinforcements is what Mowrer (1960b) calls *hope* and *fear*. By estimating the affective consequences of future events in terms of his own past experiences, the client is able to accept some solutions, reject others, and retain still others for later reexamination as events unfold in objective reality.

Effective structural planning yields a set of fairly clearly defined yet flexible symbolic behavior products that, in terms of the client's previously acquired behavior and the environmental context in which he will be functioning, have a high probability of occurring. This plan is a symbolic map of the client's psychological terrain, which permits him to chart a course between his present disordered state and his psychological destination, characterized by productivity, self-actualization, and serenity. We should more properly speak of maps than map, for structural planning yields not a single best course to satisfaction but rather a series of alternate routes, any one of which can be expected to lead to satisfaction. Human behavior and satisfactions being as flexible and multidimensional as they are, it is highly improbable that any single stream of events is the only appropriate channel for an individual. Williamson and Darley (1937) emphasize multipotentiality as a crucial factor in the guidance process.

This bare outline of the structural-planning phase of guidance raises certain theoretical and practical questions that require answers in order that the process may be understood and made to operate effectively. Among these questions we may count the following as, perhaps, most urgent:

1. What values govern the selection of structures?
2. What principles permit the counselor to select those structures which have a high probability of acceptance by the client?
3. What mechanisms operate within the client to inform him that one symbolic structure is to be preferred over another?
4. How do the counselor's personality and techniques influence the outcomes of the process?
5. Finally, how is structural planning integrated into the total problem-solving enterprise?

3. An illustrative case

In order to give this structural planning process some substance and in order to provide some context within which answers to these questions may be explored, the following case, drawn from the writer's counseling files, is introduced.[1]

THE CASE OF A. V. (VOCATIONAL ADJUSTMENT). The scrubbed, little-girl's face and the dancing eyes belied the world-weary pose she affected. She had entered the University as a competitive scholarship winner. As a second-semester sophomore she stood near the top of her class. She had been pledged early by one of the best sororities on the campus and had resigned after a year, complete with a blistering letter to the undergraduate newspaper on the evils of the sorority system. She was popular with the boys and respected by the girls. The counselor had heard about her popularity as a campus leader from both faculty and students before he met her. But family, wealth, personal popularity, and academic accomplishments seemed to leave her unsatisfied—or so she said. Yet as she described her background and achievements, a small note of pride sang through her life-weary theme.

Now, at the end of her sophomore year, she was expected to choose a major field of study. Since she appeared to do well in almost any course she undertook, she could not choose on the basis of her talents. Her interests seemed to run toward the humanities rather than the sciences, but since this was a scientific world, perhaps

---

[1] Although the essence of the client's problem, personality, and situation are retained throughout, details have been revised to safeguard the identity of the client. In introducing revisions, an attempt was made to retain the original flavor of the details, for it is frequently in the small detail that one is able to capture the significance of a behavior product.

she should major in mathematics or science? Furthermore, she could see no future in the humanities. What could you do except teach if your major were history or foreign languages? And she didn't really want to teach. Some tests of aptitude and interest confirmed her self-appraisal. A personality inventory suggested a slightly elevated anxiety level, with a mild tendency toward schizoid behavior, but no evidence of psychopathology.

By the end of the third interview, the following additional segments of the problem identification had shown themselves: She resented her mother's squandering her talents on a scheduled round of women's clubs, garden clubs, and good works and was certain (or so she said) that she wanted no part of this kind of "gracious, Southern womanhood" for her future. There were evidences of a sharp antagonism toward her mother. Her father was a somewhat distant figure, a successful professional man, whom she loved and who, in turn, dispensed material favors with a liberal hand, but who held to a clear picture of what a properly brought up young Southern woman should and should not do. There was a brother, a year or two older, equally bright, who had squandered his talents and been dropped from one of the better liberal arts colleges. After a period of psychotherapy he had returned to college, where his newly found submissiveness improved his academic performance as well as his relationships with a domineering father. The client expressed great affection for this brother and concern bordering on motherly solicitude.

This student enjoyed an active social life. She seemed to focus her attentions on young men who had or pretended to have some claim to artistic talent. At the moment she was engaged in an intimate relationship with a would-be poet who shortly was to be dropped from school for academic deficiency. (She claimed he couldn't bend his poet's will to the stupid requirements of a university, so he quit to live abroad.) This relationship colored much of her thinking about her future, for she began to see herself as the wife of an artist, supporting him and encouraging him to produce great works. She concluded that she, herself, was incapable of reaching the artistic heights she would like to achieve, but that she could achieve them vicariously through some man.

This, then, is the problem identified in the case of A. V.: a young woman of talent and drive, with artistic aspirations, operating within a family and cultural matrix that produced a reactional biography characterized by vacillation between rebellion and submission, a confusion of values, and a serious uncertainty about her own worth as a creative individual, seeking some long-term vocational goals that would provide an outlet for her talents and at the same time permit her to experience a sense of serenity she had not yet known. At this stage in the guidance process the client was not truly aware of the extent of her talents; she was not aware of the educational or vocational opportunities available to her; she was unaware of her capacity for satisfaction in socially creative activity.

The reader is, of course, aware that this description of the problem, especially the summary drawn in the last paragraph, reflects not only the facts of the case but also the reactional biography of the counselor. Another counselor, with a different set of experiences and a different value system, not only might interpret facts differently, but might actually see different "facts." This suggests that guidance is not merely a one-way process, but is an interaction between two highly active and intimately involved human beings.

But to return to the problem of vocational adjustment of Miss A. V. The problem, or rather complex of interrelated problems, having been identified, it now became necessary to create some structural plan of action that would meet the requirements of the problem and at the same time provide the client with some understanding of the problem-solving process and some skill in its application. The immediate and pressing problem was that of selecting a major field of study. Ideally, the selection of a major field is made as a means of achieving some long-term educational and vocational goal; but, university regulations being what they are, the choice must be made toward the middle of the second term of the sophomore year, and this was upon us. Alternatives in the humanities were suggested as suitable majors in terms of the client's abilities, interests, and general values as she was able to state them. The alternatives of English, history, foreign languages, and philosophy were explored collaboratively; a tentative history major with minor concentrations in the other areas seemed to be less annoying to the client than any other possibilities that presented themselves. But she was not entirely satisfied with the choice, for it seemed to her to lead nowhere except secondary-school teaching, a career for which she expressed contempt. At this point, however, career choice was deferred, for it appeared to the counselor, and soon to the client, that career choice depended basically upon the client's self-understanding.

The second problem that was attacked, then, was that of her acceptance of the values of her subculture and of herself within this value structure. The alternatives available to her here included: assuming the role of the properly nurtured Southern belle and accepting the consequences of such a role, as her mother appeared to have done; rebelling against this role and assuming the position of a dedicated career woman, with the consequences of cutting herself off from what she knew best and accepting, if only temporarily, a kind of loneliness of spirit; or attempting some compromise between these extremes and accepting the consequences of perhaps never finding a secure emotional resting place. These alternatives and others were presented and explored in the course of a number of sessions. In planning her future, the client temporarily settled on the third course, with the hope that events would decide for her, since neither of the other alternatives appeared to reduce her anxieties sufficiently to warrant their acceptance.

The third problem considered involved her interpersonal relations with her family and more particularly with men. This, of course, was the area in which the greatest stress was developed, for it was from her encounters with members of her family and with men in courtship and love relationships that she drew a confused and inadequate picture of herself. Since the identification of all the problems in this area was incomplete at this point in the guidance, it was not possible to suggest even a tentative structure, except to indicate that some extended exploration of her social behavior and emotional life might prove helpful. The possibilities of securing psychiatric assistance or counseling were considered, and she chose the latter as being less threatening and because she felt that her brother had not profited greatly from his experiences with a psychiatrist.

In the course of this general development, vocational alternatives began to emerge. The obvious plans of teaching, writing, editing, library management, and the like were discussed. None was completely rejected, yet none was chosen with any enthusiasm. This reaction from this gifted young woman was not unusual. Most gifted children have been informed by their teachers and counselors that they have the capacity to do "anything you want to do." They have heard this so often that it has become to them a ritualistic chant dismissing them from further serious consideration. The ordinary careers such as those indicated above are moderately well known to them, even if not in sufficient detail to permit a rational choice. What they are seeking and what they deserve is some course of action which is uniquely tailored to their own special talents. Such a course emerged as the vocational guidance progressed. It utilized the client's interest in history, literature, languages, and art. It accepted her present appraisal of herself as being incapable of creative artistic production, yet it laid the groundwork for her to have some opportunity to try her hand at that sort of thing. The counselor suggested that she aim toward graduate training in history in which she would focus her scholarship upon the influences of art, literature, music, and the like on historical development. In short, the area of intellectual history was recommended. Training in this area—which the counselor was able, subsequently, to arrange for—could lead to careers in college teaching, editing, research, and writing. This suggestion caught her attention. It seemed to be an answer to the question of where she was heading. With some further exploration into the details she accepted this as the structural plan for reaching a vocational goal.

This case of A. V. has been explored at some length in order to explicate some of the essential detail that must go into the consideration of preparing a vocational plan. It must not be simply a matter of "test and tell." To be sure, psychometric procedures were applied in order to verify other observations and to provide clues to the total behavioral situation. But they were simply adjuncts, if very important adjuncts, to the total guidance process. This case of A. V. illustrates, because of its relative complexity, the intricate relationships among a great number of typical behavior products which underlie the achievement of vocational adjustment. Substantially the same order of complexity exists in the case of the high-school student seeking assistance in a problem of vocational choice. Ordinarily, however, the high-school student or the less sensitive college student is incapable of bringing to light the many crosscurrents which influence his choice without the insistent aid of a skillful counselor. If a large proportion of the interrelated behavior products can be identified and accurately labeled, then some reasonably realistic structural plans can be suggested.

The case of A. V. also illustrates the active role played by the counselor in problem identification and in developing structural plans. The technique he uses may be permissive or authoritarian or some of both, depending on his personality and the ways in which it interacts with the client's personality. Whatever his technique, his focus must be on the problem-solving process as it is exemplified in the present crisis.

4. The value component in guidance

The solution of problems involves the creation of structures composed of environmental-context events interacting with the client's response repertory (either learned or newly acquired) in such a way as to evoke satisfying feeling responses in the client. To achieve this goal of guidance, appropriate stimulus objects and events of a rich environmental context must be selected, appropriate learned responses evoked, and appropriate new responses introduced. Selection of this sort involves the application of value systems, for the appropriateness of a behavior element can be measured only by the degree to which its performance meets the conditions of a system of values.

The question of whose values, the client's or the counselor's, are involved has become something of a quibble. Although early Rogerians left the student of guidance with the impression that the counselor was an entirely neutral instrument devoid of value judgments, later Rogers (1962) is able to state that "the purpose of most of the helping professions, including guidance counseling, is to enhance the personal development, the psychological growth toward a socialized maturity, of its clients." From this we may conclude as Rogers does that "the effectiveness of any member of the profession is most adequately measured in terms of the degrees to which, in his work with his clients, he achieves this goal." It matters little that the symbolic goal of *enhancing psychological growth toward a socialized maturity* conjures up such a diversity of behavioral pictures as to have no clear referent in objective reality. It is enough that this last stronghold of the neutral observer has opened its doors to the responsible professional participant in the guidance process.

The present issue seems to be not whether the counselor's values should intrude in the guidance enterprise, but rather how much. Patterson (1958) may be taken as representing one extreme when, in discussing the conscious influence of client's values, he says, "Granted that the counselor will influence the client, whether he desires or directly attempts to do so, is it therefore justifiable to attempt conscious, direct manipulation? The present writer believes not," and appends six assertions to justify this view. Williamson (1958) is representing what appears to be a more realistic appraisal of the collaborative interaction in guidance when he summarizes his argument in this way:

I have argued that counseling cannot be independent of values, whether or not we would like to make them free. Rather is counseling . . . value oriented and not open ended both regarding the goals sought through aspiration and strivings of both counselor and student within their counseling relationship. And I have further argued for making explicit our own value orientations as individual counselors . . . that we may responsibly give societal and moral direction to our individual work in terms of the explicitly desired goals chosen by our student clients. I have suggested that we accept the "teaching" of values as a function of counselors, but that we remain aware of the risk of imposing a set of values upon a student and of thus depriving him of his right to and responsibility for self-determination. (Williamson, 1958, p. 528.)

Among many present counselors and counseling psychologists there is the conviction that the counselor "cannot help conveying directly or indirectly to every client what he himself sees and feels and the perspective in which his own life is lived" (Murphy, 1955). There remains only to state, as Samler (1960) does, that "values are at the heart of the counseling relationship, are reflected in its content, and affect the process," and hence " 'intervention' by the counselor in the client's values is an actuality and should be accepted as a necessary part of the process."

If we can accept as a necessary condition of counseling that the counselor's value system, wittingly or unwittingly, must become an active ingredient in the guidance relationship, we are immediately confronted with the responsibility of making some closer inspection of values in order to estimate the ways in which certain of them are likely to influence the problem-solving process. We can, of course, conclude, as Lowe (1959) does after examining the value orientations of Naturalism, Culturalism, Humanism, and Theism, ". . . that differences in value orientation cannot be resolved, each orientation having adherents whose beliefs should be respected. We suggest that each counselor have an understanding of the values both of himself and others and that his values be known by all who are personally affected by his professional behavior." The consequence of such a position is to view each system of values as being highly idiosyncratic (which, in some respects, it is) and hence subject only to the laws of random events. The preceding discussion of the intrusion of the counselor's values in counseling would then become a rather unamusing exercise in verbal manipulations and no more. In view of the emphasis given to the role of values in guidance by practitioners and students [2] of the field, it would appear to be profitable to explore further the nature of values and their impact on guidance.

5. *The nature of values*

Values, in a very general way, may be viewed as states which individuals strive to achieve. They may be events in objective reality

[2] See for example the previously cited reference as well as: American Psychological Association 1953, Bixler and Seeman 1946, Ginsburg 1950, Green 1946, Jahoda 1950, Jahoda 1953, Meehl and McClosky 1947, Mowrer 1953, Rosenthal 1955, Taylor 1956, and Walker and Pieffer 1957.

such as wealth, power, steady employment, and the like, or symbolic events such as honesty, self-acceptance, religious devotion, and the like that may be inferred from the ways in which individuals holding these values behave. More specifically, they are stimulus functions associated with various elements of certain behavior products and certain events. They participate in all behavior products.

The individual who attends church regularly, who prays to a god with sincere fervor, who spontaneously conforms to an ethical code, who supports the "good works" of his organizations, and who seeks to communicate his faith to others is a person who may be said to be motivated by religious values.[3] What is going on here is this: through historical linkage, the stimulus object *church* has taken on the stimulus function *something to be attended regularly and devoutly*, the symbolic stimulus object *god* has taken on the meaning *requiring* or *deserving adoration*, and so forth. The important consideration here is that few if any values, as generally described, are devoid of this historical linkage through which these stimulus functions are associated with them. It is possible that certain values related to biological maintenance—such as eating, breathing, temperature control, etc.—may be viewed as having no history, as having emerged full blown, so to speak. Yet if one considers the foetal stage and even the cellular stage as part of the reactional history—as this writer is inclined to do— it becomes difficult, even in this instance of basic drives, basic biological values, to view values as independent of history.

6. *Symbolic and objective values*

One of the major difficulties encountered in considering values is the fact that some of the states we view as values exist in the domain of objective reality, whereas others exist in symbolic reality. The biological maintenance of the organism, for example, can be seen clearly as an objective value. It involves a state characterized by nourishment, stable temperature, adequate oxygen, etc. It can be described by events which have fairly specific, unspeakable referents in objective reality. Honesty, religious devotion, and self-actualization, on the other hand, are difficult if not impossible to characterize in terms of objective events which have general applicability, for behavior that

---

[3] It must, of course, be recognized that an atheistic communist performing the same spontaneous ritualistic behavior while interacting with objects and events having slightly different labels may also be said to be motivated by "religious" values.

is honest, devout, or self-actualizing for one person may not be so for another. Furthermore, the same person may view as consistent with some value two seemingly incompatible behavior segments. What honest reader of this discussion has not at some time stolen, cheated, or lied with the full conviction that his actions supported some higher value of honesty?

This suggests that symbolic values appear to be able to shift from one level of abstraction to another without always revealing their inconsistencies. This permits the soldier who values human life to take the life of an enemy, because *human life* becomes redefined as *the lives of those who support my values,* and it permits some devout Christians to refuse admission to their temples to those of a different race, because these strangers can be symbolically redefined as a different order of event hostile to Christian values.

Symbolic values, and many objective values as well, do not operate as stimulus functions in isolation; they interact with each other. Now some take precedence, now others. For different individuals at the same time and for the same individual at different times, the same value may evidence a different strength, a different rank, a different stimulus function from that shown previously. This apparently shifty character of values, especially those which have a higher symbolic component, results in part from the fact that values, as all other events, conform to the semantic principle of non-identity, which holds that each object, event, condition, etc., in nature or in symbolic reality is unique, having no exact counterpart. Human beings, however, and especially those who have enjoyed a lifetime of Western culture, expect consistency, conformity, and generalization to apply, and are surprised or even disturbed when they do not.

7. The development of values

There are, of course, other factors that contribute to the unstable qualities of values. One of these is the way in which values are introduced into the behavioral patterns of individuals.

Values, viewed as incentives, that is, states which individuals seek to achieve, become attached as stimulus functions to certain stimulus objects and events through a process of historical development. Although this developmental history differs for each individual, there is enough apparent similarity from one individual to the next to permit us to describe the process in some general terms. The reader is, of course, urged to keep in mind that this description of the way values, in general, acquire their force does not apply to the development of a particular value system of a particular individual in any detail.

At the outset, it should be noted that most values are introduced into the individual's behavior system when he is very young. The notion of dependence upon authority figures, for example, can be seen as growing out of the early feeding relationships, and the values related to the resistance to authority can be seen as growing out of early toilet and cleanliness training, for example, which tends to thwart some of the child's spontaneous responses to internal and environmental stimuli. These are, of course, highly generalized and basic values that may lead to values of patriotism and independence, depending on later developments in the individual's reactional biography. The important fact to notice here is that the acquisition of these behavior products takes place at a very early age. At this stage, the individual is incapable of making any analysis of his responses, for neither the language symbols nor the analytical methods are available to him. This is not to suggest that all values are acquired at the preverbal level; many are introduced later, but usually at a time when, although the child has a symbolic system and an analytical methodology at his disposal, it is so rudimentary and primitive as to be ineffective in coping with the semantic problems that values encompass.

As an example, let us examine the development of religious values and the notions about a god. Very early in the child's history he develops ideas, generalizations, about authority figures. These include notions of dependence on authority as well as feelings of frustration, anxiety, and aggression in the face of the thwarting of his spontaneous responses by authority figures. As the child's world grows, these values of dependence and independence become generalized and at the same time differentiated. The social matrix of the immediate family, first, and later relatives, neighbors, and strangers reinforces these values by means of rewards and sanctions. It is not long before the child learns that some responses produced by him result in satisfying stimulation, whereas others have noxious consequences. He is thus encouraged to perform behavior in which satisfying response-produced stimuli are the outcome.

For example, the child is taught to say his prayers by having his parents and others make a pleasant fuss over him when he does. Soon the process of saying his prayers itself produces internal satisfaction. Consequently, when the appropriate configuration of external stimuli is present (and not infrequently when it is not), the child will perform these responses in order to experience the satisfying response-produced stimulation. Not only does he learn to perform appropriate praying responses, but he also learns something about response-produced stimuli while acquiring a value system of devotion.

At some point in his development the child is taken to church, exposed to family prayers, told religious stories, and introduced to the relationship between an authoritarian god and ethical and moral behavior. He goes to Sunday School, where he meets his playmates. He enjoys the finger-painting he does at Sunday School, and somehow his mother's enthusiasm for his masterpieces becomes associated with the stories about the child Jesus, and both evoke in him responses which serve to recreate the satisfying stimulation. The solemnity, beauty, and emotional tone of the church ritual become associated with both his dependence and his aggression toward authority—and hence toward a god and all of his other associations with this symbolic figure. Out of this interlocking system of responses, environmental-context stimuli and response-produced stimuli, there emerges as the child develops a value system which may be labeled *religious devotion, ethical behavior, morality,* or whatever symbol seems appropriate and meaningful to the growing child. These events assume stimulus functions that interact with manipulative, feeling, and communication responses in such a way as and with sufficient reliability to form a relatively consistent, highly probable pattern, which may be revived as a system of values.

It must be obvious that this description of the development of religious values does not depend upon the actual existence of God in objective reality. (In the event that the tangible existence of God is brought into the discussion here, we need only to view the entire development as His creation, and this view may be more satisfying to some.) Neither does the development of other values depend upon the objective reality of the event held valuable. Rogers is not required to demonstrate that the "enhancement of a client's growth toward a socialized maturity" exists or can exist in objective reality in order to hold this as a prime value in counseling. It is only necessary that the child and Dr. Rogers participate in behavioral events related to the value, that they derive satisfaction from these behavioral experiences, and that they find symbols for these events that have meaning to themselves and perhaps to certain significant others, so that they can maintain a sense of social contact through their values.

The above illustration of the development of religious values indicates a further condition to the growth of values. The child in our illustration did not develop his religious values through a single kind of experience or through interaction with a single class of stimuli. Many people of many categories, objects and events from a variety of intimate and significant sources, contributed to this generalized religious value. Because of this variety, the occurrence of a particular configuration of behavior elements that will call into play responses appropriate to religious values is highly probable. If a value is associated with only a few highly specific behavior products, the probability of its occurrence in a rich and varied environmental context is limited. With only the rare occurrences of the appropriate context for the emergence of the behavior, there are many opportunities for competing behavior to be performed, with the result that the acquired value loses its force or becomes transformed. We may say, then, that IN ORDER FOR A VALUE TO DEVELOP AND SUBSEQUENTLY TO GOVERN BE-HAVIOR, IT MUST BE ASSOCIATED WITH SATISFACTIONS IN A WIDE VARIETY OF EXPERIENCES.

8. *The role of culture in values*

We cannot leave this discussion of the development of values without emphasizing the cultural influences on this development. A society is made up of individuals each of whom is basically governed by survival drives and values. Through experience each learns that his chances of survival are enhanced when he can make more effective predictions about the behavior of his neighbor and when he can profit from his neighbor's experience. Codes and customs of conduct grow up that facilitate interpersonal exchanges of experience and heighten the predictability of behavior, thus increasing the probability of individual survival. As interactions among individuals become more complex, and as physical survival becomes less pressing, aspects of psychological survival become more significant. Codes and customs are introduced to safeguard these interests. These codes and customs become crystalized into a system of values that the society has found to be successful in maintaining the physical and psychological survival of its members. This loosely codified system of values initially developed by individuals to protect themselves takes on a structure that is self-protective. In mature societies, the survival of the individual depends upon the survival of the cultural structure.

Therefore, values that support the structure are taught to the young in order that these new members of the society may contribute to the structural integrity and thus insure its survival and the survival of each of its components. This teaching of values, however, is introduced when the child is very young, often at the preverbal, preanalytic level of the child's growth. As a result, these values have a high affective component and are not easily susceptible to later verbal analyses. Furthermore, the conditions under which values are acquired by the young are often markedly different from those under which they were developed. Thus the behavior performed later in support of these values may be markedly different from what was intended at the time of teaching. In a mature and complex society there are many values governing behavior and many subcultures with substructures of values appropriate to their own demands. As members of these subcultures interact, they develop new and revised value systems that have survival value in this new context. The fact that values are learned under conditions different from those in which they were originally developed and the fact that subcultures interact to create new value structures account for the change and occasional progress in values. This also accounts for the fact that symbolic representations of value often evoke different awareness responses in different individuals.

9. *The role of stimulus function and feedback in values*

Both counselor and client bring to the structural-planning phase of guidance a system of values that have grown up in some such way as has just been described. In addition, the counselor's values have been refined and in some cases redirected by his extensive experience with other similar clients. He knows the consequences of following his values not only through personal experience but also through observing the consequences in the lives of many clients. Few counselors have had the personal experience of academic failure, yet their experience of working with many failing students has taught them new meanings for their own values related to academic aspiration. These new meanings acquired through vicarious experience are integrated into the total value structure that the counselor now introduces into the guidance collaboration.

The foregoing discussion of the source, development, and nature of values can lead us to much the same conclusion that Lowe (1959) reached: that all the major philosophies and value systems have much to recommend them and many adherents to support them. Furthermore, if values develop in the ways that have just been described here, neither the client nor the counselor can do much about controlling the values he hold or selecting the values he develops. These views of values seem to lead inescapably to the conclusion that values are highly idiosyncratic structures operating in a fairly random manner, developing according to the fortuitous experience of the individual and relying only on common cultural encounters to provide some element of consistency and lawfulness. The introduction of such a lawless element into the problem-solving process of guidance could be expected to add little save further confusion and disorder.

The unsavory fact of the matter is that this is what frequently happens. When the client's and counselor's values differ markedly, as they often do, because of the differences in the conditions under which the values were learned, differences in their subcultural origins, or differences in experiencing the consequences of certain values, etc., little in the way of effective guidance takes place. No problems are solved, no learning of problem-solving behavior develops, and the client withdraws from the situation with his confusion confounded and his anxieties heightened.

Under one set of circumstances in which client and counselor hold different values, however, there IS hope for client growth; this would be the instance in which client and counselor seek different, even antagonistic, goals, but the client has come to believe that the counselor is representative of a class or authority whose values "ought to be" or "might be" satisfying or useful to the client. This situation might be called the VENERATION OF THE MEDICINE MAN attitude. Under such circumstances, we might expect some revision of the client's values in the direction of the counselor's.

According to this formulation of values, productive guidance can take place only if the client's and counselor's values coincide, or if the client is predisposed to accept the counselor's values, or if, as in nondirective counseling, the counselor is predisposed to work only within the restrictive limits of the client's value system. Although logic suggests these restrictions, our observations of guidance in action tell us that problems are solved when initially the client's and counselor's values appear to be incompatible, and that clients do acquire new systems of values—not always those of the counselor—without necessarily holding the "medicine man" in veneration. How may this come about?

There may, of course, be a number of explanations for this state of affairs. We wish, here, to consider one that views value structures as portions of a total energy system. Such a formulation raises the concept of values to a higher level of abstraction and permits the inclusion of essential elements of seemingly incompatible value systems. It is our contention that this is the general process that goes on—in most cases unwittingly—when problems are solved and problem-solving behavior is acquired by clients despite the surface incompatibility of client and counselor values.

Earlier, we defined values as stimulus functions associated with certain states or events that evoke striving, approaching, manipulative responses in the individual. Such a definition provides only a gross description of the nature of values as they might be inferred from the general activity of an individual. For the formulation that follows, it is necessary to examine a more refined view of behavior than has thus far been presented.

The behavior product as we have thus far described it relates responses performed by the individual to stimuli impinging on him from the environmental context or from within him. The connection between these two elements is made by the stimulus function. Although this general conception of behavior satisfies the conditions of most observable behavior, it does not tell us enough about what is going on in the individual to suggest, for example, the place of values in behavior.

A more thorough examination of the stimulus function seems required here. Earlier we defined stimulus function as the meaning associated with a given stimulus object or event through the interaction of the object or event with awareness responses. This interaction and the subsequent performance of manipulative, communication, and feeling responses may be conceptualized in terms of a feedback control system.

Feedback control systems or servomechanisms are so well known by now that little needs to be said about them. The operation of the thermostat will refresh the reader's mind on the subject. The thermostatic control of room temperature is an example of a closed-loop feedback control system. The thermostat is preset to certain reference limits of temperature. Once this has been done and the loop of thermostat-furnace-temperature-thermostat has been appropriately connected, the system operates "automatically" in the following fashion: The furnace produces heat, which raises the temperature of the room. As the room temperature passes the preset upper reference limit, the thermostat is brought into action to turn off the furnace. With the furnace turned off, the room temperature falls. When the room temperature goes below the lower reference limit, the thermostat again operates to turn the furnace on. In this way APPROXIMATELY constant room temperature is maintained.

Several notions in the above description need to be emphasized. In the first place, it must be noted that the whole system is preset or programmed by some outside agency. Secondly, some of the output of the furnace (heat in the form of temperature rise) is fed back into the system through the thermostat to control the system. Third, the maintenance of constant room temperature is only approximate, for the system depends upon errors or deviations from the programmed reference levels.

This kind of feedback control system and more complex variations of it can serve as a useful analogue of human behavior, especially when we view behavior at its more basic levels. Norbert Wiener (1948) uses the example of picking up a pencil to illustrate the complexity of the behavior involved and the operation of feedback in its performance:

Now suppose I pick up a lead pencil. To do this I have to move certain muscles. However, for all but a few expert anatomists, we do not know what these muscles are; and even among anatomists there are few if any who can perform the act by a conscious willing in succession of the contraction of each muscle concerned. On the contrary, what we do is *pick the pencil up.* Once we have determined on this, our motion proceeds in such a way that we may say roughly that the amount by which the pencil is not yet picked up is decreased at each stage. This part of the action is not in full consciousness.

To perform an action in this manner, there must be a report to the nervous system, conscious or unconscious, of the amount by which we have failed to pick the pencil up at each instance. If we have our eye on the pencil, this report may be visual, at least in part, but it is more generally kinetic or, to use a term now in vogue, proprioceptive. (Wiener, 1961, p. 7.)

What appears to be going on here is this. There is a preprogrammed notion (idea, image, stimulus function) of what is meant by *picking the pencil up.* This representation or reference level is "inside the organism" and is recorded for each set of muscles involved in the enterprise. As one set begins to operate, some of the response-mediated stimuli are fed back into the system and compared with the stimulus function. If an error is observed, if the response has not reached the reference level—or has gone beyond it—corrective action is taken by the same or new sets of muscles until no further appreciable error exists; then action ceases.

In this conception of behavior, it must be noted that most of the interactions are performed within the organism. The organism's responses are evoked by deviations between response-mediated stimuli (feedback) and the internalized references. The pencil exists only as a set of proprioceptive input stimuli.

This brief consideration of feedback control systems and their application to human behavior does not, of course, tell the whole story. Mowrer (1960b) uses some of these notions to support his conception of a two-factor theory of learning (about which more later), and Powers, Clark, and McFarland (1960a and 1960b) elaborate the idea into a general feedback theory of human behavior. Both of these sources as well as the many useful references cited in both merit extended study by the interested reader. We have introduced only enough of the feedback-control-system concept at this point to throw some further light on the stimulus function and to suggest that it is this feedback-control aspect of the stimulus function in which the reference level is compared with the feedback variable that gives it its character as a value.

10. *Reference variables as values*

There remains, however, the question of where these reference variables come from. How is the organism preset with the reference images his behavior "strives" to achieve? Powers, Clark, and McFarland (1960b) suggest that some of them are part of the genetic apparatus of human organisms, whereas others emerge, through experience, from the six orders of control systems that they employ in describing the abstraction hierarchy governing human behavior. For genetically determined variables, reference limits are established at or before birth as a function of the electrochemical qualities of the organism. For the others, higher-order systems activate recorded images, which in turn serve as the reference variable for the lower-order systems' feedback. Powers, Clark, and McFarland summarize the scheme in the following way.

A system at a given order has goals given to it by higher-order systems. These goals are in the form of perceptual images of past experiences. The system acts to make its present perceptual field match the goal field as nearly as possible. It does not act on the external world but on the only environment with which it is in immediate contact, the set of next-lower-order systems. Its action is that of selecting and stimulating goals for lower-order systems; it is capable of perceiving the signals (either feedback or reference) resulting from its selection so a set of lower signals can be specified which, if achieved, would be interpreted by the system's own feedback function as the required magnitude of the perceptual variable.

Only first-order systems act directly on the (non-GNS) environment. (Powers, Clark, and McFarland, 1960a, p. 86.)

This conception has within it the possibility of specifying a central, single, high-order-abstraction value that governs the operation of all behavior. Powers, Clark, and McFarland almost touch it when they say:

In the optimum system, no significant conflict exists, so that all systems important to behavior are free to operate over their full range without internal opposition. . . . It is capable of modifying its systems as rapidly as changes in the environment may require.

If the organism is in this state, it is performing properly; there is nothing wrong with it. The person perfectly organized in this respect can still fall into conflict with himself, but the N-system is capable of finding solutions if they exist. The person is still subject to the limitations of his environment, to distortion of false information and the illusions inherent in the geometry of perception. The person may be a saint or a sinner, but he will not be mentally incapacitated.

There is no morality inherent in our theoretical structure, although the phenomenon of moralizing can be easily described in its framework. The definition of an optimum FBCS (feedback control system) hierarchy reflects our personal preferences—we prefer to see people performing "up to specs," regardless of what they choose to do, and it is toward this end that we choose to work. (Powers, Clark, and McFarland, 1960b, p. 322.)

Inherent in the idea of *people working up to specs* and the notion of a freely operating system without opposition is the overriding concept of *order*. What we wish to suggest here is that behavior systems, however conceptualized, operate to create energy and maintain it at a high level of readiness within the local system. This involves the reduction of entropy (locally), the decrease in confusion, disorder, and randomness in the interrelationships of the elements of the system. Thus increasing the available energy in a system involves systematizing and ordering the elements. It is our contention, presently no more than a belief, that the basic reference signal against which all feedback is tested is one involving order and the production of available energy.

It is our further contention that all other values represent an approximation of this central value. They simply represent the reference limits of order. Viewed in this way, values as generally conceived must be thought of as having range: honesty AND dishonesty, religious devotion AND nonreligious values, etc. Within these levels of tolerance order exists, energy for action is available, and the organism operates SERENELY. (HERE WE SEE SERENITY AS ORDERLY, ENERGETIC, FORWARD OPERATION, not simply static stability.) When behavior moves outside these reference limits in either direction, an error is automatically reported through the feedback and comparison functions, and

corrective action is taken. Thus in the properly functioning organism, dishonesty is checked, but so IS EXCESSIVELY RIGID HONEST
BEHAVIOR; immorality AS WELL AS religious fanaticism are reference
limits beyond which disorder and entropy increase and hence are to
be checked.

These reference signals that define the limits of orderly behavior
are the stuff of which values are made. In part, they are present in
the physiological makeup of the human organism, but in the main they
are learned and hence are susceptible to change.

With this general formulation in mind, then, the counselor is prepared to attack the problem of structural planning, aware that his
own values will participate in the plan but also prepared to examine
each application of value reference signals in terms of the basic value
of order and energy within the client's local system.

11. *Structural planning as the formulation of order*

Serenity, then, is the state to be achieved through guidance. There
may well be some concern that this notion of serenity contributes no
more to our understanding of guidance than do such terms as adjustment or self-actualization. In the end, where matters of definition and
semantics are concerned, taste—by which we mean the influences of
the reactional biography of the communicator—governs the situation.
And we prefer the term *serenity*. By this we mean a state of internal
psychological order, spontaneous control of spontaneous energy. It
involves, further, an orderly, controlled relationship with one's external environment, the context element. Serenity is that state of
dynamic peace that flows forward to achieve meaningful distant goals,
all the while spontaneously and effortlessly held on course by internal reference signals which in themselves have an internal consistency and order permitting them to check conflict before it arises.[4]

In formulating the structural plans, the counselor utilizes all those
elements revealed in the problem-identification phase that appear to
give promise of yielding an ordered state for the client. To these he
adds selected elements of his own experience. These are selected
according to their consistency with the client's own style of life and

---

[4] One cannot help wondering if this statement embodies any more meaning to
others than hundreds of other attempts to define similar concepts. More terrify-
ing, however, is the feeling that as time passes and new experiences are
integrated into the writer's reactional biography, this statement of serenity, which
presently seems so clear and meaningful, will evoke only the puckered-brow, the
flared-nostrils, and the hunched-shoulders (with palms spread up) response!

the degree to which they are likely to be consistent with the values of the subculture in which the client is most likely to find himself as he progresses toward his goals. Where the client's idiosyncratic values appear to be in conflict with the values of his subculture, the counselor must introduce intermediate values to serve as reference signals whose function will be to bridge the gap between the client and his subculture by partially reducing the discrepancy between the feedback variable and the reference signal, thus reducing the violence of the corrective behavior. When the core of the problem is a wide discrepancy between client values (reference signals) and cultural values, corrective action must be taken in a minimal step-by-step developmental fashion, with emphasis placed on the higher-order systems. (See Powers, Clark, and McFarland, 1960b.)

The illustrative case introduced earlier in this chapter indicates one such approach. The goals of A. V., although rather vague and formless, suggested that order could be achieved for her through some form of structure built around some core of activity related to the humanities and the notion of artistically creative work. The client's own present self-perceptions tended to minimize her own creative skills, although others qualified to judge felt she had them. She expressed more than the average adolescent aggressions toward her academic subculture, which she saw as overregulative and indifferent to the artist and his works. The structural plan which envisioned her as working toward a unique kind of competence in the area of intellectual and artistic history permitted her to express her aggressions toward the society (by studying in what was then a slightly unusual field) and made it possible for her to prepare for a field in a manner acceptable to the values of her origins, yet different enough to avoid the feeling that she was submitting to the demands of those values. At the same time these plans provided an opportunity for her to do some writing, at first as academic exercises, which she did rather well, but later of a more creative sort. An orderly plan was erected for A. V. out of elements that she introduced and elements from the counselor's experience. A. V. could not have been expected to supply these latter elements, for they were not available either to her or to her immediate circle of acquaintances.

While the structural plan involving educational and vocational goals for A. V. appeared to give promise of her orderly growth toward vocational maturity and serenity, the plans for the solution of her more personal and emotional problem did not present so clear a picture. Personal counseling, which she chose in preference to deep therapy, provided a temporary solution and a core about which a reasonably orderly life could be led. Here again, the counselor intervened by clarifying the choices available to her. Although he might have felt that more drastic therapeutic intervention was called for, he accepted the client's choice as a reasonable intermediate step.

12. *The client's acceptance of the structural plan*

The general principles governing the counselor's selection of alternatives that make up the structural plan may be summarized as follows: Those alternatives that are likely to be consistent with the client's life style and with the values of the client's subculture and that, therefore, have a high probability of introducing order into the client's behavior are selected. Thus, the general values of consistency and order determine the components of the structural plan devised by the counselor in collaboration with his client. The client now examines these alternatives and begins to make selections.

The client's selection of courses of action from among the alternatives made available to him is carried out in terms of his own perceptions of the degree to which this alternative or that will produce order in his life. These perceptions are formed through reference to his past experience and by a process of generalization.

Certain responses to certain classes of events have, in the client's past experience, produced painful stimulation; others have produced pleasure. As a consequence, those painful response-correlated stimuli become associated with the responses as "fear," and those pleasurable stimuli become associated with their correlated responses as "hope." At this stage in the response-stimulus-response sequence it is possible to evoke the sequence not only by means of external (environmental matrix) objective stimuli, but also by internal symbolic stimuli. Hence, any event that can initiate a response can also produce the "hope" or "fear" response-correlated stimulus previously associated. Thus far the argument follows very closely the general position presented by Mowrer (1960b). One needs only to note that hope and fear are feeling responses that merge in at least two points to see that this two-factor theory of Mowrer's can be conceptualized as a single energy-factor construct.

Figure 9 suggests the interrelationship between what Mowrer describes as hope and fear. In this circular conception of the feeling response we see fear blending into an aggressive state that can yield maximally stable energy (effective for attack, flight, or response inhibition and substitution). Hope can also move in the same direction. Fear, however, moving through terror, reaches the same state of dis-

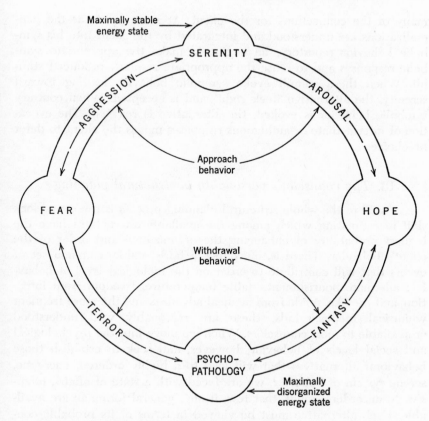

Figure 9. The Interrelationships between Drive and Energy State.

organized response patterns as those reached by hope via fantasy. This, of course, is not the appropriate place to labor the issue of a single-factor ("energy") versus a two-factor ("hope-fear") or incremental-decremental reinforcement construct of human behavior. Either formulation will satisfy the requirement of the present problem of describing the way in which the client makes his choices of alternatives.

The client, then, in terms of his previous experience tests the alternatives developed through structural planning. The testing is undertaken in the domain of symbolic reality and depends on the client's past experience in generalizing from one behavior product to another. This process of generalization is facilitated by the communication interactions of the client and counselor, in which the latter makes many of the connections for the client. At some point, as the generalizations are understood and integrated by the client into his symbolic behavior repertory, he begins to make the appropriate symbolic responses and to sense the appropriate response-produced stimuli. When these stimuli evoke symbolic behavior leading toward serenity, the alternative "feels right" and is accepted. When contrary symbolic behavior is evoked, the alternative is rejected. The evocation of intermediate or ambiguous responses moves the client to defer his choice.

13. The counselor's personality in structural planning

Essential to the whole structural planning process is the counselor's skill in estimating which among the available alternatives have the highest probability of enhancing the organization and order of the client's behavior. There is, of course, a fairly stable, common set of events that will contribute to order on the biological level of behavior: adequate nourishment, stable temperature, freedom from infection, and the like. Aside from medical advances and the more frequent whimsical medical fads, these are reasonably well understood or available to most counselors. When we move into the psychological and social levels of behavior, however, and seek to establish those behavioral alternatives that will lead to a highly ordered, energetic, serene system of behavior, we are faced with a state of affairs, offensive to an orderly mind, that few, if any, general formulae are available. Each alternative must be viewed in terms of its probable contribution to the idiosyncratic behavior organization of a unique client. The most effective tool available to the counselor for achieving this kind of understanding is his own personality.

In the process of training counselors, observing experienced as well as beginning counselors, and participating actively in the practice of counseling over a long period of time, the present writer has been led to speculate that three traits are essential to effective counseling. These traits (sets of reference signals) cause the counselor to behave in ways that demonstrate that he is secure, sensitive, and objective. THESE PERSONALITY PATTERNS OF SECURITY, SENSITIVITY, AND OBJECTIVITY SEEM CRITICAL IN THE GUIDANCE INTERACTION.[5]

What is meant by security, sensitivity, and objectivity? More spe-

---

[5] This statement and the elaboration which follows is, with minor revisions, a restatement of a point of view presented earlier by the present writer (Weitz, 1957).

cifically, how does the behavior of secure, sensitive, and objective people differ from the behavior of people lacking these characteristics?

By security we mean a frank recognition of strengths and weaknesses. The secure person is publicly aware of his limitations (that is to say, they are neither suppressed or repressed), yet is not threatened by them. His inability to play golf as well, or think as well, or even love as well as some of his acquaintances causes him no emotional pangs, although he is aware of his shortcomings. His membership in one or another religious, racial, political, or aesthetic minority group gives him no sense of inferiority that he feels must be eradicated through overaggression. His skills, his talents, his special competencies are frankly and openly accepted with equal serenity, with no feeling of pressure to display them to excess. He accepts other people as they are within the recognized limits of his perceptions, and he expects to be accepted on the same terms by them.

The sensitive person is capable of generalizing his own feelings of security to the acceptance of others. He avoids, insofar as possible, evaluating others; or, when he does, he attempts to base his judgments on their terms (which he seeks to discover) rather than on his own (which he has already intimately and critically explored). He recognizes that present behavior has its roots in past experience, so that when he reacts to the present behavior of another individual, he knows that he is responding to a total reactional biography involving an intellectual and emotional history. The sensitive person is capable of understanding and appreciating a wide range of psychological behavior.

The objective person is capable of distinguishing between objective and symbolic behavior, yet understands the intimate relationship between the two. He knows that a child is not necessarily good when he is called a "good boy" nor a criminal when he is called a bad one. He differentiates spontaneously between objective events and abstractions. He knows that no two objects are ever the same and that from moment to moment a single object or event changes its structure and character. He distrusts and fears labels, principles, generalizations, and especially absolutes. Life to the objective person is a series of discrete objects and events, each interacting with the other over vast as well as infinitesmal time and space, each influencing the other, yet each a unique entity.

These traits appear to be the ones which facilitate structural planning—as well as other guidance strategies. They permit the counselor to analyze the client's problem within the client's framework. His sensitivity and objectivity permit him to differentiate between the client's serenity and his own. His security permits him to make effective choices of alternatives from his own experiences without the need to make his selections solve some problem of his own.

14. *Structural planning and the problem-solving process*

Throughout the total guidance process, the counselor has a substantial portion of his attention focused on the transmission of information about the process to the client as it progresses. Structural planning has at its core the examination of alternatives in terms of an ordered value system. Many tricks can be used to expose and explicate this core: questioning the client, confronting him with incompatible alternatives, outlining the advantages and disadvantages of each alternative on paper, and so on. Yet experience seems to suggest that the most successful procedure with most clients is simply to proceed slowly, building the structure, utilizing as many as possible of the client's own ideas, introducing new alternatives in a tentative and hypothetical way, and all the while explaining that the purpose at this phase is not to solve the problem, but to seek possible solutions. By generalizing from this instance to other problems the client has already solved (based upon problem-identification data), it is possible to aid the client in understanding the process.

If the outcomes of guidance include the ability of the client to make self-directed, responsible decisions, then the client's understanding of how he does this may well be more important than the solution of the client's immediate problem.

15. *Summary*

The structural-planning phase of guidance is used to map out a set of alternatives that have a reasonably high probability of aiding the client in moving forward and overcoming the obstacles in his path. This mapping is accomplished by utilizing those elements available in the client's behavior repertory as revealed in the problem-identification phase and adding to them alternatives drawn from the counselor's own experience. Selection of alternatives is governed by an overriding value, which has here been viewed as *order,* leading to available energy in the client's behavior structure.

The counselor, in this formulation, participates actively in the process. His effectiveness in selecting alternatives appropriate to the client's orderly solution of his problem depends on the degree to which the counselor has achieved security, sensitivity, and objectivity in his own personality.

The client, meanwhile, selects from among the alternatives considered those that, in terms of his past experience, give promise of having satisfying consequences. He also accomplishes this selection in terms of the degree to which each alternative contributes to his sense of order. Those alternatives he selects are organized into the client's structural plan for resolving his present difficulty.

Throughout the structural planning, care is taken to insure that the client is made aware of the operation of the process, so that he is able not only to solve his current problem but also to acquire more effective problem-solving behavior.

Eight

Structural activation

◆◆◆

When effectively pursued, structural planning produces three principal results. First, a set of alternative courses of action that give some promise of leading to the solution of the client's current dilemma is collaboratively created. Second, the client selects from among the alternatives those that, in terms of his past satisfactions and frustrations, appear to have the highest probability of serving as satisfying reference signals for future action. Finally, the techniques employed in the establishment of a structure of alternatives and in the process of selection are generalized into the problem-solving procedure.

There now remains the necessity of translating the structural plan into objective reality. This process, which has been variously called therapy, counseling, adjustment, remediation, and the like, we prefer to call *structural activation*. This label is consistent with the general nomenclature used throughout this formulation, in which behavior is viewed as a dynamic structure of interacting elements, and guidance is viewed as the reorganization of structures that may have become less than maximally effective.

As far as the counselor is concerned, one of the major devices for putting the plans into action is to talk with the client about ways of doing this. To be sure, the counselor can intervene directly by actively manipulating the environmental context, and he frequently does, as when he writes a recommendation for a client, arranges a new course schedule, or takes responsibility for initiating some social action on behalf of the client. In the main, however, the consulting room interaction involved in structural activation is carried on in the symbolic domain. Here talking about the problem and the ways in which the structural plan may be put into effect is the main order of business.

1. A danger in guidance

Herein lies one of the major dangers in the guidance process. Some guidance never gets beyond the talking stage. The whole process seems to center about problem identification and structural planning, with inadequate or ineffective effort given to translating the symbolic reality of structural planning into objectively realistic structural action. The relationship between the counselor's personality and this abortion of the guidance process at the mere talking stage may be summarized as follows:

The insecure counselor may project his own frailties into (the client's) story and derive a feeling of release from (his) ventilation of his troubles. It is a kind of second-hand catharsis. Or the insensitive counselor may encourage and support this public exposure of pain out of idle curiosity, or the non-objective counselor may believe that the symbolic solution of a problem is the same as the objective solution of it. But most of the trouble at this point comes from the insecure counselor whose sense of inadequacy requires that he receive continual reassurance of his worth. (The client's) presence across the desk and the opening of his heart appears to the insecure counselor as evidence that he is needed and worthy. He will, therefore, do anything he can to retain this client. He will reassure him, and support him and explore his psychological terrain to the point of no return, meanwhile reinforcing, as best as he can, (the client's) tendency to talk about himself. If the client's anxieties are partially reduced by this verbal behavior, he may learn, in the course of counseling, that anxieties and frustrations can be reduced by talking about them. But if this is all he learns, and frequently this is all the insecure counselor can teach him, there is a good chance that irreparable damage may be done to his mental hygiene. This kind of counseling can, and unfortunately does, produce the chronic complainer, the chronic public explorer of the wounded psyche, the chronic listener-dependent. (Weitz, 1957, p. 279. Phrases in parentheses represent minor revisions in the original text.)

Utilization of the therapeutic interaction as a means of supporting the inadequately oriented practitioner is given devastating consideration by Haley (1958), who applies "Potter's principles of one-upmanship" to a hilarious but painful scrutiny of the art of psychoanalysis. "Psychoanalysis," as Haley describes it, "is a dynamic psychological process involving two people, a patient and a psychoanalyst, during which the patient insists that the analyst be one-up while desperately trying to put him one-down, and the analyst insists that the patient remain one-down in order to help him learn to become one-up." He follows this general description of the process with an instructive discussion of ploys (moves or gambits that give one an advantage in a relationship) that the analyst may use to insure his one-up position vis-à-vis the patient. These include requiring that the patient come voluntarily for help, the couch, the analyst's chair BEHIND the patient, the analyst's silence, and the like, all designed to give the client a one-down feeling.

His treatment of the nondirective therapeutic technique gives something of the flavor of this delightful essay.

Orthodox psychoanalytic ploys can be highlighted by contrasting them with the more unorthodox maneuvers. There is, for example, the Rogerian system of ploys where the therapist merely repeats back what the patient says. This is an inevitably winning system. No one can top a person who merely repeats his ideas after him. When the patient accuses the therapist of being no use to him, the therapist replies, "You feel I'm no use to you." The patient says, "That's right, you're not worth a damn." The therapist says, "You feel I'm not worth a damn." This ploy, even more than the orthodox silence ploy, eliminates any triumphant feeling in the patient and makes him feel a little silly after a while—(a one-down feeling). Most orthodox analysts look upon the Rogerian ploys as not only weak but not quite respectable. They don't give the patient a fair chance. (Haley, 1958, p. 197.)

Some of Haley's spoofing has more reality in it than counselors would care to admit. (It's always the fellow down the hall who works that way.) Yet the fact remains that counselors do misuse the relationship to meet their own needs and bolster their own inadequacies. As a result, guidance becomes bogged down at the structural-planning stage and never moves forward to structural activation.

Structural activation requires the translation of the plans created in the symbolic domain into behavior performed in the domain of objective reality. An understanding of how this takes place depends on our understanding of language, both its acquisition and its function, for the transactions between client and counselor that facilitate this translation are language transactions.

2. *The origins of language*

Speculation about the sources of language and the growth of languages appear to be without end. Philosophers, philologists, psychologists, historians, logicians, and even statisticians have had their say on how man first began to talk and to develop an understanding of what he had to say. Thorndike (1943)—to choose a psychologist as our guide—categorized the theories of language into three general classes: The "ding-dong" theories considered that objects in man's environment had the power to evoke certain sounds from man. The association of the sound with the object gave the object its label and the sound its referent. Since, in a group of men, the sounds evoked by a given object were believed to be more or less common, the common sound became, for that group, the currency of communication representing the object in question. The "bow-wow" theories, according to Thorndike, held that animals, objects, and events in man's environment produced characteristic noises. Man first used these sounds to stand for their sources and later invented other sounds as signs for other animals and things. The "pooh-pooh" or interjectional theories propose that in certain situations man instinctively makes certain noises. These spontaneous, instinctive noises, when heard by others, stimulated them to action. A cry of pain caused the hearer to be alerted to danger. From these spontaneous cries that communicated information language was developed.

Thorndike rejects these theories. The ding-dong theory requires us to believe in the magical power of objects and events to evoke common sounds from a group of individuals, a belief one would find difficult if not impossible to support by demonstration. The bow-wow theory requires the impossible (to Thorndike) circumstance that there be agreement in the ideas evoked in the members of a human group by hearing the various sounds used by individual members when they thought of a particular animal such as a cow or event such as a waterfall. The pooh-pooh theory is rejected because Thorndike and others feel that the mere attachment of meaning to instinctive sounds which are heard or uttered is not adequate to originate articulate speech.

Thorndike proposed an explanation of the origins of language behavior that he dubbed the "babble-luck" theory. This formulation relates language behavior to Thorndike's trial-and-error theory of learning and holds that in the course of his spontaneous babbling a child utters sounds which evoke reinforcing behavior from others in his environment. These terms are retained and take on meaning for the child and his hearers. Unfortunately, the expansion of these notions from an interpersonal language to a group language does not follow with any certainty, a fact which Thorndike himself acknowledges in his summary discussion.

Although it might prove interesting and perhaps even useful to have some certain knowledge of the origin of language, it is likely that the origination of language behavior is so intricately interwoven with the evolutionary process as to be inextricable from its physical, chemical, and physiological developments. Until these mysteries can be unraveled, we can expect the language hunters to discover only those tracks that lead unmistakably to their own theoretical prehistoric caves. While this leaves the bystander with an interesting vista of a mountainside of den openings leading to black, bottomless pits, he sees no comforting light at the end of any of them.

Fortunately, an understanding of the verbal exchange that comprises guidance is not dependent on a clearly formulated conception of the origins of language in human society. Contemporary man—the individual who concerns us here—acquired his language behavior in a society in which verbal communication practices were already well established. Therefore, we may focus our examination not so much on the problems of how language developed, but rather on examining ways in which individuals acquire the language behavior of their culture. The ways in which a child learns to speak and the ways in which an adult learns to modify and clarify his verbal communications throw some light on the process of translating verbal plans into action.

3. *The social nature of language*

Language behavior, as we encounter it daily, is a form of social interaction, perhaps the most significant medium of social intercourse. To be sure, some adults talk to themselves (sometimes listening and sometimes not); infants engage in a kind of babbling activity, making meaningful (to adults) as well as meaningless sounds; young children talk to themselves at play. These activities, although related to communicative language, serve other functions. In the main, language activity involves interactions between people. And it is this social nature of language that makes it such a potent tool in guidance.

4. *Language acquisition*

Theories to explain the acquisition of language behavior, as in the question of the origins of language, abound. Each such theory seems to be drawn from the author's more general notions about the learning process or personality.[1] Of the theories examined, Mowrer's (1960a and b) appears to be the most satisfactory starting point for the view to be considered here.

[1] See, for example, Miller and Dollard (1941), Thorndike (1943), Langer (1951), Sapir (1933).

Mowrer's conception of the acquisition of language behavior is tied intimately to his revised two-factor theory of learning. Mowrer makes a most interesting confession in this connection:

The autistic conception of word learning, as elucidated in this chapter, provides a particularly good illustration of revised two-factor theory in action. However, it would be a mistake to suppose that it was deduced from this theory. The truth is that the autistic interpretation of word learning came first (Mowrer, 1950, Chapter 24) and was not followed by a statement of the general theory it exemplifies until considerably later (Mowrer, 1956). The advantages of research on talking birds were even greater than originally supposed. (Mowrer, 1960b, p. 112.)

More "confessions" of this sort would not only add a human sparkle to some of the glossy formulations that reach the public eye but would also give confidence to young scientists who may not be aware that the scientific mind does not always (very rarely, in fact) follow the step-by-step procedures of the scientific method (see Greenwood, 1961, p. 77).

Adequate representation of Mowrer's revised two-factor modification of reinforcement learning theory would require at least the two volumes assigned to it by Mowrer himself (1960a and 1960b). The following abbreviated description, which is not intended to do justice to the formulation, will have to serve our purpose of providing a basis for the position we wish to put forward.

According to the revised two-factor theory of learning:

Behavior . . . consists of two types of approach and avoidance tendencies. If an *independent stimulus* arouses fear, flight is likely to follow; whereas *response-correlated stimuli* which arouse fear produce inhibition. And if an independent stimulus arouses hope, approach will occur; whereas response-correlated stimuli which arouse hope produce facilitation or "habit." And where response facilitation or response inhibition is concerned, it is not that a direct drive-behavior bond is either strengthened or weakened; instead it is a matter of the hope or fear that has gotten conditioned to the stimuli which are typically aroused by the occurrence of a particular pattern of action.

Stated most concisely, the thesis is that much of the adjustive, self-regulatory behavior of living organisms can be subsumed under four rubrics: the *avoidance* of places and the *inhibition* of responses which have been negatively (incrementally) reinforced and the *approach* to places and the *facilitation* of responses which have been positively (decrementally) reinforced. Thus the question of whether living organisms learn "responses" or "places" is resolved by the discovery that they are capable of and constantly manifest *both* forms of learning, which, however, involves one and the same set of principles: namely the conditioning of hopes and fears, under the impact of drive decrements and drive increments, to either independent or response-dependent stimuli. (Mowrer, 1960b, pp. 10–11.)

These formulations may be illustrated in the following example of a hungry child sitting near an uncovered cookie jar. Let us suppose that the child has never seen the cookie jar before and that he is unaware that it contains the means of satisfying his hunger drive. Evidence of the child's hunger is observed in his fretful manner, his whining, and his general uneasiness. He notices the jar, but since he cannot see into it, he attributes to it no special significance in his present unsatisfactory state.

His mother now reaches into the jar and provides him with a cookie. The pleasurable stimulation of the cookie momentarily reduces his hunger (decremental reinforcement in Mowrer's terms). Thus the previously neutral stimulation of the cookie jar (the sight of it) is now associated with drive satisfaction derived from eating the cookie. The sight of the jar now becomes a conditioned stimulus and under similar drive states in the future will evoke approach behavior in the child where formerly it evoked only a limited awareness response. If, on future occasions, the lid is placed on the jar, the child not only can learn to approach the jar to satisfy his hunger, but he can also learn the instrumental act of removing the lid to achieve a reduction of his drives.

This illustrates a situation in which the independent stimulus, the cookie in the jar, arouses "hope" and facilitates approach behavior. The approach behavior, in itself, produces stimuli that the child interprets as hope, and when the lid is on the jar the child can learn to remove it as a means of partially reducing the response-produced stimuli evoked by the initial approach behavior. If, after the lid-removing responses have been well established, the cookies are removed from the jar, it will be found that the child will continue to remove the lid even though no food is available to him. Lid-removing behavior may be expected to continue for some time without the primary reinforcement of cookies, for this behavior (and the pleasurable stimulation—kinesthetic, sound, and sight) has been associated with the response-correlated stimuli of "hope" aroused by the approach to the cookie jar.[2]

---

[2] Experiments on animals suggest that intermittent reinforcement with cookies during the "training trials" will result in the lid-rattling behavior in our illustration being continued for a longer period after the complete removal of primary reinforcement (extinction trials).

A similar illustration can be used to exemplify avoidance and inhibitory behavior engendered through painful stimulation (incremental reinforcement). If the child under mild hunger drive tends, accidentally, to reach for the cookie jar, which up to this point has been a neutral stimulus, and if, as he does so, his mother administers a sharp slap to his hand, the child is likely to withdraw his hand rapidly. Thus painful stimulation from an external stimulus object results in withdrawal behavior. Subsequently, when the child under similar circumstances becomes aware of the cookie jar and starts to reach for it, these awareness and manipulative responses will evoke again a sense of the painful stimulation previously administered by his mother. This response-correlated stimulus, which Mowrer labels "fear," can have the effect of inhibiting the reaching response.

Thus external pleasurable stimulation (decremental reinforcement) evokes approach behavior AND HOPE, whereas internal response-produced stimulation (hope) leads to response facilitation and habit formation. Similarly, external painful stimulation (incremental reinforcement) evokes withdrawal behavior AND FEAR, whereas internal response-produced stimulation (fear) leads to response inhibition.

The argument may be carried a step further. Habits growing out of response facilitation evoked by response-produced hope that are not occasionally given primary reinforcement tend to evoke feelings of frustration. Consequently, the habit thus acquired may be extinguished. Similarly, an inhibition evoked by response-produced fear may be extinguished by means of relief if the primary painful stimulation is not reintroduced from time to time.

From these general and basic concepts and from principles of latent learning and secondary reinforcement, Mowrer develops an argument concerning imitation, leading to the formulation of principles of language acquisition. The general outlines of the development may be briefly summarized in this way: Mowrer sees latent learning, that is, the acquisition of behavior without the performance of the specific responses in question as a process by which

. . . a stimulus which is later to be response-correlated is "baited" in advance by being "preconditioned" to hope or fear, thus predisposing the subject to make or not make some particular response or approach or avoid some particular place. Here the "transfer of training," or generalization, which is so prominent in so-called latent learning, is from the situation in which the stimulus in question is independently produced (and conditioned) to a situation in which it occurs (or is increased) as a consequence of something the *subject does*. Here, as is generally the case, the "transfer" is "mediated" by a *common element* (stimulus similarity). (Mowrer, 1960b, p. 52.)

The acquisition of language behavior may be related to the two-factor theory of learning and to the derived conceptions of latent learning and generalization in somewhat the following way. It has been demonstrated (Sanger, 1955; Rheingold, Gewirtz, and Ross, 1959) that infants are almost continuously subject to human sounds. Mothers, especially "good" mothers, talk to their children, coo over them, sing to them, and even call out to them when they are in another room. These reassuring noises accompany the mother's handling, fondling, feeding, and generally caring for the infant. These attentions are, in general, pleasurable sensations for the child. Thus the sounds made by the mother become associated in the child with rewarding experience. The sounds become a sign for the mother's care.

When the child spontaneously makes noises that have something of the same quality as the mother's sounds, he has a similar rewarding experience. This response-correlated stimulation serves to evoke more of the same behavior; thus the child continues the sound of his own voice and produces the babbling noises characteristic of infants. Infant babbling in the absence of the mother may be said to "reinstate" the mother and thus reassure the child. The first infant vocalizations, beyond the spontaneous cries of the child, may be said to be responses to the "hope" evoked by the response-produced stimulation.

Words or other human sounds [says Mowrer] are first made by infants, it seems, because the words have been associated with relief and other satisfactions and, as a result, have themselves come to sound good. Human infants . . . are vocally versatile creatures and in the course of random activities in this area will eventually make sounds somewhat similar to those which have already acquired pleasant connotations and will, for reasons indicated, have a special incentive for trying to repeat and refine these sounds.

Soon, however, the infant discovers that the making of these sounds can be used not only to comfort, reassure, and satisfy himself directly but also to interest, satisfy, and control mother, father and others. Up to this point the speech learning of birds and babies seems to be virtually identical; but before long, somewhere around 18 months or two years of age, human infants begin to do something of which birds, even the most talented of them, are incapable. It is always a big event for the rest of the family (and probably for the baby, too!) when a baby begins to "put words together," i.e., to make original, functional sentences. (Mowrer, 1952, pp. 264–265.)

It should be noted that at the outset of the language acquisition the child does not have to say a word in order to be rewarded. The person caring for the child makes the sounds and provides the rewards, thus connecting the sound and the reward. When, subsequently, the child accidently (?) produces the sound himself, the secondary (autistic) reinforcement provided by the sound alone is sufficient to insure its acquisition and further production. This, according to Mowrer, is the essence of all "imitative" behavior. The trainer or leader performs an act and rewards the imitator. The act and the reward are thus associated. When the imitator performs the act subsequently, he finds the response-correlated stimuli (already established by external reward) to be satisfying. This, of course, is simply an extension of the original concept of behavior acquisition as an organism's performing an act and being rewarded. Subsequent repetitions (imitations) of the act will be performed—under appropriate stimulus conditions—in response to response-correlated stimuli (hope).

Mowrer, however, makes an interesting distinction between habit formation and imitation:

When an organism recreates a constellation of stimuli which, as a result of past action by the organism itself, has acquired secondary-reinforcement potential by virtue of that action having produced reward of some sort—when this occurs, the organism will, of necessity, also have reproduced the previously effective *action*, which will now again be likely to produce the desired satisfaction. But what of imitation? By reproducing the pattern of stimulation originally provided by organism A, organism B may be able to re-experience (autistically) some of the satisfaction previously associated with this stimulation. But will the reproduction thereof have the same likelihood of being instrumentally effective, i.e., of producing again the desired satisfaction, as does a regular "habit"? The answer seems to be that, in general, imitative action is instrumentally effective only if a second organism is present to act as an intermediary, as in the original learning-situation, except that instead of A producing a given pattern of stimulation and then rewarding B, B now provides the stimulation and A reacts to it. Thus a child, if our analysis . . . is correct, first reproduces a word because of the indirect, autistic satisfaction which the word provides; but *then* the word may prove efficient in a more practical way in that it causes parents again to supply the satisfaction with which his original pronunciation of the word was associated. In ordinary habits the situation is a little different: since the reinforcement is initially not socially mediated, it does not have to be subsequently. But this difference does not detract from the basic similarity of the principles involved in the two situations. (Mowrer, 1960b, pp. 113–114.)

We might add to this that the similarity is even more marked when one applies behavior-product principles and notes that the stimulus event that emerges from the environmental context in the case of imitation includes the leader. Thus, in order for the response to become attached with any certainty to the stimulus function, the leader (A in the example on p. 161) must be present as a part of the stimulus function as he was in the initial performance.

This emphasis upon the essentially social nature of language acquisition has important implications for the guidance process. As the child acquires language behavior, he learns also that language may serve not only as a source of secondary reinforcement but also as a means of stimulating others to provide him more direct satisfactions.[3] It is from this social aspect of language that we begin to see a means of translating guidance plans into action.

5. Stimulus function in the acquisition of language behavior

Mowrer's conception of the acquisition of language behavior depends heavily on the notion of response-correlated stimuli. Word sounds emitted by a parent, say, are associated with the satisfaction the child experiences when the parent cares for him while making these sounds. Subsequently, when the child fortuitously produces the same or similar sound, he experiences some part of the same satisfactions he formerly experienced, because the sound has become a sign for the previous externally administered rewarding stimuli. This satisfaction encourages (causes?) the child to repeat the sound and thus to enjoy the response-produced satisfying stimuli. Since in many instances when the child produces appropriate word sounds, the parent is present—and pleasantly surprised by the child's apparent accomplishments—the parent is likely to reward the child's performance by some unusual attention, which the child finds satisfying and which, therefore, serves as additional primary reinforcement. Since this externally applied satisfying stimulation is not uniformly forthcoming every time the child makes word sounds (the parent is not always present when the child's babbling produces appropriate sounds), the intermittent primary reinforcement serves to permit the secondary

[3] The learning of negative words takes place in much the same way as that of positive. "No!" associated with punishment evokes a fear response and withdrawal. Subsequent stimulation by "No!" said by the child evokes fear and inhibition of the response, followed by relief because of no punishment. Soon the child learns that not only can he control his own behavior by this negative verbalization, but, more important, he can control the behavior of others in the same way.

reinforcement of response-correlated stimuli to perseverate for a considerable period without extinction. However, the occasional primary reinforcement by the parent is essential to insure that frustration does not contribute to the extinction of the word-sound response. This social aspect of language acquisition leads to the second step of utilizing language as a means of environmental control. In securing reinforcement for the word response, the child learns not only the word response but also the use of it as a means of securing rewards. He finds the word a useful command device for manipulating persons in his environment, and thus he moves his language behavior forward from a mere word-sound production to a highly developed system of social communication.

As one follows this formulation of the acquisition of verbal behavior, one must become impressed with the idea that from moment to moment, in the process of producing word sounds, stimuli and responses appear not only to interact but actually to interchange. Consider, for example, a single instant in the language-acquisition event. These are some of the things going on in the case of an infant who has not been fed for several hours, and who is, as a consequence, mildly hungry: The biochemical state of the organism (the level of sugar, the enzyme secretions, the waste content, etc.) and the muscle activity of the digestive system represent responses to the food previously eaten and the degree of general activity in which the organism has participated up to the moment of observation. These internal responses serve as stimuli to other actions—perception of this internal state, for example. The perception, in turn, serves as stimulus for other activity, for example: gross bodily activity, tentative sucking movements of the lips, and sound making (crying, whining, or babbling, depending on the intensity of the stimulation). Meanwhile, the sounds made by the child, blended with the environmental sounds, serve as aural stimuli; the child responds by hearing, perhaps differentiating between his own and external noises. Light from many sources stimulates the child's visual apparatus, which responds by transmitting these signals to other centers. These stimuli cause the child to adjust the size of the pupil, move his eyes, change the focus, move his head, etc., and each of these responses produces stimuli that evoke new action. At the same time, the mother is fondling the child, changing his diaper, preparing to feed him, and all the while talking to him. As she turns him this way and that, the child makes the necessary corrective movements to maintain his sense of balance and internal order. He responds to the sound of his mother's voice and the sight of the bottle being placed in the warmer.

All these actions and more take place in the infant and in his environment in a very short space of time. Stimuli from the environment evoke responses in the child, which in turn become stimuli to new internal responses. Some of the child's responses alter his relationship with external events and evoke responses from environmental objects, as when his squirming causes his mother to grasp him more tightly. These responses from outside become stimuli to the child's further action. Thus the total event in which the child experiences word-sound stimuli produced by his mother as well as fortuitous word sounds simultaneously produced by himself, both accompanied by satisfactions resulting from fondling, diaper changing, and feeding, is a highly complex and tightly interrelated structure of behavioral events. This structure of interrelated stimuli and responses is the *meaning* of the event to the child. This is the expanded conception of the stimulus function. Thus, to speak of response-correlated stimuli or response-produced stimuli may leave the notion that a particular response produces a particular, equally identifiable stimulus, which may then be conditioned to a new response. What we wish to emphasize here is that behavior, even a relatively small temporal segment of it, is made up of a highly complex structure.

Some of the internal responses made by the child in the above illustration are feedback responses designed to keep the organism in some state of serene activity. These feedback responses are compared with internal reference signals, many of which are simple, unlearned, inborn conditions of the organism. Thus, if the mother's manipulation of the child places him in an uncomfortable position, some of his responses to the excessive pressure on his arm, say, will feed back to tell him the amount by which his response has relieved the pressure. Other reference signals are acquired. In his babbling he occasionally makes sounds similar to those made by his mother. When he does, the mother generally provides some stimulation—usually pleasant—which differentiates these sounds from nonword sounds, and the two kinds of signals (the sound of his own voice and the stimulation from the mother) are combined in a single reference signal, which identifies a state of order and appropriate organization within the organism. On subsequent occasions when he emits noises, some of this response is fed back and compared with the previously established reference signal, so that as differences appear between feedback and reference signal, corrections are made until some adequate approximation of the reference signal—a word sound—is achieved.

Language acquisition, in this formulation, can be seen as taking place within the structure of the stimulus function. Word sounds become a part of the total stimulus function of each behavioral event in which word sounds were initially a part. Since a large part of an infant's and child's early adaptive behavior takes place in the presence of other human beings, and since this social circumstance is almost invariably accompanied by word sounds, it should not be surprising to find that words are a part of most stimulus patterns and hence of most stimulus functions.

6. Repetition in context

During his early development the child repeatedly experiences approximately the same set of stimuli and responses over and over again, as when he is fed, dressed, cleaned, and put to sleep. These events are repeated many times a day. Although no single event completely matches any other event, certain elements recur. In feeding, for example, the place may change, the light stimuli are likely to be different, the way in which the child is fondled and held may vary, and so on, but certain elements are fairly standard. The mother is usually present; the bottle is warm; the nipple has a certain feel; the milk has a certain taste and odor; sucking produces certain kinesthetic and aural stimuli; and the satisfying stimuli from a full stomach repeat themselves. The sounds made by the mother have a certain similarity from feeding to feeding.

Those stimuli and the responses they evoke that tend to be repeated most often are the ones that come to stand for the total event. These interactions that are common from feeding to feeding are abstracted and become the generalized stimulus function. Through this repetition process, reference signals are clarified, and corrective actions taken to approximate them are refined, so that discrepancies between reference signals and feedback are minimized.

While word sounds are being refined and associated with particular stimulus functions by means of repeated occurrence in close temporal contiguity with the events they ultimately come to symbolize, they also occur in other contexts. Thus "baby," which becomes associated with the feeding enterprise, is also a part of the dressing and fondling activity. The word thus gets associated with the other elements common to the events; as elements from one context to another are removed, only those that are constant are associated. In this case the word "baby" and the thing baby itself remain constant from event to event, whereas other elements with which the word might have been associated are withdrawn.

7. Discrimination in language

At the outset of language-behavior acquisition the sounds themselves adhere to the total event in which they were uttered. Fortuitous production of sound in general, at first, and then later of particular sounds by the child have the power of symbolizing the total function. Through refinement by differential repetition, certain sounds symbolize certain stimulus functions and become words with meaning.

Words acquired in this way carry with them a double value. Thus *baby* symbolizes baby, but also symbolizes not mama, and *bottle* is at the same time something containing food and not rattle. Each word we learn and use differentiates between the *this*, which it symbolizes, and all of the *not that*, which is antithetical to its meaning. The double value of words is closely related to the feedback system, which depends upon differences between the reference signal and the feedback stimulus. The thermostat set at 72 degrees is also set at *not* 68 or 76 degrees. In the closed feedback system, as the room temperature drops below 72 by some discernible amount, the furnace is turned on; when the room temperature passes the reference signal of 72, again by some discernible amount, the furnace is turned off. It is the discernible difference—preset in the case of the thermostat—that activates the mechanism.

It is this two-valued aspect of language that permits it to be used in a symbolic feedback system. When words come to stand for stimulus functions through a process of repeated association with events, they bring with them their negative meanings as well. Thus, when the word is used to call up the event, and the organism reacts to the symbolic event, any intrusion of the negative aspects of the word into the organism's reaction will show up through the feedback mechanism as an error and will evoke corrective action.

The nature of feedback is such, however, that the error needs to be fairly large in order to call for remediation. If this were not the case, very small deviations from the reference signal would evoke corrective action and as a result the organism would find itself in a perpetual state of corrective oscillation. Thus the human analogue of the feedback principle is arranged in such a way as to tolerate considerable error before remediation is introduced. This same principle of error tolerance applies to language behavior and results in a fairly large measure from the way in which language is acquired. As a consequence it is not uncommon to find an individual performing symbolic behavior—writing or talking—in which the symbols appear to another person with a different set of tolerances to be self-contradictory nonsense.

8. *Word learning and predication*

Mastery of word sounds and the association of word sounds with internal and external objective events is not the whole of language acquisition. Word acquisition involves embedding the word in the total matrix (stimulus-response interaction) of the stimulus function in such a way that the word alone, when uttered by the individual or produced from some external source, can evoke the stimulus function again and recreate the total behavior product of which it was an essential element. Language behavior, however, involves more than this. It involves combining word symbols in ways that can produce new stimulus functions. This process has been called predication.

A baby may see a bottle of milk and say, "Milk," meanwhile exhibiting all the outward signs of enthusiasm for feeding. The mother may say, "Milk," without presenting the feeding bottle immediately, and have the child exhibit the same enthusiasm. The child may even say, "Milk," himself and perform the same behavior, indicating that he understands the meaning of the symbol. It is a long step from this, however, to the child's saying, "I'd prefer orange juice to milk for lunch today." The former behavior represents word acquisition; the latter, predication.

Predication emphasizes the social notion of language. In word-making behavior, the individual is simply associating a word with an event—usually present—and thus giving it meaning. If two persons have had similar experiences with similar events in which the word was embedded, they are able to respond similarly to the word, and communication may be said to take place. In predication, however, we do not depend exclusively upon common experiences, but attempt instead to create experience by associating new meanings with old words. Predication expands the notion of communication and gives language behavior its uniquely human quality. Mowrer discusses communication in these terms:

Let us explore now, instead, the proposition that in communication we are not transferring meanings from person to person as much as we are transferring meanings *from sign to sign* within a given person, within a single mind. Said a little differently, the suggestion is that in order for us to communicate effectively with another person, he must already *have* the meanings with which we shall be dealing and that in the communicative act we are, for the most part, merely changing the signs to which particular meanings are attached, merely shifting or transferring meanings from one sign to another. One person, by the use of appropriate words or other signs, can *arouse*, or "call up," particular meanings in the mind of another person; but he does not "transfer" or implant them there. The communicative act, in its most salient aspect, lies rather in the combination, juxtaposition, or association of the meanings thus aroused in *novel, "informative" ways.* (Mowrer, 1960b, p. 139.)

Mowrer's argument in support of this view, although too extended to reproduce here in full and too subtle to permit any meaningful digest, will be rewarding reading for those concerned with theories of language and theories of learning.

The concept that meanings are transferred from sign to sign within a single mind rather than from person to person can be illustrated in the following experience: A friend on returning from a European tour brought back a gift which the recipient felt to be too generous. His concern about how he might return such generosity caused his appreciative comments to be somewhat muddled. The giver, however, saved the situation for him by observing that the graciousness of the recipient was ample return to the giver. This clothing of the symbol *recipient* with the new meaning *graciousness* changed the course of this recipient's behavior in all subsequent gift-exchange events. Thereafter such gifts as he received were accepted without embarrassment but with as much grace and courtesy as he could project, and such gifts as he gave brought him additional satisfactions as he observed and appreciated the graciousness, not gratitude, of the recipients. New meanings, previously known in another context, had become associated with old symbols, and behavior was changed thereby.

Perhaps the most generally accepted criterion as to whether a sentence has or has not done its work [says Mowrer] is this: If, as a result of hearing or reading a sentence, an individual's behavior, on some future occasion, with respect to some person, thing, or event not present when the sentence occurred, is different from what it would otherwise have been, then that sentence may be said to have been "understood" and to have functioned effectively. If, for example, John tells Charles, in the absence of Tom, that Tom is a thief, and if, when Charles subsequently encounters Tom, he reacts toward Tom with distrust and apprehension, communication has clearly taken place.

But this criterion of linguistic action poses an interesting problem for the behavioral scientist. Everyone is familiar with situations in which an organism learns, or is taught, to react to a sign more or less *as if* it were the thing or the event signified. In the vernacular of the conditioning laboratory, the organism, after conjoint exposure to the conditioned stimulus and the unconditioned stimulus reacts to the CS somewhat as if it were the UnCS. Or, as we may equivalently say, the meaning of the UnCS "moves forward" and becomes anticipatory.

This phenomenon seems to occur in language, true enough, as when the predicate meaning of a sentence "moves forward" and gets connected to the sentence subject. But in language something else, of a different nature, is also involved. This is the remarkable, and indeed somewhat paradoxical, phenomenon of an organism, after exposure to a sentence, reacting to some thing, event, or person as if *it* were the corresponding sign or symbol which was the subject of the sentence. In other words, the new meaning attached by means of predication, to the sign constituting the subject of the sentence has a tendency to shift or transfer "back," so to say, to the thing, event, or person which the subject of the sentence represents, or "stands for." This phenomenon—sometimes referred to as *semantic* generalization—has received comparatively little attention, but can be accounted for on the basis of well-known principles (latent learning and mediation). (Mowrer, 1960b, p. 143. Parentheses added.)

We have here, then, the process of predication formulated in terms of the mediation process via secondary reinforcement wherein the meaning associated with the symbol becomes associated with the objective event. Thus by changing, first, the stimulus functions of symbols, it becomes possible to change the stimulus functions—and hence the responses they evoke—of events in objective reality. Herein lies the mechanism whereby the symbolic behavior of the consulting room becomes transformed into structural activation.

9. *Structural activation in guidance*

James Miller (1956) in commenting on the applications of various behavior theories to the solution of a hypothetical case of maladjusted emotional and social behavior, summarizes his analysis in terms of a general behavior-systems theory. This summary is so clearly related to the formulation being considered here as to make the following extended quotation desirable.

General behavior systems theory is a sub-category of such (general systems) theory, dealing with living systems, extending roughly from viruses through societies. A significant fact about living things is that they are open systems, with important inputs and outputs. Laws which apply to them differ from those applying to relatively closed systems.

All behavior can be conceived of as energy exchange within an open system or from one such system to another. Any exchange of energy across a boundary results in some alteration or distortion of the energy form. Those specific functions of systems which we can stipulate and whose magnitude we can measure in a relative scale, we will call "variables" if they are within the system and "parameters" if they are in its environment. Each system except the largest of all—the universe—has its environment. The system and its environment together constitute a supra-system. Each system except the smallest has sub-systems, which are any components of an organism that can affect a variable.

Inputs and outputs may be either coded or uncoded. Coding is a linkage within sub-systems whereby process A_1 is coupled with process A_2 so that either will elicit the other in the future. Coding involves conditioning, learning, or pairing of two processes in a system and the memory or retention of this union over a period of time. Any action is uncoded unless—like speech or gesture—it has some added significance as a result of such a bond. It then conveys information.

All living systems tend to maintain steady states of many variables, by negative feedback mechanisms which distribute information to sub-systems to keep them in orderly balance. Not only are sub-systems usually kept in equilibrium, but systems are also commonly in balance with their environments, which have outputs into systems and inputs from them. This prevents variations in the environment from destroying systems, either by collapse or by explosion. There is a range of stability for any parameter or variable in any system. It is that range within which the rate of correction is minimal or zero and beyond which correction does occur. Inputs (or loads), either coded or uncoded, which, by lack or excess, force the variables beyond the range of stability constitute stresses and produce strains within the system. These strains may or may not be capable of being reduced, depending upon the equilibratory resources of the system.

The above general statement can be translated approximately into the characteristic terminology of several behavioral sciences. In individual psychology, for instance, the system has generally been known as the organism; the input, as the stimulus; the output, as the response. Uncoded inputs can result in strains or disequilibria within the organism which are known as primary or somagenic drives. Coded inputs result in secondary, learned, acquired, or psychogenic drives. Reduction of strains is called drive satisfaction. When inputs or loads create strains great enough to call into play complex sub-systems to restore equilibrium, we sometimes refer to such processes as "defense mechanisms" or "adjustment mechanisms." When these processes fail, severe disruption of the steady state of the organism, known as mental or physical illness, or ultimately death, occurs. The total of the strains within the individual resulting from his genetic input and variations in the input from his environment is often referred to as his values. The relative urgency of reducing these individual strains determines his hierarchy of values. (Miller, 1956, pp. 120–121.)

If we can view the stresses and strains of the Miller system as lack of correspondence between feedback stimuli and reference signals in the comparator function, we can see the applicability of this formulation, in the present context, to the structural activation process. What takes place is something like this: Structural planning provides symbolic alternatives which appear to be appropriate in solving the client's problem. These symbols are now associated with symbols already a part of the client's repertory of symbolic behavior in such a way as to provide new meaning for these symbols. This permits (requires?) the client to begin responding in new ways. At first these responses will be the symbolic responses involved in the client-counselor interchange.

As these symbolic responses are reinforced by the counselor, they will become reference signals for subsequent behavior. Some of this subsequent behavior, of course, will still be verbal exchanges with others outside the counselor's office. If the feedback on these occasions demonstrates that the client tends to achieve the equilibrium of Miller or the serenity previously considered here, the state of affairs symbolized by the new word meanings learned in counseling will become established as effective reference signals for maintaining the desired state. Thus, as conditions develop over time to the state where the appropriate stimuli are available, the client will translate the talk of the consultation room and the social gathering into action. The meanings of the words will move to the events the words symbolize.

This process of structural activation may be viewed as a kind of behavior programming, in which the counselor provides the instructions by combining processes already available in the client's system in ways which give them new meaning. This is analogous to instructing a computer that has been wired for a variety of computational processes. The instruction cards (input) reorganize the prewired structure into new patterns, thereby producing new output.

10. The need for gradual change

Since structural activation takes place by having new meanings—stimulus functions or reference signals—associated with events that, therefore, evoke new and more appropriate responses from the individual, and since these new meanings depend upon the organism's having these signs already available in his repertory, it must be clear that no behavior change could occur unless the required signs were already available to the client. Expecting to reorganize meanings or to give new meanings when the signs are not available would be like expecting a computer to perform the squaring operation without insuring first that it had been wired to perform the process of multiplication. To apply the Mowrer illustration (see page 168) we could not expect Charles to react to Tom with distrust and apprehension after he was informed by John that Tom was a thief if Charles had never had any experience either direct or vicarious with the concept of thief. Only after the appropriate meaning for the word *thief* has been integrated into Charles' behavior repertory can the reorganization of *Tom* ⟷ *thief* be made.

The counselor must, therefore, proceed in a gradual step-by-step manner to build up the semantic generalizations appropriate to the kind of structural activation essential to the solution of the client's problem. This means that when new meanings not previously available in the client's repertory are required, these must be built up. This may be accomplished either by reorganizing meanings already available and associating them with the new sign or by associating the new sign with closely related satisfying behavior presently being performed by the client. The first of these methods involves manipulation of symbols alone and is common in the guidance consultation. The second, however, involves manipulation of the environmental input in such a way as to produce the essential conditions for the acquisition of the necessary understandings. This latter procedure is not so frequently possible or, if possible, utilized in guidance.

Illustrative of the way in which structural activation may be accomplished through reorganization of meaning is the case of the reasonably able college student who was failing in his academic work because of his apparent unwillingness to do the academic assignments required of him. This student came for counseling with a view to securing some assistance in developing better study habits. Problem identification revealed that effective study methods were already well known to the student. He also was well acquainted with various methods of study scheduling. He needed no guidance, then, to provide him with knowledge of how to study. What he seemed to need was some help in putting to use what he knew and what he was capable of doing.

At this point, there may be a temptation on the part of the counselor to "instruct" this delinquent scholar in the joys of scholarship and send him on his merry way with some heartfelt comment about "all you need to do is stick to it and apply the very sound principles you already have." The dean had already tried this approach, to no avail.

Further exploration revealed that this young man was experiencing many difficulties in achieving independence from a domineering father. This parent enforced his wishes by curtailing the boy's privileges when he was at home and by limiting his allowance when he was at school. The father had always insisted upon a high level of academic performance from the boy, not infrequently expecting grades that the boy was incapable intellectually of achieving except under the most favorable circumstances. These facts, presented by the client, were confirmed in a conference with the father. The father justified his continued extensive control over the boy's activities on the ground that he was certainly not able to make major or even minor decisions for himself if he couldn't at least do passing work at college. The father boasted that the student had been admitted to the school only because of the influence that the father had used.

The student, for his part, began to view satisfactory academic performance as a "knuckling under" to his father and failure to do his assignments as a means of expressing his aggressions toward his father and thus achieving a kind of independence. He spent much of his time hanging around the fraternity house, the university canteen, or a small beer parlor with the few students who were willing to put up with his constant complaining.

Here we have a situation in which certain of the crucial elements have acquired meanings that were incompatible with the student's professed goals of passing his college work. Study had come to mean *submission to his father;* thus when he did study, and he did occasionally try, his anxiety was heightened by a feeling of loss of independence. On the other hand, failure to study had come to have the sign of *independence.*

In the course of the counseling which subsequently took place, the student expressed the view that he would like to become a lawyer. Considering the grades he was earning, it seemed improbable that he would ever graduate from college, let alone gain admission to a law school. The idea of going to law school, however, served as the needed lever by means of which certain of the meanings could be reorganized. Gaining admission to a law school on the basis of his own merit might serve as an equally satisfying means of achieving independence from his father. (The father had started college, but because of financial reasons—he took pains to explain to anyone who would listen—he had been unable to finish.) Furthermore, there was reason to believe that if the student did begin doing better in school, his father might be somewhat less oppressive. It was all worth a try. With this new view of study as a means of achieving the independence he sought, the student was prepared to begin to apply some of the study techniques he already knew.

Unfortunately, however, he had given so many excuses for his failure to turn in his papers on time that his professors were reluctant to give him any further extensions. At this point the counselor actively intervened and persuaded several of his key instructors to accept his overdue work. When the work was submitted, it proved to be of an acceptable standard, thus providing reinforcement for the new meaning being associated with work and study. As time went on and the student's new efforts began to pay off—not without several setbacks—he began to consider the study of law as a serious possibility. This now had changed its meaning from a way of expressing aggression toward his father to a constructive goal. Luck took a hand at this point. (No counselor should exclude luck from his essential bag of tricks.) The father expressed strong approval and pride when his son informed him that he planned to go on to law school. The son now found himself in the position of having the prideful support of his father, whom he had long viewed as an antagonist. The meaning of this relationship now changed. Ultimately the student graduated from college, an event that could not have been predicted on the basis of his earlier performance or on the basis of the meaning of the reference signals that were then governing his behavior.

Here is a case of changes in meaning of signs both through the reorganization of the verbal symbols and through direct manipulation of the environment in such a way as to increase the probability that the new meanings would be reinforced.

11. *Summary of structural activation*

Guidance has achieved its first goal when the client translates his plan into action and thus overcomes the obstacles to his ongoing behavior.[4] The immediate problem that drove the client to seek guidance begins to be solved when the client learns new modes of attack not previously available to him. The process by which the counselor and client collaboratively achieve this translation of plan into action relies heavily on language.

In the process of structural activation new meanings are first asso-

---

[4] The ultimate goal, of course, is generalizing the problem-solving process.

ciated with symbols already available to the client. These new meanings are then moved forward to the events they symbolize, so that the client can now respond to these new meanings (stimulus functions) of objective events in new ways. These new meanings associated with external events and internal responses become the reference signals required by the individual to guide his behavior toward effective, active organization—that is, toward serenity.

196

good quote

200

203

Nine

Generalization and evaluation

◆◆

Our examination of the nature of human behavior thus far has led us to the view that man actively seeks to attain a state of serenity. This state may be characterized as ordered, dynamic movement toward distant goals. These goals, and the intermediate steps to their attainment, serve as reference criteria against which the individual's immediate behavior may be tested and evaluated. Under normal conditions deviations of behavior from the reference standards become stimuli for corrective action. Ordinarily the corrective action thus instituted is adequate to maintain the serene state.

From time to time, however, environmental and internal events threaten the ordered flow of the individual's activity. He finds his available response repertory inadequate to cope with these new stimuli. The painful disorganization that results from his unsuccessful attempts to master these intrusions drives him to seek aid in making more effective corrective responses. The aid he may receive in the form of guidance makes it possible for him to examine the nature and sources of the new and threatening stimuli and to assess the peculiar inadequacies of his own response repertory. Guidance also provides a collaborator who is trained to help the client plan for the acquisition of new behavior patterns capable of coping effectively with the new situations, a collaborator who can manipulate environmental stimuli—particularly symbolic stimuli—to facilitate the acquisition of the required new behavior patterns. In this manner the behavior of the individual is changed, and the problems that faced him are resolved, returning him to the goal state of serenity.

Resolution of the problems originally presented by the client cannot, however, be viewed as the ultimate objective of the guidance process. To be sure, the client who finds solutions to the problems that drove him to seek the assistance of a counselor has made some progress toward reestablishing a serene behavioral flow. The modification of behavior to achieve the solution of immediate or even distant problems is an important first step in the guidance process; but it is only a first step. Unless, in addition to rectifying his immediate disorganization, the client finds the means for solving new problems as they arise, he is left in the defenseless position of being the victim of each new pattern of stimuli confronting him from a rich and varied environment. Under these circumstances the client's only recourse is to seek further aid. Such a client becomes a dependent individual, running for help each time some new configuration of demands disrupts his system of automatic controls. Many clients become victims of incomplete guidance, depending on a counselor or some other collaborator throughout their lives, and fail to develop those traits of maturity, responsibility, and self-direction that are the marks of a self-regulating individual.

Effective guidance, then, seeks not only to change the behavior that is essential to the solution of the immediate problem, but also to reorient the entire problem-solving behavior of the client. Ultimately guidance aims at aiding the client in acquiring behavior essential to making self-directed, rational decisions. Thus, the counselor must direct his energies toward the modification of the client's more general problem-solving behavior while attending, incidentally, to the solution of the immediate problem. He uses the solution of the immediate problem as a means of instructing the client in the elements of the more general behavior. In this way the client learns to make self-directed, responsible decisions and to accept the consequences of his decisions. The processes used in achieving the behavior modification necessary for the solution of the immediate problem—problem identification, structural planning, and structural activation—are generalized into procedures that are applicable to a wide variety of problem situations.

1. Behavior generalization

Behavior generalization, in the broadest terms, is a process by which responses associated with one stimulus may be evoked by other similar stimuli. The child who learns to say, "Kitty," when she sees a cat may make the same response when she is confronted by other four-legged animals. Dogs, mice, horses, and what not may evoke the response, "Kitty," from the child by a process of stimulus generalization. This process differs from simple conditioning in that the new stimulus has never been paired with an unconditioned stimulus, nor has it been linked with the unconditioned stimulus by means of secondary reinforcement. Behavior generalization depends upon some basic—but not always obvious—similarity between the original stimulus and the new one.

In its simplest forms, behavior generalization takes place within a single sense modality. An animal that has been conditioned to salivate at the sound of a tone of a given frequency will subsequently salivate when a tone of a different but similar frequency is presented. An animal that has been trained to favor the arm of a T-maze that is painted white over one that is painted black will later favor the arm painted gray over one painted black. Here we have examples of stimulus generalization in the auditory and visual areas. It should be noted that the animals respond to the new tone or the new color in the same way that they responded to the originally conditioned tone or color despite the fact that the second tone and the second color had never been directly associated with the unconditioned stimulus.

One possible explanation of this behavior may be inferred from the fact that the nervous system is a highly excitable structure. Thus, when a stimulus excites certain nerve endings in the eye or ear, for example, adjacent neural tissue is also stimulated. This general state of neural excitation spreads out from the initial point of contact between the stimulus energy and the receptor mechanism. The response repertory of the organism functions in the context of this general excitation rather than in response to a unique energy input level. Consequently, when later stimuli of a different but similar input level activate the proprioceptors, the same kind of excitation-spread effect occurs, even though it may be initiated from a slightly different starting point. Again the organism interprets the total effect, which appears in the mass stimulation, to be the same stimulus as the original one. Of course, what has been generalized in this instance is not the stimulus but the stimulus function. Different stimulus objects and events have taken on the same meaning by reason of the overlapping excitation in the neural system of the receptors. Miller (1951) believes that stimulus generalization is more natural than discrimination, which must be learned.

So long as we view stimulus generalization as taking place within a single sense modality, it is possible to explain it in terms of the spread effect in neural excitation. When, however, we consider behavior generalization as encompassing more than one of the sense areas, and especially when the stimuli to be generalized are higher-order abstractions, this simple neural model does not suffice.

Mowrer (1960b) moves us along a little further in our understanding of this process of generalization by introducing the notion of mediation. In this concept of mediation, a response may become associated with a formerly neutral stimulus through the mediation of a response-correlated stimulus that has been associated with the formerly neutral stimulus. The experiment by Shipley (1933) illustrates the point. The subject is presented with a dim light stimulus and at the same time receives a tap on the cheek. This pairing results in the blinking response, which is the unconditional response to the tap, becoming associated with the dim light stimulus. After the appropriate number of presentations, the dim light alone will produce the blinking response. Subsequently, the tap on the cheek is administered at the same time as a mild shock is administered to the finger, resulting in a withdrawal response. In time, the tap on the cheek is sufficient stimulus to result in the withdrawal response. Now the dim light stimulus, which has never been paired with the finger-withdrawal response or the shock stimulus that evoked it, can be shown to be able to produce the withdrawal behavior.

Mowrer (1960b) interprets the Shipley experiment in the following way: In the first step of conditioning the light and the blinking response are linked: (1) Light—blink. In the second step, the tap on the cheek is linked with the finger-withdrawal response, but since the tap on the cheek is the unconditioned stimulus for the eye blink, this latter response is produced along with, and probably preceding, the finger withdrawal response: (2) Tap—blink—withdrawal. The light, which had previously been conditioned to the blink response in step one, is now capable of evoking the withdrawal response by reason of the mediating effect of the response-correlated stimuli from the blinking response: (3) Light—blink—withdrawal. The generalization of the stimulus effect in this illustration, where both the light and the shock have the effect of evoking a withdrawal response despite the fact that they have never appeared in a joint pattern, may be accounted for on the basis of the mediation effect of the blink response.

Up to this point we have been dealing with fairly simple and usually publicly observable response-correlated stimulus-mediated generalizations. Stimulus generalization, which gives two unique events their apparent similarity, is accomplished by means of a mediating behavior product. This permits us to generalize stimuli from one sense modality to another. Even here, however, we are dealing with relatively simple events whose elements are reasonably susceptible to specification: the light, the tap, the blink, and so forth. When the kind of generalization that takes place is a symbolic process rather than an observable event in objective reality, the explanation of what takes place becomes more difficult.

An example of this sort of process generalization is seen in an experiment carried out by M. R. Kuenne (1946) with a group of young children.

A group of children ranging in mental age from three to six years were taught to secure small toys from one of two boxes which were identical in all respects except that white squares of different sizes were placed on top of each box. One square had a surface of 68.0 square inches, and the other had a surface of 37.8 square inches. The apparatus was arranged in such a way that the identifying squares could be assigned to the two boxes randomly from one trial to the next. The box identified by the smaller of the two squares was the one in which the children could find the toys. The children soon learned to select the box with the smaller square.

Subsequently the children were divided into two groups and tested, in counterbalanced order, on similar problems, but with identifying squares of a smaller size. The pairs of test squares were 21.0 and 37.8 square inches for one pair and 2.0 and 3.6 square inches for the other pair. It was found that all the children did about equally well in generalizing the selection process from the original problem to the larger pair of squares. The older children, however, did much better in applying the principle to the smaller squares than did the younger children.

The first question that needs to be raised is, "How did the generalization take place at all?" The stimulus that evoked the response in this case had to do not with the size of the identifying squares but with the relationship of the sizes. It is, of course, possible that this relationship—large vs. small—is reflected in the visual adjustments made by the eyes, and that these responses serve as stimuli to later action through the process of excitation spread. If this were the case, the response-correlated stimuli of the eye muscles would be acting as mediating stimuli. A different interpretation, however, has been made of these findings (Mowrer, 1960b, p. 245). In view of the fact that the older children could make the generalization to a remote situation much better than the younger children, it was postulated that the mediating stimuli were verbal. The idea the smaller one was verbalized and served to control the subsequent choices. Of course, some of this verbalization, if not all of it, could well have been subvocal.

The implication here appears to be clear. When stimulus generalization involves process abstraction, the mediating stimuli are symbolic.

This kind of principle would need to apply to the Harlow (1949) demonstration of the generalization skills of monkeys. A group of these animals was trained to find food under one of two similar objects that differed slightly from each other. The position of the two objects was varied in a random manner from right to left. After the monkeys had learned to make the appropriate choice for one pair of objects, they were trained on a second pair, and so on through a fairly long series of discrimination experiments. The principle involved, of course, was that, from trial to trial in any single problem, the food would always be under the same object in the pair as it was on the first trial. Thus, if the monkey lifted object A on the first trial and found the food, he could expect to find it under the same object on the next trial. On the other hand, if he did not find it under object A on the first trial, he would need to go first to object B on the second trial. During the first part of the series of problems of this sort it was found that the monkeys' performance on the second trial of each problem was not much better than chance, but that as the number of problems increased, the monkeys' second trial choices improved so that as the series of problems reached the end, the proportion of correct second-trial responses exceeded 95 per cent. This suggests that the monkeys had established the principle. If we wish to hold to the stimulus-mediation concept of generalization here, we must also accept the notion that these animals were performing some sort of verbal or at least symbolic behavior.

Behavior generalization appears, then, to occur in several ways. In the simplest instance we have classical conditioning. Here a formerly neutral stimulus takes on the quality of being able to evoke a response formerly evoked only by the unconditioned stimulus by the process of joint presentation of the conditioned and unconditioned stimuli. The stimulus function of these two stimuli is thus generalized. In the case of similarity of stimulation within the same sense modality, it is likely that the generalization takes place as a function of the general excitability of neural tissue. When stimulus generalization occurs across the lines of sense modalities, and when direct or second-order conditioning has not been introduced, it is likely that the generalization is achieved by means of some mediating stimuli. When the stimulus to be generalized is a process, relationship, or principle, the argument that the mediating stimulus is verbal or at least symbolic seems to hold.

2. *Generalization in guidance*

In guidance we wish the client to apply the principles of problem solving learned in one situation to new situations as they arise. If he has acquired the responses necessary to solve one problem and has mastered them adequately to perform them with skill, we need to insure that new problems as they arise produce stimuli that are similar to those found in the original problem, so that they will evoke these previously learned problem-solving responses. It must be obvious, however, that the stimuli from one human problem to the next rarely have even a superficial similarity. In real life—even in the real life of a monkey outside Dr. Harlow's laboratory—generalization of stimuli must be subtly mediated, generally by means of symbolic stimuli. The student who has learned to make satisfactory decisions about the courses he takes in high school may find himself in a relatively similar context when it comes time to choose his college major. Many of the stimuli—the body of courses from which he may choose, the administrative demands of the curricula, his own academic strengths and weaknesses, and his ultimate vocational goals—have a kind of generality that can call up stimulus functions similar to the ones evoked by the high school situation and thus result in satisfying interactions with the responses acquired in the former situation and applied to the present one. What appears to happen here is that stimulus generalization is established from a single encounter with a somewhat similar stimulus configuration in the past. In the main, and even when we include the impact of the mediating influence of language, stimulus generalization is not such a one-shot affair.

In human experience, what appears to be the application of generlizations derived from a limited number of encounters with similar stimuli turns out to be the abstraction, by means of symbolic processes, of principles drawn from a wide variety of experiences that have embedded in their contexts a few similar elements. Unless this were the case, we would be unable to account for the fact that a student learns something about choosing courses from his high school experience and then applies this information to the new problem of selecting a major field of study in college, meanwhile acquiring additional problem-solving skill which he can later apply to the problem of vocational selection or social orientation; the stimuli, on the surface at least, show little evidence of similarity. In a lifetime an individual encounters many problems and faces many decisions, no two of which ever appear to have the SAME external elements. Even such similarities as they may have are rarely obvious or clearly identifiable on the objective level. Yet man manages to survive these crises, in the main, and to maintain a serene progress toward his chosen objectives. How does he manage to do this when the stimuli he encounters in each new situation appear to be so uniquely dissimilar?

In part, he is able to make the shifts from one situation to another by reason of his ability to abstract and symbolize. His main aid, however, is his ability to generalize about behavior generalization. He learns that certain basic principles appear to function effectively in a variety of situations. In short, the stimuli that generalize from one situation to the next are not the events of objective reality but, rather, symbolic events of a high order of abstraction, organized into a structure that conforms to the individual's generalizations about generalizations. This is, in effect, a two-step process. Elements in a situation are given a more general form through the processes of symbolization and abstraction; they are, then, reorganized in terms of the generalizing principles appropriate to problem solving. The organizing principles that permit stimuli to generalize from one decision problem to the next are those that we have been considering thus far in this book: problem identification, structural planning, and structural activation. In this way the total problem-solving behavior product becomes the stimulus, which is first abstracted, given meaning, and then generalized to new situations. The ways in which the three previously mentioned steps in the guidance process may be generalized are considered in the sections that follow.

3. *Behavior generalization in problem identification*

However much one human problem may differ from the next, all problems require that a common first step be taken in seeking their solution. Before a problem can be solved, it is necessary to have some clear understanding of what the problem is. What appears to be a truism is not so obvious to some of the troubled souls who carry their burdens to the counselor's office. Many clients have at their disposal the resources for solving their problems without assistance, but fail to do so because they are directing their energies toward the solution of the wrong problems (problems that do not exist in objective reality) or because they are focusing their efforts upon some limited aspect of a more general problem and are thus having little impact upon the central issue. The failing student who views his failure as the result of the teacher's prejudice against him, and who, as a consequence, attempts to avoid further failure by "apple polishing" instead of by devoting the same amount of energy to getting his

assignments done, is a well-known example of faulty problem iden-
fication to most experienced counselors. Usually the student has at his
disposal the resources necessary to the solution of his problem, but
the problem will never be solved in the way he has chosen to solve
it, because he has chosen the wrong problem to solve. More accurate
identification of what the problem is would make it possible for him
to apply his resources appropriately.

Problem identification involves the description of the nature of
the problem and the specification of the possible sources of difficulty
both from within the client and in the environmental context in
which he is expected to function. Two major processes are involved in problem identification (see Chapter Five)—the detailed
cataloguing of significant events by means of extensive description
and the analysis of the resulting structure of events to identify those
that appear to be inconsistent with the overall structure. Regardless
of the nature of the problem, this is the place to start in seeking a
solution.

In the day-to-day business of living we do not appear to solve
each problem as it arises by any such elaborate procedure as we have
considered here. Despite appearances, however, this is precisely what
is done in the case of relatively new configurations of stimulus patterns emerging from the environmental context. Our awareness responses provide us with extensive descriptions of the situation, and
these are matched against our total reactional biography to provide
us with stimulus functions with which our behavior repertory can
interact. The process of extensive description and structural analysis
usually takes place so rapidly that we are unaware of it, but it takes
place nonetheless.

What we wish to accomplish, then, in the process of guidance is to
insure that the client acquires the behavior essential not only to solving his immediate problem but also to generalized problem solving,
which involves the extensive description and structural analysis we
have been discussing here. Certain obvious difficulties are found in
effecting this behavior generalization. In preparing a catalogue of the
factors that are relevant to his problem, the client will often suggest
information that he needs to know but that is not presently available
to him. In the illustration of the failing student, such a client may be
uncertain of his ability to do the necessary academic work even if he
were to apply himself with diligence. It is, of course, possible to draw
some reasonable inferences about his academic capabilities from his
previous scholastic record. This, however, may not be enough. For
example, a college freshman may be adequately informed about his

capacities relative to his former high-school class, but unable to make any satisfactory estimates of his academic potential relative to his present classmates. In such an instance the counselor can refer to available test data or can secure the data if it is not already available. Securing data that is not readily available to the client but that the client knows is necessary to the identification of his problem provides an opportunity to instruct the client in the desirability of utilizing a variety of resources for securing a variety of information that he may require in subsequent problem situations.

A more serious difficulty is encountered, however, when a client is in need of certain significant information for the solution of his problem but is unaware of this need. The failing scholar in the illustration needs to know something about his own study procedures. If, however, the focus of his attention is on the imagined prejudices of his teachers, he is not likely to become aware of the need for this kind of information in the present context. The counselor has the responsibility, under these circumstances, of redirecting the client's attention to the need for this sort of information. So far as the immediate problem is concerned, this is all that may be required to secure the essential information. It is not enough, however, to accomplish behavior generalization. What seems to be required here is the generalization of the need to seek information when the nature of the information sought may not even be known. One way to accomplish this is to relate the whole process to the structural analysis, which is designed to reveal inconsistencies. Identification of a group of inconsistencies all of which seem to point in a given direction can provide clues to the nature of the needed information.

Another approach to this problem may be derived from what appears to be an essential quality of human nature, namely, that the individual is likely to look outside himself for the sources of his misfortunes. Man seems to learn to be fearful of his own inadequacies and delinquencies and to enjoy certain satisfactions when he can assign responsibility for a troubling state of affairs to someone or something other than himself. In the process of problem identification the counselor can take pains to point out to the client that many of the sources of his difficulty were found among his own stock of behavior products and that most of the resources for overcoming these difficulties were found in the client's own behavior repertory.

In order to effect behavior generalization it is necessary to establish some similarity of stimuli from one behavior product to the next. Stimulus generalization in the problem-identification segment of guidance takes the form of abstracting from the problem-solving situation the processes of extensive description, structural analysis, and resource utilization in such a way as to insure that these concepts become associated with responses made by the client when he is confronted by a problem. These concepts then become stimulus functions associated with the response-produced stimuli as the client attacks his problem from the first. The techniques that the counselor may apply in order to accomplish this kind of linkage are examined later in this chapter.

4. *Generalization of structural planning*

As in the case of problem identification, structural planning represents a fairly high-order abstraction that can serve as a generalized stimulus function in the generalized problem-solving situation. Within this broad procedure of structural planning there are certain sub-elements that can serve as generalized stimuli for decision making and problem solving. Among these, perhaps the most important are the evaluation of plans in terms of broad value structures, the examination of value systems in terms of probable consequences, and the achievement of serenity through the ordered relationship of behavior to values.

Throughout the collaborative process of structural planning, alternative courses of action are constructed, examined, and evaluated in terms of the client's value system. This performance takes place in the domain of symbolic reality, where the client tests the possible behavior against his values and estimates the degree to which this behavior or that is likely to yield satisfactions and serenity. The reference signals that he uses as guides in this testing process come mainly from his past experience. To this extent the behavior to be generalized is the reinstatement of affective states that, in the past, were the consequences of certain types of behavior and the evaluation of the degree to which the planned behavior is similar to the previous experience. The planning and selection of alternative courses of action depend to a large degree on the client's skill in estimating the consequences of behavior and in evaluating these consequences in terms of similar previous experiences.

To the extent that the planned behavior has a high similarity to behavior previously performed by the client, and to the extent that the value system involved in the new behavior is the same or similar to value systems previously used as criteria for behavior, the generalization process has a kind of built-in automatic quality. It is acquired as it is performed. For many clients requiring guidance, however, the crucial issue is a system of values that appears to be inconsistent with their ever achieving anything resembling a state of serenity. In such situations the counselor intervenes to the extent of redirecting the client's attitudes toward values that he is likely to find more satisfying. In generalizing, then, we are again faced with the problem of trying to help the client seek the sources of his difficulty within himself, in this case within his value system. The procedure that would appear to be relevant here, as in problem identification when the client is unaware of the need for certain types of information, is to aid the client in establishing a mood of exploration, an attitude of open-mindedness, in the face of a problem of this sort.

5. *Generalization of structural activation*

The central issue in structural activation is providing situations in which the client can carry out his plans and enjoy satisfactions in carrying them out. At the core of this procedure is the client's willingness to accept the consequences of his actions. The principal device to be used here is the gradual approach to goals that, at the outset, differ fairly markedly from the client's original goals. By insuring that the client can have a high probability of satisfaction by performing behavior that is only slightly different from his current behavior but that is, at the same time, more closely related to his goal behavior, it is possible to move him at an accelerating rate toward his own chosen goal. It is this progress toward goals in small steps that needs to be generalized. Unfortunately, many clients expect to resolve their difficulties, solve their problems, and rid themselves of their troubles in one decision. Thus, as new problems arise and as they attempt to solve them, if resolution is not instantaneously achieved, they lose heart and begin to apply what seems like random behavior as a means of reducing their difficulties. In guidance, the client should learn that solutions are not so readily found and that by gradual exploration of the structural plan, new and generally more effective behavior products can be developed. As a corollary to this gradual process, the client should learn that in order to achieve his goals he must accept the consequences of his own decisions, some of which may prove to be temporarily distasteful. These, then, are the elements of structural activation that need to be generalized in order to insure that clients can achieve the ultimate objective of guidance: the ability to make self-directed, rational, responsible decisions.

6. *Some techniques for achieving behavior generalization*

Generalizing problem-solving behavior requires that similarities be established among stimuli from one problem-solving situation to the next. In effect, this means that events in one situation need to take on the same or similar stimulus functions as events in another situation. Thus stimulus events having the same or similar stimulus functions will evoke the same types of responses from the response repertory. The problem for the counselor then becomes that of devising means by which he can facilitate this transfer of meaning from events in the present problem-solving situation to events in some future problem situation that neither he nor the client can imagine with any degree of clarity.

Since the counselor cannot estimate the nature of the configuration of events in the client's next problem, and since the client is more than likely unconcerned about this matter because he is so intently absorbed in the current crisis, the only way in which the stimulus generalization can be established, other than by chance, is by means of abstraction. This is the process by which essential elements in a situation are symbolically detached from the event, grouped together, and provided with a label that can subsequently be applied to similarly abstracted elements in another event. In the case of the failing student referred to earlier in this chapter, the process might work out in somewhat the following manner. During problem identification, the student first reports that the cause of his failure is the teacher's prejudice toward him. This matter is explored at some depth, with the result that it is found that other students also receive failing grades. These students are identified as students who don't study. As this line of investigation progresses, the client recognizes that perhaps he has drawn the wrong conclusion from the events in which he has been participating. From this experience, the counselor generalizes the notion that it is possible to interpret events in many different ways and applies the label *possibility of misperception,* or some similar label appropriate to the vocabulary of the client, and indicates that this general sort of behavior can occur in many problem situations. What the counselor has done, of course, is detached selected elements from the client's total description of his interactions as well as the interactions of other failing students with the teacher and abstracted from these detached elements a common event, namely failure to study, resulting in poor grades. He compares this abstraction with the client's interpretation *prejudiced teachers* and finds a discrepancy, which the client can accept. This is labeled *possibility of misperception.*

This kind of label, representing a fairly high-order abstraction from the original events, can become associated with other problem situations. The association takes the form of response-correlated stimuli. Thus, when a new problem situation confronts the client, he produces a variety of behavior, some of which involves making interpretations of the events in which he is participating. In the process of making these interpretive responses he also produces the stimuli that have previously been identified as *possibility of misperception.* The stimuli have thus been generalized by the process of abstraction, and the similarity of the two stimulus situations increases the probability of the evocation of problem-solving responses acquired in a previous situation.

The underlying technique for the generalization of problem-solving behavior, then, is that of abstraction. Care must be taken, however, to insure that the client not only understands the abstraction but also actively accepts it. Unless he does both, the abstract label is unlikely to operate as a stimulus function in a new situation. It must serve as an affective reference signal against which the client can evaluate his subsequent problem-solving activities. During the process of solving a problem in guidance, the client must also acquire a set of problem-solving reference signals such as the ones indicated here. This acquisition of reference standards having drive qualities depends on the relationship that can be established between the client and his counselor on the one hand and the client's previous experience in solving problems on the other. Under conditions of strong favorable interaction between counselor and client, the former can use the relationship to engender, by appropriate selective reinforcement, the responses he seeks to establish. He can also utilize the client's previous problem-solving experiences as a source of the necessary abstractions.

There appears to be substantial evidence that the kinds of verbal responses made by a client in the guidance interview can be considerably modified by the actions taken by the counselor (Greenspoon, 1954; Verplanck, 1955). Through appropriate reinforcement of certain parts of the client's verbal behavior, the counselor can increase the probability of the occurrence of the reinforced behavior. Reinforcement may take place by the counselor's simply making the appropriate noises—"Uh-huh," for example—when the client produces verbal behavior that is likely to lead to the solution of the present problem and is likely to contribute to behavior generalization, and to withhold any comment when the client's responses are irrelevent or unproductive. Or, when the relationship between the client and the counselor has been established upon a firm footing of warm mutual acceptance, the counselor may use the relationship as a means of more direct intervention by the expression of approval when the client hits upon meaningful associations between his own behavior and his current crisis, and by evidencing disapproval when the client devotes the time available to him in rehashing details over and over again or in discussing obviously irrelevant matters.

Special attention needs to be given to responses that embody the sort of abstractions that were discussed above. Thus, when the client produces a generalized label that can prove useful in the present problem and that also has implications for subsequent problem-solving activities, the counselor should take pains to identify this response and to reinforce it in such a way as to increase the probability of its subsequent reproduction. In this way, the client begins to associate the approval of the counselor with the kinds of responses that have the qualities necessary for generalization. Hence, when the client produces this sort of behavior subsequently, the satisfactions initially provided by the counselor's approval will be reinstated by the generalizing responses themselves, thus acting to preserve and continue them. Since the result of making such generalizing responses should be problem solution, this should serve as additional reinforcement to their continuation.

There are, of course, many instances where the client does not hit upon the appropriate responses "on his own" despite all the skillful manipulations of the counselor. The client just does not seem to see the right elements, or the right relationships, or the right way to put them together and label them for subsequent generalization. Under such circumstances, the counselor can do no better than to present the necessary combination of elements to the client in such a way as to avoid threat—to which the client will react by rejection—and to insure that the client will at least try to imitate the counselor's verbal activity. When the imitation takes place, the counselor can introduce reinforcement by approval, and the process suggested above is under way.

Previous problem-solving activity of the client also can serve as an effective source of stimuli to be generalized for the acquisition of problem-solving behavior. Prior to coming for counseling, all clients have faced problems and made decisions in ways that have afforded them satisfactions and that could serve as reference criteria for their present and future behavior. In most instances, however, the behavior performed in these previous situations has not been adequately generalized so that it can be made to apply to the current crisis; the counselor, therefore, needs to relate the present situation to these former events. To do this he must first detach those elements from the earlier events that appear to be appropriate to the present situation and must provide this configuration of detached events with a generalized label that can be transferred to the situation at hand. By demonstrating that the client has already coped successfully with situations having stimuli that are common to the present situation, the counselor is able to give these stimuli the quality of generality necessary to the evocation of appropriate problem-solving behavior products already available in the client's reactional biography. This procedure of calling upon previously performed behavior has the same effect as reproducing the total experience and reinforcing the appropriate responses. It is a kind of conditioning exercise that takes place in symbolic reality instead of in the objective domain. While we do not at this stage have adequate data on the relative effectiveness of reinforcement in which both the responses and the reinforcement occur in the symbolic realm as compared with objective responses and reinforcement, we do know that verbal approval can serve quite adequately for learning to take place. Since, in the guidance process, it is not possible to establish a sufficient number of repetitions of problem-solving behavior under a wide variety of circumstances and thus permit the common elements to emerge on their own account, it becomes necessary to produce the necessary abstractions and to generalize the necessary stimuli by drawing upon the client's previous experience.

The effectiveness of the reinforcements introduced by the counselor in the generalizing process depends, to a large extent, on the relationship that can be established between the counselor and his client. In general, we are inclined to expect that approval will serve as an effective reinforcement if the client views the counselor as a person whose approval he seeks. The need for establishing a warm, friendly collaboration (Rogers, 1957) becomes evident as we see the importance of it to this crucial aspect of the guidance process. Fortunately, the collaborative relationship that obtains in guidance has built into it certain factors which increase the effectiveness of the counselor's reinforcing procedure. When the client comes for guidance, he brings with him certain expectations. Among these are his expectations about the counselor. Most clients come to the counselor with the expectation that he can do something for them; otherwise there would be little cause for their visit. Clients, then, see in the counselor a kind of secure authority. To many clients he represents their society. Thus, what the counselor does from the outset of the relationship has the endorsement, at least the tentative endorsement, of the client. The counselor's approval will facilitate the acquisition of the approved behavior; his disapproval or his neutrality will retard such acquisition. To be sure, the role which the client first assigns to the counselor must be confirmed or modified by their subsequent interactions; but it must be remembered that the counselor starts out in the guidance process in a favored position, which he can utilize from the outset to achieve the goals of guidance.

7. A question of values

Certain embarrassingly insistent questions confront us at this stage of the discussion. How, for example, does the counselor know which of the client's responses to reinforce? How does the counselor know when the client is rehashing some irrelevant detail and when he is struggling for self-understanding? How can the counselor be certain that this rather than that stimulus is likely to be more effective in generalizing problem-solving behavior? How does the counselor know when the client is integrating a generalized label into his total reactional biography—affective content and all—and when he is simply aping the word-noises produced by the counselor? In short, how does the counselor know when he is doing any good? To these and similar questions that might be raised in connection with the foregoing argument, the simplest and most direct answer is: He doesn't.

This, of course, is not the whole answer, simple as it may be. To be sure, the counselor can have no certain knowledge of these things. Guidance research will give scant comfort to the counselor seeking final answers to these questions. The Pepinskys (1954) have outlined in shockingly intimate detail the shortcomings of research in the field of guidance, and a reading of their document leads one to the inescapable conclusion that answers to questions like those raised above will be a long time in coming if we seek them in the guidance research now being pursued.

One source of answers, of course, is the client himself. We may simply ask the client whether or not he feels that he is making progress toward solving his current problem and at the same time learning techniques for the solution of new problems as they arise. More subtle approaches to determining client's evaluations of their experiences in guidance have, of course, been devised and used, including Q-sorts and other self-report devices. Interview inquiries into clients' appraisals of the impact of their guidance experiences on their subsequent behavior, especially a substantial number of informal interviews, have convinced this writer that clients are either unaware of the relationship between their behavior and their guidance experiences or that they have suppressed any knowledge they may ever have had of the relationship. This is particularly true when the time interval between the guidance experience and the interview is a long one. Follow-up interviews after several years prove to be very damaging to the counselor's professional self-concept.

Illustrative of this state of affairs is the case of a college freshman who sought the aid of a guidance counselor to estimate his chance of success in a physics major. In the course of making the educational and vocational appraisal, the counselor suspected the possibility that the student might have a considerable potential for the study and practice of music. With the approval of the student, the counselor pursued this line of investigation to the point where he felt that there was a high probability that this student might find a career in music both satisfying and profitable. Politely, but firmly, the student rejected the counselor's suggestion and enrolled in a program leading to a degree in physics, where his performance was sufficiently good to earn him, in his senior year, a nomination for a Woodrow Wilson Fellowship. In the course of preparing his credentials for the Fellowship competition, he returned to the counselor to secure a recommendation and to take certain tests required by the screening committee. When the counselor asked him what university he was planning to attend for his graduate study, he replied, "The Julliard School of Music." Upon further inquiry, the client indicated that although he had majored in physics in order to satisfy his father, he had always had an interest in music and had participated in as many as possible of the musical extracurricular activities, where he had won a number of distinctions. He had also carried as many formal music courses as his heavy science program would permit. Now he was planning to go to a professional school of music and to devote the remainder of his life to a career in music teaching and performing.

When he was asked how he happened to make this sort of a decision about his career, he replied that he didn't really know, but that he had always been interested in music, so that once he had decided about his undergraduate major, he just naturally drifted into the glee club, the orchestra, and the band. He had no recollection of having been encouraged by the counselor to explore these extracurricular activities, and when pressed on this point, denied that they had ever discussed the matter. Nor did he have any recollection of the counselor's having made suggestions about the ways in which he might go about choosing a career and a program of graduate studies. The student was so sure that all the counselor had done was "give him a few science tests to check his aptitude for the study of physics" that the counselor began to have some misgivings about his own recollections of what went on during the guidance program in which this client had participated. Upon checking his case notes, however, the counselor discovered that the situation was as here described.

This, of course, is not an isolated instance of a client's failure to relate his present behavior to events which took place during guidance. If it were, there would be no point in mentioning it. In a follow-up study of high-school graduates of a college-preparatory program (Weitz, 1942) it was found that few students listed the school counselor as a major influence in the selection of their post-high-school educational program or their vocation, despite the fact that the school had had highly qualified and effective counselors. We may, of course, draw several conclusions from illustrations of this sort. On the one hand, we may conclude that the counselor, in fact, had little influence on the decisions of these students or on the ways they made new decisions. Under these conditions we could say that the students would have made substantially the same decisions with or without the counselor's intervention. We have no way of definitely demonstrating the truth or falsity of such a conclusion. On the other hand, we may infer that the counselor had been especially effective from the facts that the courses of action pursued by the clients were in keeping with the recommendations of the counselor and that the clients did not remember the source of their decisions. Thus, we may conclude that the clients had integrated the guidance experience so effectively into their total reactional biography as to view the counselor's suggestions as their own decisions. This is the kind of gold star some counselors give themselves when confronted with former clients who do not have the foggiest recollection of what went on in the guidance interaction. But, again, no presently available research model will tell us whether Counselor A deserves the star because he is the forgotten man.

How, then, can the counselor evaluate his effectiveness? How can he know if he is doing any good? He can not depend on his own certain knowledge in the guidance situation itself, for only if his own reactional biography and that of his client exactly coincided could he know the essence of this element or that. He can not depend upon the recollection or self-reports of his clients, for these are known to be pitiably unreliable. Research methodology can provide the counselor with more information than he wants to know about minute details of counseling, but in its present immature state it can tell us all too little about the factors that influence the long-term global behavior of individuals. And this is precisely what we wish to know.

Under these sad circumstances the counselor can do no better than make such observations as he can of the long-term behavior of the individuals it has been his privilege to guide. In making such observations the counselor needs to ask the following kinds of questions: Does the client appear to be achieving a degree of serenity? Is he moving purposefully, and without undue stress, toward goals which are meaningful to him and realistic in terms of his strengths and weaknesses and the opportunities provided by the subculture in which he finds himself? Is he meeting new problems as they arise with self-directed, rational decisiveness? Does he accept, with good grace, the consequences of his decisions? Having made these observations and asked these questions, the counselor can now return to his case notes and try to identify the relationship between what went on in guidance and the present state of affairs of his client. In the long run the counselor seeks to identify those steps he took in the guidance process that may have contributed to the client's present serenity, for this is the value he seeks to attain in his counseling.

The counselor who is strongly motivated by drives toward professional competence and who, at the same time, has developed qualities of serenity, objectivity, security, and sensitivity himself will find satisfactions in those observations that relate certain of his guidance practices to the achievement of serenity by certain of his clients. The discovery of these relationships and the consequent satisfaction experienced by the counselor will tend to reinforce the more effective of his procedures. Meanwhile, the recognition that some of his most prized techniques had no impact or, worse, had a deleterious influence on the behavior of the client should cause him to reexamine his efforts. Occasional informal chats with former clients will, however, not serve the purpose of evaluation here. The counselor must make a purposeful effort to seek out former clients regularly and observe their progress.

In the long run it will be the counselor's values that determine the evaluations made of counseling. His, not the client's, view of the matter will influence subsequent practice. Only the blind counselor, however, will overlook what the client may have to say about his counseling experience. But the counselor will still want to evaluate the client's statements in terms of the client's behavior in objective reality. In doing this the counselor applies his own value standards.

It all comes down, then, to a question of values. Rogers (1961), after reviewing opinions from a variety of schools on what constitutes the essential moment in therapy, concludes that there may well be a hundred acceptable points of view on the matter. What is true of psychotherapy is equally true of guidance, for the aims and goals of these two helping practices differ very little. Rogers seeks the solution to this muddle in finding more facts and in developing more effective research methodologies. Rogers suggests a number of places to look for the facts—the therapeutic interview, controlled follow-up interviews, laboratory situations, more sophisticated means of measuring subjective behavior, and the like—and he indicates the kind of instrumentation that will be needed to make accurate observations. He concludes with this summarizing statement:

Psychotherapy at the present time is in a state of chaos. It is not, however, a meaningless chaos, but an ocean of confusion, teeming with life, spawning vital new ideas, approaches, procedures, and theories at a rapid rate. Hence the present is a period in which the most diverse methods are used, and in which the most divergent explanations are given for a single event. This situation makes inevitable the development of a new fact-finding attitude—a more objective appraisal of different types of change in personality and behavior, and a more empirical understanding of the subtle subjective conditions which lead to these changes. Only on the basis of such facts can the therapist of the future select the way of working which is most effective in achieving his own deeper aims and those of his client. Only out of such a fact-finding attitude can a reasonable order again emerge in this crucially significant area, and bring us again to some clarity in our understanding of the ways by which constructive personality change may be facilitated. (Rogers, 1961, pp. 15–16.)

Semantic differentials, Q-sorts, and phenomenological descriptions to the contrary, we can not dispel the insistently gnawing feeling that the pursuit of new and better instrumentation and better and more sophisticated research methodologies may lead us to know more and more about matters that are only tangentially related to the central core of the issue. The influence of guidance, if it has any influence, is on the global behavior of the individual performed in a social context. Thus, only by knowing the nature of this social interaction and ONLY BY ESTABLISHING SOME MEANINGFUL CRITERIA FOR SUCH INTERACTIONS can we get some inkling of what is going on. We need, then, not better instruments and better methods, but rather to know what it is we are looking at.

We hope that the behavior product described here will provide some clue for the focus of our attention and that the concept of serenity, related as it is to maintenance of energy levels, may provide a unit of measure for our long-run observations. We are, of course, not entirely satisfied with these conceptions, for they do not lend themselves with ease to the quantifications necessary for precise observations. Meanwhile, however, they provide a framework within which effective guidance can be carried on.

Ten

Perspective

◆◆

Guidance is thought to have had its origins in the first decade of the twentieth century, with the establishment at the Civic Service House in Boston of a vocational bureau, although Jesse B. Davis had been carrying on some guidance activites with high-school students in Detroit as early as 1898 (Brewer, 1942). Davis' educational and vocational guidance involved a considerable element of moral guidance (Davis, 1914). In Boston, however, Parsons (1909) and his colleagues centered their efforts on bridging the gap between school and employment for those young people whose education had been terminated or was about to be. A third focus of attention among the early workers in the field of guidance was that of educational guidance, represented first and most vigorously by Brewer. His *Education as Guidance* (Brewer, 1932) summarized this point of view and took the stand that all education is guidance, a point of view which profoundly influenced the organization of guidance services in the schools and the general practice of guidance.

We would be mistaken, however, if we considered Davis, Parsons, Brewer, and their distinguished contemporaries as the originators of the basic notions that underlie guidance. What these workers did was to provide a public structure, technical labels, and direction for an activity that became a flourishing enterprise shortly after the birth of Adam's first offspring. Parents, tribal chieftains, and their educated agents have assumed the responsibility for the direction of the young, the enfeebled, and the troubled in such areas as moral development, vocational choice, and training since the beginning of time. In a major way, it is especially because of this general involvement in guidance that practitioners today find it difficult to identify their special role and to claim unique competence. This recognition of the long history and general practice of guidance is not to minimize the contributions of the founders of the public (professional?) branch of the guidance movement, for they and the many devoted practitioners and scholars who followed them have left a rich legacy of understanding of both the public and private applications of the guidance process.

1. *Themes in the structure of guidance*

Three themes in the structure of guidance are readily identifiable: philosophical, vocational, and educational. The philosophical theme relates to the nature of man and the society in which he lives. Underlying all guidance activity—and all other human activity, for that matter—are some basic notions of values and ultimate goals. Whether consciously expressed or implicit in the ways in which the activity is carried out, convictions about the role of man in his universe govern what the guidance practitioner does. The vocational theme in guidance suggests something more than a focus on the matter of vocational adjustment. This early emphasis on vocational adjustment and the subsequent reaction against such an emphasis suggest a concern about the immediate objectives of guidance. This second theme, then, may be examined more effectively under the rubric of the immediate goals of guidance as contrasted with, but intimately linked to, the long-term values and objectives. The third theme, education, as initially introduced by Brewer and subsequently expanded by educational leaders who followed him, relates less to what we have come to think of as educational guidance—assisting students to develop more effective educational experiences—and more to the means employed in achieving the long-term values and immediate objectives of guidance. These three themes—values, immediate objectives, and methods—were the major elements in the design of guidance from its primitive, private beginnings and were evident in the earliest foundations of guidance as a public enterprise.

With the development of guidance as a public, professional function, subthemes began to emerge. Psychology and its applications in psychometry and mental hygiene became part of the fabric, now related to values, now to immediate objectives, and now to methods. Professionalization and the training of guidance workers is a subtheme belonging, in basic substance, to the more general theme of means for achieving the goals and values of guidance, but the vigor, intensity, and sheer volume of the instruments carrying this subtheme cause it to overwhelm, from time to time, all other aspects of the melody. See, for example, reports on professionalization and training issued from time to time by committees of the American Psychological Association and the American Personnel and Guidance Association (APGA, 1961, and Division of Counseling Psychology, 1961 and 1962). Matters of organization, administration, and operation of guidance services and their relationships to other contiguous activities are, of course, subelements of the methods theme; but they also have implications for other major themes in the symphony (Hahn and Maclean, 1955, Chapter 13; Weitz, 1958).

An examination of these major themes and some of their elements may throw some light on the present state of guidance; it will provide us with a convenient way of placing the formulations discussed in this book in a more meaningful perspective, and it may suggest the direction of possible future developments. To the extent that man and his society change little and change slowly, the examination of history may be instructive.

2. *Values in guidance*

Davis clearly identifies the value theme in guidance when he says:

> From the moral standpoint, the idea of "guidance" is particularly essential in the development of the pupil. Ethical instruction that merely informs the brain does not necessarily produce better character. It is of most value when it is in some way applied to the actual thinking and acting of the pupil. In this connection, guidance means the pupil's better understanding of his own character; it means an awakening of the moral consciousness that will lead him to emulate the character of the good and great who have gone before; it means a conception of himself as a social being in some future occupation, and *from this viewpoint* the appreciation of his duty and obligation toward his business associates, toward his neighbors, and toward the law. (Davis, 1914, p. 17.)

These values, which are in the Judaic-Christian tradition, involve the emulation of good and great men (not clearly specified, but certainly well known to all right-thinking persons) and the maintenance of a high standard of ethical business practice. Brewer seconds this view of man and describes man's purpose as being a reflection or manifestation of God.

Clearly man's being is a philosophical and religious fact. Hence, if the reader likes to do so, he may hold, with the writer, that man derives his life and activity and the ultimate character of "what he shall be" from his reflection or manifestation, moment by moment, of the Infinite. (Brewer, 1932, p. 11.)

To a large extent, the general view of man and his society held in the early days of twentieth-century America involved a picture of man doing God's work. Man's purpose was seen in terms of performing good and moral acts, a reasonable inventory of which could be found in the religious documents available to all. The fact that other philosophies and value systems—humanism, for example—were available to the culture and were, in fact, held and practiced by a not inconsiderable segment of the population is of little consequence here. The beliefs and practices of the broadly based majority of the population run behind, often far behind, the thinking and writing of the culture's intellectual minority. It is the stable, almost rigid, majority that determine by their acts the texture of their society's values. Davis and Brewer were simply giving voice to these views.

Despite small, but continuous and progressive, revisions, there was little change in the PROFESSED values of the culture for almost thirty years after the first stirrings of organized, formal guidance. The standard virtues of honesty, charity, respect for authority, brotherly love, and the like continued to be honored in the texts of sermons, political speeches, and social studies syllabi. As time went on, however, the "Infinite" appeared less and less frequently in these official expressions of society's values. These virtues, over the years, came to seem good in themselves, without needing to be associated somehow with a god. Man achieved status in the eyes of his fellows by practicing these virtues in all aspects of his life. Not only were these virtues preached; among some segments of the citizenry they were even practiced. But not in all, and even in those segments of the population where the practice could be observed, there developed considerable evidence of flexibility of interpretation. The segment of the culture that seemed to adhere most tenaciously to these values, the lower middle class, also seemed to provide the largest proportion of the teaching force, and hence the guidance force, of the nation. It is not surprising, therefore, that guidance had built into it, and to a large extent still retains, a middle-class religious, moral system of values.

Many persons, including many guidance practitioners, were forced by the events of World War I to reexamine their value systems. "Immoral" demands made in the name of a "higher morality" were forced upon some citizens by the war. Furthermore, following the war there was considerable evidence to suggest that personal gain and advantage were available to those who repudiated or at least bent the standard virtues. This was the beginning of the break with the moral codes of the past, although large segments of the citizenry continued to hold their old standards of value. The "Roaring Twenties" were followed by the Great Depression of the thirties, which brought the standard virtues still further into question. This economic crisis seemed to teach many the lesson that the virtuous suffered as painfully as their sinful brethren and made many wonder if man's purpose really was to live the virtuous life, since it appeared to lead to no better end. Furthermore, society, through its government, gave succor to all alike regardless of apparent merit. The WPA worker leaning on his shovel became the symbol of business ethics and industry. The social legislation of the thirties and the years to follow World War II gave considerable substance to the notion that man's purpose in being was simply to be. Virtue, effort, and merit appeared to many to be truly their own reward; mere existence earned further perquisites.

World War II, which touched more lives than its precursor, accelerated the shift in values. Again we saw the transmutation of "immoral" actions (murder, deceit, enmity, aggressiveness) into a golden morality by reference to the "higher moral values" of patriotism and loyalty to allies. (The situation grew even more confusing when former enemies such as Russia became our great and good friends, and then after the war returned to a kind of ambiguous enemy status.) What was the bulk of society to think? To be sure, clergymen made it quite clear that the fighting and the winning of the war was God's work, for it confronted evil and drove it back. Unfortunately, clergymen on both sides took the same view, differing only in their personification of the Devil. For many, this war confirmed the notion that the central value in life was simply to live. While the survival value was most staunchly held by those whose survival was most directly threatened, the concept of existence for the sake of existence seems to have spread to those only tangentially threatened by the war.

The aftermath of the war, the Bomb, the reconversion of friend to enemy and of enemy to friend, the almost incomprehensible and hence frightening advances of science, made the world seem to be a very small and inhospitable place to many. The systems of regimentation and bureaucracy, made necessary first by the demands of a worldwide military operation and later by the similar demands of worldwide reconstruction, forced individuals into unpleasantly intimate contacts with their cultural comembers. The primary value of survival that emerged during the war was translated, with little loss of meaning, from physical survival to psychological survival. Man's purpose since the war appears to have been to maintain his phenomenal self, to achieve physical and psychological survival through freedom and security.

The twin values of freedom and security are seen in operation through the so-called "drift to the left" and through the emerging nationalism of former colonies throughout the world. It is seen in the surge for equality among America's Negroes and in the militant resurgence toward domination among the normally serene and unworldly Buddhists of Ceylon and Vietnam. It is as if each individual were saying, "Look at me! I'm somebody. I am! Therefore, I am entitled to freedom and security!" Van Kaam applies this system of values to guidance in a piece entitled *Counseling from the Viewpoint of Existential Psychology,* in which he says:

> Counseling is essentially a process of making-free, a humanizing of the person who has lost his freedom in sectors of his existence where he can no longer transcend his life situation by freely giving meaning to it. (Van Kaam, 1962, p. 403.)

This brief sketch of the shift in values from the beginning of guidance in the United States until the present time suggests that in the short space of a little over half a century, large sectors of the population have changed markedly with respect to the kinds of ultimate goals they strive to achieve. Note further that in the period covered by the history of formal guidance a new generation has come into adulthood and is shaping the value structure of the society. The forces that have given this new generation its direction include two major wars, many minor wars, a major economic depression, overwhelming scientific advances, and, of course, the necessary aggressions that each generation feels toward the ideas and standards of its parent generation. These events have led to the emergence of at least two major ideologies in the world, which appear to be in mortal grips with each other. Small wonder, then, that the values held dear at the opening of the twentieth century should have been transformed. In America, at least these changes may be summarized as a shift from a value system centered on moral responsibility to a higher law to a system centered on individual freedom, security, and self-actualization. The significant fact here is not that there have been changes, nor that the changes were as great as they may appear to some, but that both systems of values represent society's appraisal of what the times required to insure the survival of the society and of the society's comembers.

Changes in the value system of a society have significant implications for the practice of guidance. The client seeking solutions to a problem must find solutions that are compatible with the culture in which he finds himself. The counselor whose efforts are directed toward achieving the ultimate goals of an earlier generation may be doing serious damage to his client. Gilbert Wrenn, in discussing the culturally encapsulated counselor and his "tendency to be surprised or even unbelieving regarding changes in truth," describes his attitude toward his values in this way:

Certainly the values that I hold—convictions of the worth of things and of people—are culture bound. They are also time bound. The virtue of "work for its own sake," of "being mature before you marry," of "knowing what you want to do and then hewing closely to the line" may be far less significant values for our children than for us. If the youth of tomorrow seek work, marriage, and vocational decision in different perspective than do the youth of yesterday (us), who is to say that we are nearer the truth than they will be? They are reared for different worlds and for different values associated with these worlds. So if I rest secure in the cocoon that what I know is an ultimate truth or what I believe is an ageless value, that cocoon will betray me. My values are for *now* and for *me*—not for all time or for all people. (Wrenn, 1962b, p. 447.)

Events over time bring changes to the values of individuals and of societies. With the change in values, there must be a change in the relative appropriateness of one mode of behavior or another for achieving them.[1] Thus, counselors need to modify their guidance practices to meet the demands of the times in which they function.

3. *Immediate goals of guidance*

From its inception, guidance has been viewed as a means of helping persons solve problems. The change in focus over the years has not been in terms of this central function, but rather in terms of the kinds of problems given priority.

[1] One is tempted to speculate that values may simply be a symbolic respresentation, at a high order of abstraction, of the behavior we are impelled by our circumstances to perform in any case. Discrepancies between the symbolic statement of the values and the acts that are performed—which we usually identify as hypocrisy—may be intentional fantasy for the "instruction" of the young or the confounding of our enemies and competitors, ritualistic unsanity, or insane self-delusion.

Parsons gave priority to vocational problems. The immediate concern of the early guidance work in Boston was assisting young people in making more effective vocational adjustments after leaving school. Solving the problem, then, of fitting human talents to job demands, of "placing square pegs in square holes," was the immediate objective of guidance practice at its inception. This focus was a reflection of the then current value system, which held that action and production, especially economically and socially useful production, was an effective means of representing moral standards. Davis, for example, expressed his moral emphasis by significant attention to vocational adjustment. Since man spent almost one-third of his time in gainful employment, any influence that disrupted this activity or any circumstance that reduced the individual's productivity had profound effects upon his total life. Thus it became crucial that disruptive influence and obstructing circumstances be removed from man's vocational path.

At about the time of the beginning of the guidance movement, Binet was producing his first intelligence tests. Other psychologists also turned their attention to psychometry, so that by the time of World War I there was a substantial inventory of testing instruments available. This growth in measurement influenced not only the means by which guidance was carried on, but also the immediate goals. In a sense, measurement served as one bridge, an important one, between vocational and educational guidance. Psychological measurement, after it had developed beyond the psychophysics stage, was intended initially to assess the educability of school children. The initial applications were to the school situation. Subsequent applications during World War I were to the classification of men in ways having not only educational but also vocational implications. This handy similarity of application of measurement to both educational and vocational problem solving emphasized the relationship—which was already becoming apparent for other reasons—between these two kinds of problems and hence between the two immediate objectives of guidance.

Of course, other influences accelerated the growth of educational guidance as well. Principal among these was the fact that most of the young people who received help in vocational adjustment had recently left school or were still in school and the fact that many of the solutions to vocational problems involved further education and required guided educational choices. It was natural, therefore, for vocational guidance work to flourish best in school settings and, once established there, to extend its services to the educational area.

The immediate objective of vocational guidance was to assist young people to select, train for, enter, and progress in vocations suited to their talents and tastes. This objective grew into the distribution function of guidance, which sought to move students into occupations for which they seemed best suited. This distributive objective was soon adopted by educational guidance, which was viewed as the process of selecting students for those educational programs that would best utilize their skills. Until the early 1930's, however, the emphasis of guidance remained on the solution of problems (both educational and vocational) of individuals.

The transition from a fairly specific individualized function to a broad philosophical conception was given impetus by Brewer (1932). He saw all of education as guidance. Through individualized instruction, the problems of individual students could be solved. The economic depression of the 1930's gave support to this point of view, for it seemed unrealistic to center the school's guidance efforts on occupational guidance if employment opportunities were so limited that few young people could choose vocations on the basis of their talents and interests. They took what they could get, if anything. The economic disasters facing the families of many of the students in the 1930's aggravated many other problems of adjustment, so that the concept of education as guidance was interpreted to mean that all aspects of student adjustment—social, personal, community, family, emotional, etc., as well as educational and vocational—were the province of guidance; at the same time all the functionaries of the school became guidance workers. Again, we are concerned here not with the means used for solving problems, but rather with the nature of the problem tackled. During this period, all human problems—with the possible exception of medical problems, including deep psychopathology—were viewed as being in the school's domain and hence in the domain of guidance.

During this period, the mental hygienic movement, encouraged by the writings of Freud's followers, began to flourish. Experience with the emotionally disabled of World War I gave the movement greater drive. This interest in psychopathology reawakened interest in the structure of the normal personality, which found expression, insofar as guidance was concerned, in the additional emphasis given to the more general aspects of adjustment. By the time the United States entered World War II, interest in psychological counseling was so well established that Roger's *Counseling and Psychotherapy* (1942) found a ready audience. The need for professionally trained psychologists during this second war of the century led to the employment of guidance workers in classification offices and medical centers. It led also to a number of quickie training programs for psychological personnel in the armed services. These persons were frequently employed in psychological positions in medically oriented settings. After the war, many of them entered Veterans Administration guidance center and hospital work. With the increased demand for counseling personnel after the war, the Veterans Administration provided support for doctoral-level training programs in counseling and clinical psychology and made available to these students practical and internship training facilities in the psychiatric wards of Veterans Administration hospitals. Subsequently many of these people found their way into college and university counseling centers and training programs, where they brought with them their early interest in personality adjustment. Thus, for some time after World War II, the guidance leadership and the guidance training responsibilities were assumed by persons who had had some experience with the Veterans Administration counseling and mental-health services, where educational, vocational, and social problems were given a secondary role and problems of personal adjustment were given the center of the guidance stage. Thus the attention of these guidance leaders became fixed on personality redirection as the most significant immediate objective of guidance.

Since World War II there have been a series of shifts in the immediate goals of guidance. Perhaps the most striking has been the effort to identify students with special talents and to aid them in making unique socially significant applications of those talents. Several provisions of the National Defence Education Act gave particular encouragement to this immediate guidance objective. Despite these shifts, exemplified by the special attention to the problems of the gifted, guidance has, since the war, maintained a fairly steady focus on the solution of problems of personal adjustment. All other problems are viewed by a considerable sector of the guidance fraternity as manifestations of some personal or emotional malaise. Vocational maladjustment, for instance, is seen as a manifestation of basic choice frustration.

4. *The methods of guidance*

The early methods used in the resolution of vocational problems included vocational orientation, personal analysis, and counseling (Parsons, 1909). In view of the limited measurement facilities available for vocational appraisal, and in view of the relatively limited understanding of the dynamics of the counseling process as we know it today, vocational guidance became principally a matter of providing vocational information and making available opportunities for occupational exploration.

With the growth of the testing movement and the development of a greater variety of measuring instruments, the principal technique of guidance became appraisal. This approach to problem solving fit nicely into the philosophy that viewed guidance as the main apparatus through which the distributive functions of the school could be carried out. The appropriate distribution of society's intellectual resources by means of appraisal, selection, and placement (in both the educational and vocational spheres) seemed most easily accomplished through what has more recently been labeled—often in a derogatory sense—directive or authoritarian guidance.

As the value system shifted from moral standards based on societal norms to highly personalized values, and as the immediate goals of guidance shifted from vocational to personal adjustment, psychometric techniques—which depend upon broadly based norms—and counseling techniques that depended upon the authoritarian responsibility of the counselor seemed less appropriate as problem-solving devices than they once had. The problem had changed, and so had the right answers. By the middle of the twentieth century, the conception of personal adjustment put forth by many involved the notion that the best judge of personal adjustment was the individual himself. Since, furthermore, it was additionally held that all the resources for achieving adjustment resided in the individual, it followed naturally that the major responsibility and authority for guidance and its outcomes should rest with the individual (Rogers, 1942 and 1951). The logical consequences of a phenomenological view of behavior are guidance practices centered on permissiveness and counseling techniques which are nondirective (Snygg and Combs, 1949).

5. Summary of major themes

This brief look at the major themes of guidance from its inception in the first decade of the twentieth century to the 1960's suggests that the values that have governed guidance, the immediate goals of the profession, and the techniques and methods that have comprised its practices have moved from an external, objective, society-centered model to an internal, subjective, individual-centered model. The subthemes of psychometery and mental hygiene have contributed to and supported this shift. Even the subthemes of professionalization and training reflect the changes. In a sense the striving toward professionalization of guidance workers and their efforts to separate themselves from other contiguous professions in terms of practice and professional training parallels society's shift in values toward the freedom-and-security motif.

Of course, it becomes an act of consummate nonsense to believe that all guidance practitioners, or even a substantial portion of them, view their profession in just this way. It is equally unlikely that even those who see guidance in this light would describe their views in just these terms or evaluate the changes in just this way. Yet the fact remains that professional papers presented at the annual meetings of the American Personnel and Guidance Association and of Division 17 of the American Psychological Association give the distinct impression of this trend. The reorganization of the major professional associations—the change from the National Vocational Guidance Association to the American Personnel and Guidance Association and the change in name and emphasis of APA Division 17—lend some support to this interpretation. A look at what now goes on in the guidance offices of schools and colleges across the country suggests that what is now being done differs markedly from what was done thirty to fifty years ago and that the difference is in the general direction of what has been described here.

This is not to suggest that what has happened is either good or bad nor that there is some internal imperative that guidance must follow the course outlined above. This is merely to suggest that a social event such as guidance changes its structure over time and that the changes that do occur emerge from the stern necessity imposed on the structure by the interactions of individuals with their culture.

Guidance represents one of the instrumentalities by which a society attempts to insure its survival and concurrently provide for its growth and development. Since a society is merely an institutionalized expression of the efforts of individuals to maintain themselves biologically and psychologically, society's instrumentalities must conform, in significant ways, to the aggregate of individual views of ultimate purposes and immediate goals. Natural and social phenomena, however, may impose massive modulations on the long-term standards and the immediate objectives of individuals seeking survival. Thus, the instrumentalities used by the culture to maintain the standards and achieve the objectives must of necessity be transformed or be discarded and replaced. The substantial changes imposed on the culture of twentieth-century America by wars, depressions, scientific and technical growth, and the shrinking of the world's size due to communication advances have forced, in turn, modifications in the values, goals, and methods of guidance.

6. *Extrapolation*

Any attempt to predict the nature of the world for the next x number of years, even when x is small, is foredoomed to failure. Our predictions of the future of a culture, or even of a small part of it as found, say, in the United States, are improved very little by the present state of our statistical or decision theories, for the crucial variables in the processes are unknown and perhaps unknowable; therefore, to predict the future of guidance as it will be or is likely to be over the next reasonable number of years becomes a hazardous if not foolhardy undertaking.

If, however, it is possible to make and accept certain assumptions about the nature of man and his interactive role in a society of men, then we can make some educated guesses about the ways in which guidance can make its most effective contributions to the survival and growth of the culture such a man controls. We must assume first that man's physiological mechanisms remain substantially as they are or change so slowly as to make it possible to absorb the changes into the ongoing behavioral context without undue stress. (Even so conservative an assumption as this may be suspect in the light of the increasing levels of radiation in man's environment.) We must assume, further, that man's nature is such that, regardless of changes in his natural or social environment, he will continue to strive toward a state of dynamic serenity characterized by purposeful, unimpeded progress toward goals that he finds satisfying. We must assume, finally, that society does, in fact, represent individual man's means of enhancing his chances for biological and psychological survival. These assumptions are drawn from such descriptions of man's personal and social behavior as are found in the field theories of Lewin (1935), the bio-social theories of Murphy (1947), the learning approaches to behavior acquisition of Dollard and Miller (1950) and Mowrer (1950 and 1960a and b), the organismic conceptions of Kantor (1933), the semantic ideas of Korzybski (1948), and feedback models such as the ones presented by Wiener (1961) or Powers, Clark, and McFarland (1960a and b).

If these assumptions hold, we may predict with reasonable confidence that the goals toward which individual men strive will differ and that the interactions of the individual and frequently conflicting strivings will become obstructions in the paths toward these goals. We may, furthermore, predict that large-scale natural and social phenomena over which the individual has little or no control will interfere with his strivings to achieve dynamic serenity and hence will pose problems requiring resolution. We may predict, also, that many individuals, goaded by social forces they neither recognize nor understand, will seek goals that are barred to them by reason of their own incapabilities. All these factors lead to the inescapable prediction that, within the framework of the earlier assumptions, individual, unique, and personal man will face unique and personal problems crying for solution. Guidance workers, with their special competence in problem solving, are the most likely collaborators in this essential effort to resolve problems. Thus we may conclude that if guidance is likely to make an essential, long-term contribution to the survival and salvation of individuals and of the culture they represent, it can best achieve this by focusing its attention on those behavior changes that involve the firm acquisition of general problem-solving behavior. Guidance, then, as seen from this perspective, is problem-centered behavior change.

Bibliography and author index

❖❖

American Association for the Advancement of Science (1958) *Identification and guidance of able students*. Washington, D.C.: American Association for the Advancement of Science.

American Personnel and Guidance Association (1961) The policy statement on counselor education. *Personnel and Guidance Journal*, 40, 401–407 [200].

American Psychological Association (1953) *Ethical standards of psychologists*. Washington, D.C.: American Psychological Association [132].

Bachrach, P. B. (*see* Super and Bachrach, 1957).

Ballantyne, R. H. (*see* Weitz, Ballantyne, and Colver, 1963).

Bennis, W. G., Benne, K. D., and Chin, D. (eds.) (1961) *The planning of change*. New York: Holt, Rinehart, and Winston.

Bixler, R. H. and Seeman, J. (1946) Suggestions for a code of ethics for consulting psychologists. *Journal of Abnormal and Social Psychology*, 41, 486–490 [132].

Brewer, J. M. (1932) *Education as guidance*. New York: Macmillan and Co. [198, 200–201, 206].

Brewer, J. M. (1942) *History of vocational guidance*. New York: Harper and Bros. [198].

Brunswick, E. (1944) Distal focussing of perception: size consistency in a representative sample of situations. *Psychological Monographs*, 56, No. 254 [39].

Buros, O. K. (ed.) (1941) *The 1940 mental measurements yearbook*. Highland Park, N.J.: The Mental Measurements Yearbook [98].

Buros, O. K. (ed.) (1949) *The third mental measurements yearbook*. New Brunswick, N.J.: Rutgers University Press [98].

Buros, O. K. (ed) (1953) *The fourth mental measurements yearbook*. Highland Park, N.J.: Gryphon Press [98].

Buros, O. K. (ed.) (1959) *The fifth mental measurements yearbook*. Highland Park, N.J.: Gryphon Press [98].

Carroll, J. B. (1953) *The study of language*. Cambridge, Mass.: Harvard University Press.

Chernoff, H. and Moses, L. E. (1959) *Elementary decision theory*. New York: John Wiley and Sons, Inc.

Clark, R. K. (*see* Powers, Clark, and McFarland, 1960a, 1960b).

Clendenen, D. M. (*see* Division of Counseling Psychology, 1961).

Cohn, R. (1961) Language and behavior. *American Scientist*, 49, 502–508 [1, 28, 29].

Colby, K. M. (1961) Research in psychoanalytic information theory. *American Scientist*, 49, 358–369 [29].

Colver, R. M. (*see* Weitz, Ballantyne, and Colver, 1963).

Combs, A. W. (*see* Snygg and Combs, 1949).

Cronbach, L. J. (1960) *Essentials of psychological testing.* New York: Harper and Bros. [104, 109].

Darley, J. G. (*see* Williamson and Darley, 1937).

Davis, J. B. (1914) *Vocational and moral guidance.* Boston: Ginn and Co. [198, 200].

Division of Counseling Psychology, American Psychological Association (D. M. Clendenen, Secretary, Div. 17) (1961) *The current status of counseling psychology.* New York: The Psychological Corp. [200].

Division of Counseling Psychology, American Psychological Association (1962) The scope and standards of preparation in psychology for school counselors. *American Psychologist,* **17,** 149–152 [200].

Dollard, J. (*see* Miller and Dollard, 1941).

Dollard, J. and Miller, N. E. (1950) *Personality and psychotherapy.* New York: McGraw-Hill Book Co., Inc. [210].

Easley, H. (1937) The curve of forgetting and the distribution of practice. *Journal of Educational Psychology,* **28,** 474–478 [93].

Field, F. L. (*see* Tiedeman and Field, 1962).

Froehlich, C. P. (1950) An investigation of precounseling orientation. *Vocational Guidance Quarterly,* **4,** 103–105 [96].

Gaffron, M. (*see* Zener and Gaffron, 1962).

Galanter, E. (*see* Miller, Galanter, and Pribram, 1960).

Gewirtz, H. L. (*see* Rheingold, Gewirtz, and Ross, 1959).

Ginsburg, S. W. (1950) Values of the psychiatrist. *American Journal of Orthopsychiatry,* **20,** 466–478 [132].

Ginsburg, S. W. and Herma, J. L. (1953) Values and their relationship to psychiatric principles and practice. *American Journal of Psychotherapy,* **7,** 546–573.

Green, A. W. (1946) Social values and psychotherapy. *Journal of Personality,* **14,** 199–228 [132].

Greenspoon, J. (1954) The effect of two non-verbal stimuli on the frequency of two verbal response classes. *American Psychologist,* **9,** 384 (abstract) [189].

Greenspoon, J. (1955) The reinforcing effect of two spoken sounds on the frequency of two responses. *American Journal of Psychology,* **68,** 409–416 [189].

Greenwood, E. (1961) The practice of science and the science of practice. In Bennis, W. G., Benne, K. D., and Chin, R. (eds.) *The planning of change.* New York: Holt, Rinehart, and Winston [157].

Guthrie, E. R. (1952) *The psychology of learning.* New York: Harper and Bros. [35].

Hagen, E. (*see* Thorndike and Hagen, 1961).

Hahn, M. E. and MacLean, M. S. (1955) *Counseling psychology.* New York: McGraw-Hill Book Co., Inc. [200].

Haley, J. (1958) Obiter dicta: the art of psychoanalysis. *Etc.: A Review of General Semantics,* **15,** 190–200 [153–154].

Harlow, H. F. (1949) The formation of learning sets. *Psychological Review,* **56,** 51–65 [181].

Herma, J. L. (*see* Ginsburg and Herma, 1953).

Hilgard, E. R. (1948) *Theories of learning.* New York: Appleton-Century-Crofts, Inc.

Jahoda, M. (1950) Toward a social psychology of mental health. In Senn, M. J. E. (ed.) *Symposium on the healthy personality, Supplement II: Problems of infancy and childhood*. New York: Josiah Macy Foundation [132].

Jahoda, M. (1953) The meaning of psychological health. *Social Casework*, 34, 349–354 [132].

Jones, A. J. (1951) *Principles of guidance*. New York: McGraw-Hill Book Co., Inc.

Kantor, J. R. (1933) *A survey of the science of psychology*. Bloomington, Ind.: Principia Press [15, 18, 24, 25, 28, 35, 210].

Kilpatrick, F. P. (ed.) (1961) *Explorations in transactional psychology*. New York: New York University Press.

Koch, S. (ed.) (1959) *Psychology: a study of a science, Vol. 3*. New York: McGraw-Hill Book Co., Inc.

Koch, S. (ed.) (1959) *Psychology: a study of a science, Vol. 4*. New York: McGraw-Hill Book Co., Inc.

Koch, S. (*see* Zener and Gaffron, 1962).

Kohler, W. (1958) The present situation in brain psychology. *American Psychologist*, 13, 150–154 [113].

Korzybski, A. (1948) *Science and sanity*. Lakeville, Conn.: The International Non-Aristotelian Library Publishing Co. [8, 13, 79, 81, 210].

Kuder, G. F. and Richardson, M. W. (1937) The theory of estimation of test reliability. *Psychometrika*, 2, 151–160 [104].

Kuenne, M. R. (1946) Experimental investigation of the relationship of language to the transposition behavior of young children. *Journal of Experimental Psychology*, 36, 471–490 [180].

Langer, S. K. (1951) *Philosophy in a new key*. New York: Pelican Books [156].

Lepley, W. W. (1954) Variability as a variable. *American Journal of Psychology*, 37, 19–25 [120].

Lewin, K. (1935) (Zener, K. E. and Adams, D. K., translators) *A dynamic theory of personality*. New York: McGraw-Hill Book Co., Inc. [210].

Lindsay, R. B. (1959) Entropy consumption and values in physical science. *American Scientist*, 47, 375–385.

Lowe, C. M. (1959) Value orientation, an ethical dilemma. *American Psychologist*, 14, 687–693 [132, 138].

McClosky, H. (*see* Meehl and McClosky, 1947).

McFarland, R. L. (*see* Powers, Clark, and McFarland, 1960a, 1960b).

McGowan, J. F. and Schmidt, L. D. (1962) *Counseling: readings in theory and practice*. New York: Holt, Rinehart, and Winston, Inc.

McLean, M. S. (*see* Hahn and MacLean, 1955).

Marquis, D. G. (1948) Scientific methodology in human relations. *Proceedings of the American Philosophical Society*, 92, 411–416.

Mathewson, R. H. (1955) *Guidance policy and practice* (revised edition). New York: Harper and Bros.

Mead, M. (1937) *Cooperation and competition among primitive peoples*. New York: McGraw-Hill Book Co., Inc.

Meehl, P. E. and McClosky, H. (1947) Ethical and political aspects of applied psychology. *Journal of Abnormal and Social Psychology*, 42, 91–98 [132].

Meehl, P. E. and MacCorquodale, K. (1953) Drive conditioning as a factor in latent learning. *Journal of Experimental Psychology*, 45, 20–24.

Mendelssohn, K. (1961) Probability enters physics. *American Scientist*, 49, 37–44.

Miller, G. A. (1951) *Language and communication*. New York: McGraw-Hill Book Co., Inc. [178].

Miller, G. A., Galanter, E., and Pribram, K. H. (1960) *Plans and structure of behavior*. New York: Henry Holt and Co. [95].

Miller, J. G. (1956) General behavior systems theory and summary. In Shoben, E. J. Behavior theories and a counseling case: a symposium. *Journal of Counseling Psychology*, 3, 120–124 [169–171].

Miller, N. E. (*see* Dollard and Miller, 1950).

Miller, N. E. and Dollard, J. (1941) *Social learning and imitation*. New Haven, Conn.: Yale University Press [156].

Mowrer, O. H. (1950) *Learning theory and personality dynamics*. New York: Ronald Press [157, 210].

Mowrer, O. H. (1952) The autism theory of speech development and some clinical applications. *Journal of Speech and Hearing Disorders*, 17, 263–268 [160].

Mowrer, O. H. (1953) Some philosophical problems in mental disorder and its treatment. *Harvard Educational Review*, 23, 117–127 [132].

Mowrer, O. H. (1956) Two-factor learning theory reconsidered, with special reference to secondary reinforcement and the concept of habit. *Psychological Review*, 63, 114–128 [157].

Mowrer, O. H. (1960a) *Learning theory and behavior*. New York: John Wiley and Sons, Inc. [2, 156, 157, 210].

Mowrer, O. H. (1960b) *Learning theory and the symbolic process*. New York: John Wiley and Sons, Inc. [2, 125, 141, 146, 156, 157–158, 159, 159–160, 161, 167–168, 169, 179, 180, 210].

Murphy, G. (1947) *Personality, a biosocial approach to origins and structure*. New York: Harper and Bros. [210].

Murphy, G. (1955) The cultural context of guidance. *Personnel and Guidance Journal*, 34, 4–9 [132].

Parsons, F. (1909) *Choosing a vocation*. Boston: Houghton Mifflin Co. [198].

Patterson, H. C. (1958) The place of value in counseling and psychotherapy. *Journal of Counseling Psychology*, 5, 216–223 [131].

Peiffer, H. C. (*see* Walker and Peiffer, 1957).

Pepinsky, H. B. and Pepinsky, P. N. (1954) *Counseling theory and practice*. New York: Ronald Press [192].

Pepinsky, P. N. (*see* Pepinsky and Pepinsky, 1954).

Powers, W. T., Clark, R. K., and McFarland, R. L. (1960a) A general feedback theory of human behavior; Part I. *Perceptual and Motor Skills*, 11, 71–88, Monograph Supplement 1–VII [2, 141, 142, 210].

Powers, W. T., Clark, R. K., and McFarland, R. L. (1960b) A general feedback theory of human behavior; Part II. *Perceptual and Motor Skills*, 11, 309–323, Monograph Supplement 3–VII [2, 141, 142, 145, 210].

Pribram, K. H. (*see* Miller, Galanter, and Pribram, 1960).

Rheingold, H. L., Gewirtz, J. L., and Ross, H. W. (1959) Social conditioning of vocalization in infants. *Journal of Comparative Physiological Psychology*, 52, 68–73 [160].

Richardson, M. W. (*see* Kuder and Richardson, 1937).

Rogers, C. R. (1942) *Counseling and psychotherapy; newer concepts in practice*. Boston: Houghton Mifflin Co. [68, 206, 208].

Rogers, C. R. (1951) *Client-centered therapy; its current practice, implications and theory*. Boston: Houghton Mifflin Co. [208].

Rogers, C. R. (1957) The necessary conditions for therapeutic change. *Journal of Consulting Psychology*, **21**, 95–103 [191].

Rogers, C. R. (1961) Psychotherapy today or where do we go from here? *American Journal of Psychotherapy*, **17**, 5–16 [196].

Rogers, C. R. (1962) The interpersonal relationship, the core of guidance. *Harvard Educational Review*, **32**, 416–429 [131].

Rosenthal, D. (1955) Changes in some moral values following psychotherapy. *Journal of Consulting Psychology*, **19**, 431–436 [132].

Ross, H. W. (*see* Rheingold, Gewirtz, and Ross, 1959).

Samler, J. (1960) Change in values: a goal in counseling. *Journal of Counseling Psychology*, **7**, 32–39 [132].

Sanger, M. D. (1955) Language learning in infancy: a review of autistic hypotheses and an observational study of infants. *Harvard Educational Review*, **25**, 269–271 [160].

Sapir, E. (1933) Language. In *Encyclopedia of Social Sciences*. New York: The Macmillan Co., 155–169 [156].

Schmidt, L. D. (*see* McGowan and Schmidt, 1962).

Schmidt, P. F. (1957) Models of scientific thought. *American Scientist*, **45**, 137–149.

Seeman, J. (*see* Bixler and Seeman, 1946).

Shipley, W. C. (1933) An apparent transfer of conditioning. *Psychological Bulletin*, **30**, 541 [179].

Shoben, E. J. (1949) Psychotherapy as a problem in learning theory. *Psychological Bulletin*, **46**, 366–392.

Shoben, E. J. (1953) A theoretical approach to psychotherapy as personality modification. *Harvard Educational Review*, **23**, 128–142.

Shoben, E. J. (1961) Comment on guidance as behavior change. *Personnel and Guidance Journal*, **39**, 560–562.

Snygg, D. and Combs, A. W. (1949) *Individual behavior*. New York: Harper and Bros. [208].

Stanley, W. O. (1953) The collapse of automatic adjustment. *Education and Social Integration*. New York: Bureau of Publication, Teachers College, Columbia University, 192–206 [3].

Super, D. E. (1955) Personality integration through vocational counseling. *Journal of Counseling Psychology*, **2**, 217–226.

Super, D. E. (1957) *Psychology of careers*. New York: Harper and Bros.

Super, D. E. and Bachrach, P. B. (1957) *Scientific careers: vocational development theory*. New York: Teachers College, Columbia University, Bureau of Publications.

Taylor, C. P. (1956) Social and moral aspects of counseling (letter to the editor). *Personnel and Guidance Journal*, **35**, 180 [132].

Thorndike, E. L. (1943) *Man and his works*. Cambridge, Mass.: Harvard University Press. [155, 156].

Thorndike, R. L. and Hagen, E. (1961) *Measurement and evaluation in psychology and education*. New York: John Wiley and Sons, Inc. [104].

Tiedeman, D. V. and Field, F. L. (1962) Guidance: the science of purposeful action applied through education. *Harvard Educational Review*, **32**, 483–501 [51].

Tolman, E. C. (1951) *Purposive behavior in animals and men*. Berkeley, Calif.: University of California Press.

Tolman, E. C. (1958) *Behavior and psychological man.* Berkeley, Calif.: University of California Press.

United States Office of Education (1918) The cardinal principles of education. *U.S. Office of Education Bulletin, Number 35* [49].

van Kaam, A. (1962) Counseling from the viewpoint of existential psychology. *Harvard Educational Review,* 32, 402–415 [203].

Verplanck, W. S. (1955) The control of the content of conversation: reinforcement of statements of opinion. *Journal of Abnormal and Social Psychology,* 51, 668–676 [189].

Walker, D. E. and Peiffer, H. C. (1957) The goals of counseling. *Journal of Counseling Psychology,* 4, 204–209 [132].

Weitz, H. (1942) *An evaluative study of the instructional and guidance services in the college preparatory curricula of the Rahway High School.* New Brunswick, N.J.: Rutgers University (unpublished dissertation) [194].

Weitz, H. (1954) Semantics in diagnosis. *Journal of Counseling Psychology,* 1, 70–73 [78].

Weitz, H. (1955) Instruction and guidance in education. *Educational Forum,* 19, 169–177 [44].

Weitz, H. (1956) Education is a science. *Educational Forum,* 20, 293–301 [44].

Weitz, H. (1957) Counseling as a function of the counselor's personality. *Personnel and Guidance Journal,* 35, 276–280 [148, 153].

Weitz, H. (1958) The role of the guidance worker in the schools. *Personnel and Guidance Journal,* 37, 266–272 [61, 64, 65, 200].

Weitz, H. (1961) Guidance as behavior change. *Personnel and Guidance Journal,* 39, 550–560 [22, 99].

Weitz, H., Ballantyne, R. H., and Colver, R. M. (1963) Foreign language fluency, the ornament of a scholar. *Journal of Higher Education,* 36, 443–449 [46].

Wiener, N. (1961) *Cybernetics.* New York: The M.I.T. Press and John Wiley and Sons, Inc. [141, 210]

Williamson, E. G. (1958) Value orientation in counseling. *Personnel and Guidance Journal,* 36, 520–528 [131, 132].

Williamson, E. G. (1959) The meaning of communication in counseling. *Personnel and Guidance Journal,* 38, 6–14.

Williamson, E. G. and Darley, J. G. (1937) *Student personnel work.* New York: McGraw-Hill Book Co., Inc. [125].

Wrenn, C. G. (1962a) *The counselor in a changing world.* Washington, D.C.: American Personnel and Guidance Association.

Wrenn, C. G. (1962b) The culturally encapsulated counselor. *Harvard Educational Review,* 32, 444–449 [204].

Zener, K. E. and Gaffron, M. (1962) Perceptual experience: an analysis of its relations to the external world through internal processings. In Koch, S. (ed.) *Psychology: a study of a science, Vol. 4,* 515–618. New York: McGraw-Hill Book Co., Inc. [39].

Subject index

◆◇◆